EXPERIENCE

Desmond MacCarthy.

EXPERIENCE

Essay Index Reprint Series

BOOKS FOR LIBRARIES PRESS
FREEPORT, NEW YORK

First Published 1935
Reprinted 1968

LIBRARY OF CONGRESS CATALOG CARD NUMBER:
68-54357

PRINTED IN THE UNITED STATES OF AMERICA

TO CLIFFORD SHARP

DEAR CLIFFORD,

You will not be surprised at this dedication :
most of the items in this book were contributed to
The New Statesman while you were editing it ;
and if you were not the first editor (Cecil Chesterton
had used me sometimes in this way) you were at any
rate the last editor to encourage me to write about
what I had observed instead of always about books
or plays. If you turn to my adventures on the night
of August 4th 1914, you will find there a confession
that I have cherished in my time hankerings after
the life of a "Special Reporter." Indeed, it was
one of my many dreams that you should become
the editor of a great daily paper (a post for which
you were admirably fitted) and I the apple of
your reporters. To record my impressions of
trials, strikes, public characters, disasters ; to
define "situations" whether they arose in East
Ham or Abyssinia ; to live with a packed bag
ready to dart to the scene of any crisis once seemed
to me a most enviable lot. I have, too, an immense
respect for the Art of the Reporter, so much respect
that I have often been extremely dissatisfied with
the manner in which that sort of work is done.
The main function of the Press is to make vivid
to us everything important or interesting that is
happening everywhere at a given moment. Yet it is
in the presentation of actualities that the Press
most often fails us. Editors seldom employ
imaginative men for this purpose, and consequently
their Reporters are usually at their best when they

DEDICATION

confine themselves strictly to news. But facts by themselves are dead; the reporter's art lies in making them credible and in interpreting them. Two contemporary novelists have shown that they were also born-reporters, Rudyard Kipling and H. G. Wells; but few who have made description their profession have attained high excellence in it. At the moment I can only think of three notable exceptions in our life-time, George Stevens, Henry Nevinson, William Bolitho—and, yes, there is a fourth, an Italian, Ugo Ojetti. He, too, creates the scene.

William Bolitho was one of those zestful men who feel that only by drawing upon every faculty—heart, intellect, imagination, eye—can anything approaching justice be done to the interest of current events. I would rather celebrate his work, so brilliant and so apparently evanescent, than that of many a finer writer among my contemporaries. It reminds one that Journalism also is an art. Journalism differs from Literature in that it must be interesting at the very moment at which it is written, and be addressed to the inattentive as well as to the concentrated reader. Hence the contemptuous use of the word "journalism" and the invidious distinction implied in such judgments as "He's only a journalist." Yet we can still read pages of Nevinson or Stevens' account of the Diamond Jubilee, or Bolitho's description of Landru's trial with the emotions of one actually on the spot. What they have done is precisely what the historian is praised for achieving—they have made dead facts live, and made them comprehensible.

After looking through the following pages, you may decide that my aptitudes never lay in that direction, but rather in that of meditative retrospection. Well, I shall bow to that verdict, for I never worked for an editor who had a surer sense of what

viii

each contributor could best supply. Doubtless in the happy event of your having occupied the editorial chair of a great daily paper, I should have pled to be transferred from the Theatre of Art to the Theatre of Life ; perhaps (for where editing was concerned you were a hard man) in vain. But I would have insisted that you had never fairly tried me ; that I had been compelled to exercise my faculties of observation and description only on events which had accidentally come to my notice, and then only for the purpose of a review or an essay on some general topic. Whose fault was it, I would have argued, that I had so seldom been " on the spot," so seldom " present " to use the words of Pater, which describe, oddly enough, the life of the Special Reporter, " at the focus where the greatest number of forces unite in their purest energy " ? You would have shrugged your shoulders and reminded me that the *New Statesman* had been a poor paper, unable to afford sending me or anybody else travelling for copy. That, I hasten to say, was the only sense in which it ever was " poor," and I take this opportunity of paying a tribute to you who made that paper.

Let me say what the *New Statesman* meant to me when it started. I had written dramatic criticism for the *Speaker*, but when that paper turned into the *Nation*, the new editor, Massingham, had no use for me. It was an enormous relief to get regular work again, and, too, work better paid. The *Speaker* had only been able to afford thirty shillings for dramatic articles even when they ran, as mine often did, to two thousand words. The *Eye Witness*, on which I had next depended to save me from nibbling away too fast my small capital, had been most erratic in its remunerations. We were all of us, Belloc, G.K. and Cecil Chesterton, Maurice Baring and I, paid at irregular intervals, and we racked our brains to think of an explanation which would account for those incalculable but blessed spates. Oddly enough, they appeared to coincide either with our employer buying yet another paper, or with his starting a publishing business, or with his abrupt disappearances abroad. In short, with moments when anyone might have expected money to be tight. We entertained the notion that he must be the illegitimate son of a wealthy Russian countess living on the Riviera, whom he could periodically tap or blackmail. He was an open-handed, kindly, rather wistful man. The only benefit that he ever got out of feeding us, as far as I could see, was one review of his own book of verse which all other papers had ignored. It was a difficult review to write, but we had three men of genius on the staff and, with Cecil Chesterton also pulling his weight, that review got written. However, the real explanation of the money-situation proved to be different. Suddenly our employer was charged with bigamy and embezzlement. Knowing nothing of this, I went down to the office one morning and to my amazement found several strange men lounging about with their hats on. I learnt on the spot one little fact about human nature; that just as men instinctively bare their heads to show respect for the dead, they keep them obstinately covered to show contempt for the bankrupt. I was left with a stuma of thirty-odd pounds (two months' earnings); a sum which I gratefully recall was made up to me by subscription among my friends. So I lost nothing —not even my job, for the paper turned into the *New Witness* and continued to employ me till it lost the Marconi Libel case, after which it became a shakier support.

You can imagine therefore how glad I was when in the spring of 1913 you invited

me on to the staff of the *New Statesman* as
dramatic critic ; it meant security (in so far as
that is obtainable by journalists), and it was
opportunity. I had a high opinion of myself as a
critic, which was only occasionally shaken, and I
knew I sometimes wrote well, though at other
times with an involved limpness most distressing
to me. I thought I could hold the job ; two
guineas per thousand plus ten shillings extra for
time wasted in attending theatres (extracted from
you, you may remember, while strolling on the
cliff-top of Beachy Head) and reviewing at the
two-guinea rate. It was a beautiful prospect. It
promised not only security but the delight of
expressing oneself before an audience which would
see when one had hit, or missed, a mark. And there
was another aspect agreeable to me. The *New
Statesman* was out to improve the world, to correct
the injustices of the social system, to stick up for
the have-nots. I had, and have, the vaguest
notions as to the best means of accomplishing these
ends, but provided that I am not obliged to help
myself, I like to be associated with others intent
upon them. It was therefore delightful to me that
Shaw and the Webbs should be directors of this
new paper and that you yourself were a Fabian.
The atmosphere of the other papers for which I had
worked had been radical, not socialistic. Tempera-
mentally, they suited me better. But so far as I
gave social questions a thought (and I did so only
in connection with the study of human-nature) I
was prepared to believe that the Fabians knew
what was what, that genuine statesmanship was a
prosaic grammatical kind of business (I still believe
this), and that all sorts of rules and regulations (and
prohibitions alas !) were absolutely necessary if
more people were to have elbow-room and a fairer
chance on this over-crowded competitive planet.

The *New Statesman* was destined sometimes to shock me by its recommendations, or, more accurately, to prompt the reflection, " Oh dear, that would mean the end of a good many things I care about. What a world we shall end up with—if they get their way ! " However, the paper cared about *justice*, and that was all important.

I found, when I got to know them, that the Webbs were less unfair to my friends, though they were decidedly firm about them, than my friends were about the Webbs. In their company I came across a purposeful magnanimity—not at all imposing, indeed almost mechanical—which, however, impressed me in the end as one of the most genuine things I had struck in human beings ; also, a persistence of purpose which, though it arranged experience in a perspective not alluring to me, made some flashes of generous indignation, to which I responded readily, look rather cheap. And then there was Bernard Shaw ! For him I had—and still have—a hero-worship ; one which no amazed exasperation, either at some of his utterances or at the limitations of his genius, seems to make the slightest difference. In the hey-day of his narrower but more select fame, he was known as the " inimitable G.B.S." ; to me he was, and is, the " indispensable." What shall we do when there is no one gaily and truculently to blow the gaff !

Of course to some extent I was a fish out of water in such company—or rather not out of water, for I was always easy and interested, but a fish in a strange tank. When I used to lunch with the Webbs, the talk took for granted much knowledge I did not possess. References by means of initials often bewildered me. I remember once inquiring what " the L.G.B." was, and the note in Webb's voice when he replied—I will not call it either impatience or contempt, which were absent from his conversation—nevertheless fixed for ever the information in my memory.

Do you recall a week-end at Beachy Head, shortly before the paper started, to which the Webbs had invited its future staff? Squire, the literary editor, whom I already knew well from working with him on the *New Witness*, was there, and Robert Lynd, whom I then met for the first time, and others. What has remained with me are the two scraps of conversation. H. G. Wells, as we were all aware, had guyed the Webbs in *The New Machiavelli*, and he had recently published another novel. I remember Beatrice Webb saying cheerfully, " I'm in it ; I'm the woman whose voice is described as ' a strangulated contralto,' but *you* are not, Sidney." " Oh yes, I am," said Webb, speaking from a sofa on which his legs and feet looked absurdly small in comparison with his broad brow and head, " Oh yes, I am, I'm described as one of those supplementary males often found among the lower crustacea." This smiling serenity made me feel that I was in high and good company.

Late that evening Bernard Shaw arrived, and I remember his remarking, à propos of his mother's funeral, on the soundness of the military instinct regarding such ceremonies ; on the way to the grave one wanted solemn music, on the way back, a rousing march. But divining that I was slightly startled by this detachment, he turned to me and—with a casualness which made a deeper impression—added " You mustn't think I'm a person who forgets people." I instantly knew that to be true. What had interested me was not the apparent heartlessness of such a comment, but the light it threw on Shaw the artist—on that extraordinarily objective attitude towards emotions which is the source of the penetration in his plays, and, in spite of his tolerant sympathy with such a variety of types, of their imaginative limitations.

These memories strike me as throwing light on the *New Statesman* during its early years—its high dry detachment from personal and (above all) from self-delighting emotions, which if bracing was certainly austere. I was to feel on occasions an inclination to apostrophise my paper, " Come down O Maid from yonder mountain height." The *New Statesman* invariably emphasized the least gratifying reasons it could for any generous policy. In this respect it contrasted with its rival, the *Nation*, now happily united to it in holy wedlock. Both papers often moved in the same direction, but while the *Nation* supplied arguments which encouraged its readers to feel that they were the salt of the earth, the tone of the *Statesman* in arguing the same point would be, " If you want to escape being a short-sighted fool, this is the line you must take." This austerity was as marked in your own admirable articles—taut arguments released with a whizz like a steel spring, as it was in the atmosphere you created in the office. We were never permitted to forget that whatever our own work might be doing for the paper, it was nothing compared with what the paper was doing for *us*. This was salutary for writers like Squire, Lynd and myself whose contributions were signed. We were never encouraged to think ourselves indispensable ; a persuasion to which journalists of our type are too prone. True, this made the atmosphere sometimes a trifle wintry, and Jack Squire, Robert Lynd and I used occasionally to give each other little warm shower-baths of praise—as a relief. At the same time we felt complete confidence in our editor's loyalty, while every week in your and in C. M. Lloyd's anonymous articles we had before our eyes an example of the possibility of keeping apart satisfaction in doing one's best and the desire to get credit for it—a dicotomy upon which civilization itself depends.

Looking back I see that you possessed in an extraordinary degree two of the rarest editorial qualities : Creativeness (the power of blending a whole paper into a publication of homogeneous character) and Decision. The *New Statesman* never waited for the cat to jump, but sprang to its own conclusions. After I became Literary Editor in 1920, this business of maintaining a pervasive tone sometimes led to differences between us, when I would be often exasperatingly elusive and you would be often very rude. Seated opposite each other at the make-up hour, you would glare and I would despair—but not reform. You wanted the literary side of the paper to be readable from beginning to end. I did not care if there were items in it which the average intelligent educated person would skip, provided most of the paper appealed to him. It seemed to me, in the long run, better for our prestige that a good author should say " Of course, all the reviews have been piffle—except perhaps one in the *New Statesman* which showed that the man knew what my book was about," than that the A.I.R. (the Average Intelligent Reader) should be deluded on every page into supposing himself interested in, and instructed in, subjects about which he would really remain for ever as ignorant and indifferent as an owl. Again, you were all for a firm macada-mized surface, while I liked it to be broken by those wild green sprouts of folly which are apt to appear when writers care about their work. I didn't mind (or even notice) a little bad grammar, especially when it seemed due to a quiver of sensibility, and to call Housman " Professor " in one sentence and " Mr." in the next, did not, if I observed it, seem to me to matter. But to you these were *blots*, symptoms, too, of a confounded inefficiency which I am afraid I exhibited in other departments of my work. Still, we always had in common a strong dislike of brilliant pretentious nonsense, and a well-concealed respect for each other which made our collaboration interesting. Besides this tug between us was, I believe, good for the paper. If it had not been for you, the literary side would have been slovenly ; if I had not been—well, what I was, readers of that part of the paper might have sometimes hardly known whether they were reading a current issue or one a month old. But as it was, our combination sometimes resulted in a paper which, from the first note to the last shorter notice, was more remarkable than any item in it, and that might be saying a lot.

I have met few men who could do their work as well as you without being praised for it, who were yet genuinely pleased whenever its value was recognized. I hope that this Dedication—the only practical tribute I can pay your gifts as a journalist and an editor, will at least bring you pleasure. —Yours always,

DESMOND MACCARTHY.

CONTENTS

CONTENTS

CONTENTS

OF HUMAN NATURE

THE ESSAYS OF MONTAIGNE

THE sleepless are often advised to court drowsi-
ness by giving their minds to some monotonous occupation, such as counting imaginary
sheep jumping a hedge-gap or staring at a visionary
sheet of brown paper. I doubt if these expedients
deserve their repute as sedatives ; they are too
boring to compete with random thoughts and
recollections. Rather let one who lies awake with
the stale ache of some anxiety at heart, or with
a blunder rankling in his memory (for anger and
remorse there is no poppy or mandragora), picture
to himself a scene from the life of somebody, real
or imaginary, with whom he is familiar. Let it be
the picture of an existence interestingly—that
is the point—interestingly safe. It matters not
of what kind the interest is ; it may be trivial :
Sherlock Holmes and Watson travelling down together (first class) on a cold, early morning to the
scene of some mystery, " Holmes's tall spare
figure looking even taller in his long ulster " ; or
David Copperfield safe at last with Miss Trotwood
at Dover. Any scene will serve, from Mr. Wood-
house, surrounded by everyone he is used to,
saying, " Let us all take a little gruel together,"
to men carousing in the belly of a fort, provided
only that it inspires a peculiar sensation of security.
Everyone who mountains mole-hills in the dark
should have many of these imaginative anodynes,
for fancy exhausts each in turn, and new ones
must be found. Let me not therefore be suspected
of paying a dubious compliment if I mention

3

first among the merits of this book the fine sedative virtue it exhales.

Montaigne in his tower library, across the threshold of which no cares or obligations in material form of bailiff, wife or visitor were allowed to pass ; Montaigne surrounded by his books, amulets against the more insidious approach of trouble, seems to the imagination as satisfyingly safe as ever Crusoe was behind his palisade, when once he had drawn his ladder up. And this art of life which Montaigne so genially, so casually, so persistently explains, never with the gestures of a preacher, but taking you by the arm like a friend and telling you candidly where it has profited himself—how like it often is to the shifts of one addressing himself to sleep, gently disengaging the clutch or worry from his soul !

Imagine him, then, in his tower among his books, looking out with tranquillity upon a distant angry world, reading just as the fancy takes him, making a *fagotage* of human extravagances, preparing with a lazy leisure *une fricassée que je barbouille*, choosing with care, but not with moroseness, the words which fit the thing, revelling sometimes in the coquetries of language—even to the point of committing to paper " certaine verbal wily-beguilies whereat I shake my ears "—yet feeling, happy man ! that after all, writing is not his business : *"Mon métier et mon art, c'est vivre."*

He was confident that his philosophy was important, yet that he need not proselytize ; there were " meddlers enough already." He was aware, perhaps, that those very means of convincing others which his temperament suggested were in the end more effective than to roar, thump, blaze as a prophet, " lighting such a candle as would never be put out." It is probably a more effective way of combating intolerance in others

4

to insinuate into their minds a *Que sais-je?* than to thunder for the liberty of thought. Once instil into men that misgiving, and they too will come to think that " after all it is setting too high a value upon our conjectures to have a man roasted alive for them." They may stick to those conjectures, but the sceptical humanist will have attained his end.

This famous " scepticism " of Montaigne— what does it come to ? We have perhaps read him too often with the eyes of Pascal, who took Montaigne's doubts far harder than Montaigne himself, and used them as a vaulting-block to faith. You must first doubt, Pascal insists, passion- ately, persistently, universally, or you can never believe ; then, *humiliez-vous, raison impuissante, taisez-vous, nature imbécile, et entendez de votre Mâitre votre condition véritable que vous ignorez : écoutez Dieu.* Was Montaigne a sceptic ? He who takes for his motto " I doubt," but is by no means sure of that, is not a sceptic in Pascal's sense. Such a man will take probability as his guide, and doubt will not be an uneasy pillow for his head. Montaigne had neither the passion nor the curiosity of a philosopher, but the interests of a moralist and an historian. He was an observer and a painter of human nature. He lived in times of ferocious duplicity, massacre and religious war ; cruelty and self-deceived pre- sumption were the qualities he most detested. Ah, if he could only soften and modify " the temerity of propositions," responsible, on both sides, for so much hatred and ambition ! . . . He had the gift of natural candour, and we are still under its spell. His mind was also open to every quality in others. To one who declared that he had " often heard fools say things far from foolish," it was natural that pedantry and conscious superiority should seem to be regrettable barriers between

5

human beings. He rejoiced to think that, under
the solvent of a little doubt, even moral standards
might lose something of their finality and dividing
power.

We must think of him as the friendliest of
men. "*Je m'aime trop*" he admits, but he had the
right to boast himself a perfect friend. He lived
for this intimate and natural converse with others.
It is not therefore surprising that he discovered
the literary form which approximates to that
converse—the Essay. He was a paragon of friendship. Separated from his friend by death, he
tries to discover why they have been so dear to
each other, and after describing Étienne de La
Boétie in a manner which should lay for ever the
suspicion that he was blind to goodness, he can
find only the lover's answer, " Because it was I,
because it was He."

Yet Montaigne was an " egoist " ; indeed, the
word was invented by the Port-Royalists to describe
him. To most people, since they too are egoists,
this should be a comforting thought. " The
greatest thing in the world," he wrote, " is for
a man to belong to himself . . . this he cannot
achieve if he is not to some extent others' also,
but it is a bad, unnatural course to lose health
and gaiety of life in others' service." Here we
have got very far away from the Christian virtue
of charity, and there is no sign that Montaigne
found any place for that in the scheme of things.
Though he could say " crawling on the face of
the earth, I cease not to mark in the clouds the
inimitable height of some heroic souls," he dis-
trusted heroic aspiration in ordinary men. For
them he recommended rather a certain easy way
of taking things as more likely to make life better
for themselves and others. He was quite sure
such a way of living suited him. " I love a gay

6

and civil philosophy. There is nothing more
cheerful than wisdom ; I had like to say, more
wanton." We must, in short, live among the
living, and let the river flow under the bridge
without our care, above all things avoiding fear,
that great disturber of reason. "The thing in
the world I am most afraid of," he adds character-
istically, " is fear."

One critic has compared her impression of
Montaigne's attitude towards life to the sensation
of watching a tiger-tamer " playing with the wild
beast Nature. Fascinated, repelled, she looks
at him, and fascinated, repelled, we look at her
coerced by Montaigne's will." This gives an
altogether false idea of him. He seems rather
to be playing an easy, a perhaps too easy, game—
not a dangerous one. His counsel to us is never
to forget that we have roots in earth, and not
to be afraid. " The prize for which the soul
maketh is not to walk on the heights but to walk
orderly. It practiseth not its greatness in greatness but in mediocrity." Montaigne is so en-
amoured of an ideal within reach of ordinary
sturdy human nature that he is often inclined
to rank it above those heroic virtues he sometimes
wonderingly admired. . . . It is what he understood best himself, for a supernatural view of the
world " made too many things compulsory and
momentous for his inclination." Of romanticism,
of mystical self-reliance and faith in will and
action, he had not a touch. He was an Epicurean
at bottom, though, unlike Epicurus, he did not
turn away from life but faced it stoically. His
relish of it was robust and constant, and he had
an exquisite sense of human relations.

His first essays are commonplace-books in
which he copied down any passages which struck
him as he lazily read, also his reflections upon

7

them. But as time went on these essays began to fulfil more and more completely an avowed intention, that of drawing an impartial portrait of himself. Such an occupation served him in two ways. In studying himself minutely he drew for us a diagram of the human species, and by dwelling curiously upon each experience he made his own life more rich. Thus we learn to know human nature better through knowing him so well, and if we can acquire his habit of self-investigation we too can enrich our lives.

No man ever pervaded more completely his own book. He is there on every page before your eyes. You can watch him ; now he smiles, now he shrugs his shoulders ; now you are listening to the elaborate elocution of a man of letters, now to the racy accents of a rustic Gascon nobleman.

One word of advice to those who read Montaigne's Essays for the first time. Read the book as they were written, by snatches. There are some writers whom you must read consecutively in order to get their full flavour. Montaigne can be read by fits and starts. Once you have made his acquaintance, his book will always open at the right page ; but since it is in the later essays he paints himself most clearly, turn first to them.

GOOD TALK

I

FRIENDS of mine in the country have sometimes been romantic enough to say they envy,
so they tell me, the life I lead in London—what
they are pleased to call "being in the heart of
things "; and I notice that what they have most
often in mind are social opportunities, chances
of meeting people whose fame makes them loom
gigantic at a distance. They imagine that these
encounters, acquaintances, friendships, constantly
afford me the privilege of hearing wonderfully good
talk. Well, I have met, I do meet, many remarkable people, and, occasionally, I do hear good
talk—these things I reckon among my blessings ;
but they are quite mistaken if they suppose that
the occasions on which I meet celebrities are usually
those on which I hear the best talk.

Remarkable men and women often practise
in company an intellectual economy which would
both surprise and disappoint my country friends.
Good talk arises out of happy situations, and social
occasions do not often produce these, even when the
company has been carefully selected with that
hope. In the first place, people seldom meet
each other at dinners and in drawing-rooms in
moods sincere enough to stimulate the mind ;
and, then, topics change too quickly for anyone
to become really interested in them. People
are so haunted by the fear of being bored—or of
becoming bores themselves, which is worse—that

9

EXPERIENCE

the talk flitter-flutters about too restlessly. The
man or woman who shines most is the one who
can say quickest something passably amusing
and pointful about anything.

I have just read the last literary success.
Rather rash ; it would have been safer to postpone it for another three months. Think of
the immunity I have enjoyed hitherto ! Everybody
has been reading it, and if I have been asked
once I have been asked a hundred times, " What
do you think of it ? " Hitherto I have been able
to turn, " with the most civil triumph in the world,"
on my interlocutor, and reply truthfully that I
have not read it yet. Now, however, I think I am
fairly safe ; several months have passed since the
book's publication, and it is more likely that the
same question will be put now about Mr. Aldous
Huxley's new novel ; and in half a year's time I
shall be able to read that also with impunity.

Of course I understand people wanting to
know what others think about the books they have
read ; I often want to myself, but this zest for
collecting bare statements of opinion from miscellaneous people puzzles me. " Oh, I thought
it *very* good," " Don't you think it is *rather* over-
rated ? " " I enjoyed it *immensely*," " I was a
little disappointed "—such comments do not seem
worth collecting. They may express what was
felt in each case, but they get one no further.
The only possible reply is " O . . . " What people
seem to want from you is a neat little pellet of
an opinion which can be flipped across a table,
amusing if possible and repeatable. But *I* like
the company of people who go hacking on at the
same subject, even if that is only how to get a lawn
in good order. If they go on long enough the
subject is usually illuminated, but I notice that
most people begin to get bored just when I am

10

becoming interested. I suspect I was born a bore myself; I prefer so distinctly the persistent to the hop-skip talker. I should very much like to hear two or three people discuss some new book of importance. Though I have heard such a topic mentioned and dismissed hundreds of times, I have seldom heard such a discussion in society. After A. has said he thinks it remarkable, B. has said she enjoyed it enormously, C. has said he thinks it much over-rated, A. has gone on to say that he thinks future generations will take no interest in Shaw's plays, B. that she detested *Lady into Fox*, C. that he has been trying to re-read Henry James : I don't call that literary conversation. It is not conversation at all. I seek two solid, long-winded, labyrinthine-minded, pertinacious bores, with whom to discuss a book, and who, when started on a subject, cannot let it alone.

II

The discreet bow-window in Ebury Street had not arrested my steps as I passed it, although I had *Conversations in Ebury Street* under my arm, and what should have been more delightful than to discuss the book with Mr. George Moore himself ? Yet I passed by. In the Mall I stopped and thought of returning, but felt again an inhibiting premonition. Of what ? I will amuse myself, I said, in Mr. Moore's own manner, and reflect very slowly and carefully upon this strange reluctance. Strange it was, for could I not have told him that I had enjoyed many charming moments of literary pleasure while reading his book ? Besides, had I been obliged to add that the criticism in *Conversations* had fallen far below the interest of the criticism in *Avowals*, was not Mr. Moore the one author of my acquaintance who really

11

could discuss with literary detachment what he had just written? In the course of colloquies, held in that very room, but colloquies certainly less urbane and Landorian than those recorded in the book, how often I have been struck by this surprising suspension of vanity in him just at the very point where men much less vain invariably grow touchy. No craftsman ever forgot himself more completely in his work. Issuing late at night into Ebury Street I had often said to myself: " Now I know where to go when I want to be reminded that the art of writing is important."

I had an excellent excuse, too, for calling, for I appeared in *Conversations in Ebury Street* myself, though only, I am sorry to say, as the most negligible and futile of those interlocutors who attempted to put in a good word for the work of Thomas Hardy. Still, it was an excuse, and I wanted, too, to lodge a gentle protest at being made to say in the book that Landor's *Pericles and Aspasia* was the noblest work in the English language. And yet I had passed by! Why? Alas! I could not, in his own manner, luxuriously delay coming to a conclusion. No sooner had I asked myself the question than pat the answer came: " Yes, he *is*, sublimely, detached from his own stories, but what a bate he gets into over his estimates of other writers." There's the rub; I shall have to listen to conclusions to which I cannot assent, while my respect for the artist will withhold me from the relief of shouting, " Bosh!"

In the book I had just been reading Mr. Moore, Mr. de la Mare, and Mr. Freeman are discussing what is the test of pure poetry, and Mr. Moore suggests that they should compile an anthology. What is his criterion? That a true poem is something which a poet creates outside his own personality. Ignoring the vagueness of such a test,

12

for whatever a man creates is coloured by his personality, it is clear that Mr. Moore means that subjective poetry is not " true poetry," because Mr. de la Mare next observes that " many of the most beautiful poems in the language would have to be barred—Shelley's *Lines Written in Dejection in the Bay of Naples*, for instance." But it is when Mr. Moore turns to explaining where he will discover, and where he will not discover, examples of true poetry, that his reader—and if the reader, how much more his listener!—will find himself thrown into a state of incredulous dismay. " Milton does not abound in objective poetry, Pope still less, but we shall find several poems that come within our definition in the *Songs of Innocence*, none, I am afraid, in the *Songs of Experience*." Imagine a respectful visitor, many years his junior like myself, being left with a statement like that on his hands! Milton a subjective poet! who with the exception of few brief restrained references to his own feelings as a blind and lonely man, is the most objective poet in English literature, unless you range beside him—could my ears have deceived me just now ?—Pope or Dryden.

Mr. Freeman is then made to remark : " We shall find very little in Keats," and Mr. de la Mare to add : " I doubt if we shall find anything " (I suspect this attribution) ; while Mr. Moore continues : " Keats never attracted me . . . I think of him too frequently as a pussy-cat on a sunny lawn." Imagine your feelings if a venerable writer, for whom you felt an admiration which prevented you from being visited by the humour of Ham, told you that what strikes him most about Keats is a resemblance to a curled and comfortable cat !

What is the explanation ? The reader will find it in the confession, recurring in Mr. Moore's later personal works, that he has lost the power of reading. I doubt if he ever possessed it. On page 175 you will find a reference to a certain Augustus. We are given only one remark of his, but, as in the case of the one recorded utterance of Juliet's nurse's husband, it makes us wish to know more of Augustus. Whenever Mr. Moore used to expound a general idea, Augustus, after listening to him, invariably asked : " What about the poor chap in the café ? "—for it was his joke to assume that Mr. Moore was entirely café-educated. Substitute conversation-educated, and there is much point in the joke of Augustus. Now education by conversation leaves a good many gaps. Nothing is more characteristic of Mr. Moore than his discovering the Bible and *The Sentimental Journey* when he was past sixty, and his amazement at the density of a world which had not drawn his attention to their merits. He has an independent, whimsical, creative mind, and the truth is he has always read to stimulate his own talent. The writer who helps him most at the moment is consequently exalted above all others. At one time it was Landor ; some years back it was Flaubert. This is, of course, not only legitimate but wise in a creative writer, but it is not a proceeding which trains the critic, who must yield himself to an author, and not follow his own fancies across the page, or hunt for corroborations of his own literary methods in a book. Mr. Moore laughs at me for being anxious about his literary education, and for writing " a long, pathetic letter," urging the merits of Thomas Hardy. I am sure the pathos was not misplaced. He changes his view of authors when his own work takes a new direction. He once dismissed Stevenson as merely the smartest young literary buck in the Burlington Arcade ; now he speaks of his " radiant page," for Mr.

Moore happens to be now more interested than he was in the craft of constructing sentences. He has read Thomas Hardy in the spirit in which he read Newman, when he read Newman in order to discover that no Catholic could write. Of course Newman is a good writer. But Mr. Moore discovered some weak sentences in the *Apologia* and cried : " There you are ! " The results of this method are naturally surprising. I might apply it with the same results to Mr. Moore himself, to Pater, to Landor. I recollect an unfortunate sentence or two in " The Confessions of a Young Man "—one comes back to me, about a piano leaning its melodious mouth towards a lady. Pater was not happy when he described Marius as being " always as fresh as the flowers he wore," a phrase more suitable to a society paragraphist ; Landor's monumental skittishness is often utterly unworthy of him. Mr. Moore, is, of course, absolutely without literary snobbishness. In this book he draws attention to a delicious passage in *Agnes Gray* where one vulgar little girl appeals to her sister to bear her out that she looked beautiful at the ball. " Middling," replies the younger. We are grateful to Mr. Moore for pointing out the delightful quality of that bit of dialogue, but when he goes on to declare that *Wuthering Heights* is poor compared to the novels of Anne Brontë, gratitude is not what we feel.

III

I am exceedingly fond of controversy, not as a participant, but as a spectator. Indeed, I have never taken part in a dispute which was long enough to be called a controversy. My own exploits in that direction have never amounted to more than a brief blow, parry, and counter-blow, but I have watched others at the game ; I imagine that I have learnt something about the noble art of self-defence. One's method should vary with the strength of one's case and the character of one's opponent ; that is the basic principle. For instance, suppose you have an unanswerable point to make, and this point, though it does not cover the whole of your case, is the most central one in the controversy, the character and gifts of your adversary should make you decide whether it is wiser to confine yourself to that single point, or whether you had better go for him all round and try to finish him up completely. (I am taking for granted that on all other points except the central one you have not such an immediately convincing case.) It will also depend upon his character and gifts how far it will be prudent to attempt to show that he is a coxcomb, an idiot, an ignoramus or an ignominious person. It is unsafe to stray beyond your best point when you are dealing with an adversary of great mental agility. He will meet your weaker points, and pass over, as comparatively unimportant, your vital contention. He may indeed succeed in answering your minor arguments so well that the world at large will get the impression that the fight was drawn on " points," when in reality he ought to have been counted out.

I know it requires great self-control not to caper about triumphantly after you have delivered a knockdown blow. Yet the more exuberantly triumphant your war dance round the prostrate body, the more likely are you to lay yourself open to a counter-blow, and the more delighted the spectators will be at seeing the tables then turned against you. And if you kick him when he is down, then, if he is a wily controversialist, he will instantly revive ; his spirits will rise, and his wit, if he has any, will be displayed to the delight of all beholders. If, on the other hand, you have a weak case, you cannot do better than to lead off by being insulting. This may make your adversary lose his hair, and, forgetting he has the best case, he will perhaps turn the argument into a scrap in which you may be able to hold your own. But, if you have the best case, it is folly to let him stray away from that case into personalities.

IV

In a book on spectres by Le Loyer, written in 1586, I came on the following passage :

" Of all the common and familiar subjects of conversation that are entered upon in company, of things remote from nature and cut off from the senses, there is none so ready to hand, none so usual as that of visions of spirits, and whether what is said of them is true. It is the topic that people most readily discuss and on which they linger the longest because of the abundance of examples, the subject being fine and pleasing and the discussion the least tedious that can be found."

The same might be said of conversation to-day, only perhaps all would not agree that such conversations are " the least tedious." If not tedious, they are at any rate sometimes embarrassing ; one is left with such startling statements on one's hands. Still more inexplicable than the spiritualistic wonders retold every day, is the way in which people take them. One dines out ; one sits next a lady whose aunt has seen a table levitate to the ceiling, and a medium walk out of one top-storey window and in at another. The lady herself has been to a necromancer in Bond Street, who has told her things about herself which he could not

17   C

possibly have known by natural means, and others about her future which she is convinced will come true.

This starts off a man at the other side of the table telling, with impressive reserve, a story about a friend to whom a little grey woman appeared one night warning him that he must never leave the country—his friend thought nothing of it, but he went down in the *Titanic*. One then asks the lady if she has sat with her aunt's medium, and discovers that she not only has not done so, but does not even know his name. Fancy having had within grasp the chance of seeing a man walk on air and not seizing it ! What is flabbergasting is the casual way in which people take experiences which ought to shatter that whole framework of reason to which we trust whenever we turn to the right to go out of a door on the right. If one evening a necromancer drew the moon out of the sky for me, and it turned out to be a flat silver platter about the size of an offertory-plate— this would not be a whit more disconcerting than seeing a man walking upon air—I should be beside myself until I had assimilated the occurrence to my general conceptions of the world. What makes me suspect that people really do exaggerate a little when they report marvels (it is so hard to astonish !) is not the apparent frequency of such events, but the comparative scarcity of gibbering sceptics.

V

I don't think the social atmosphere was always as unfavourable to good talk as it is at present. People used to be more patient ; dread of the monologue or of prolonged discussion was not so intense ; the ban upon the longer story was less severe. I can hardly doubt that some of the famous talkers of the past like Coleridge, Carlyle or Oscar Wilde, would still dominate their company ; but I am less certain that they would be so much admired and encouraged.

The fame of talkers, alas, is as unsubstantial as the fame of actors. The recorded scraps of old discourse give us little sense of the brilliance of conversation in the past—as little as the specimens which travellers bring home suggest the fertility and wonder of distant lands.

The tradition of Coleridge's amazing and unique powers of discourse is part of the history of English Literature. His talk has been described by many contemporaries. Carlyle's description, too well known to quote, in the *Life of Sterling*, is the most famous. But we must remember that this is a description of his talk in Highgate days, when a preaching tone had crept into his voice, and he was less inspired and more diffuse than when in his youth he astounded Hazlitt and De Quincey. In youth and middle-age talk had been his refuge from disappointment, bewilderment, and shame. In the glow of it, in the wonder he excited, he could forget that he was a gigantic failure (how absurd this verdict sounds now !) in his own eyes, and in those of all who loved him. But under the care of the good Gillmans he had become more or less reconciled to his own nature, while his allowance of opium had been restricted to an amount which gave exhilaration and relief, but did not incapacitate. A modern critic is right when he says " he had been so ecstatic a talker because he was in flight from a fiend, and when the fiend ceased to pursue him he tended to lapse into a sententious amble."

Carlyle, when he visited Highgate, had too many undelivered lay sermons in him to find satisfaction as a passive bucket to be pumped

19

into. But though he did not admire, he wondered at " those sunny domes, those caves of ice " which Coleridge built in air. " Glorious islets, too," he says, " I have seen rise out of the haze ; but they were few and soon swallowed in the general element again. Balmy, sunny islets, islets of the blest and intelligible."

There is a half-forgotten, anonymous little book called *Conversations at Cambridge*. The author was an old school-fellow of Coleridge, C. V. Le Grice, who is mentioned by Lamb in that essay on Christ's Hospital which contains a much more sympathetic description than Carlyle's of Coleridge's extraordinary gift. In the summer of 1833, a year before his death, Coleridge paid a visit to Cambridge. In 1793, distracted by debt and love, he had run away from Cambridge and enlisted in a dragoon regiment. " My emotions," he wrote, " on revisiting the University on this occasion were at first overwhelming. I could not speak for an hour ; yet my feelings were, upon the whole, pleasurable and I have not passed, of late years at least, three days of such great enjoyment and healthful excitement of mind and body." He was put up in Trinity. He did not rise till the afternoon, when he held a crowded levee, and he seems to have talked all night.

It is this talk which Le Grice endeavours to recapture. Unlike Carlyle, he cannot imagine anyone wishing " to punctuate by a single question that rich musical discourse." Although he took notes while the poet's voice was still in his ears, it is seldom we can hear that voice. Sometimes, however, we do : " How the heart opens at the magic name of Milton ! Yet who shall, in our day, hang another garland on his tomb ! " I fancy that is verbatim. It has Coleridge's soaring effectiveness. But when the reporter goes on, recording the excellent criticism which follows, the words have no longer a spoken quality, only a stately tameness. It is almost in every case only in the exordium we hear the living voice : " And why should I not call Taylor a poet ? Is not ' Holy Living and Dying ' a sacred and didactic poem in almost as wide a sense as the ' Commedia ' of Dante ? What bard of ancient and modern times has surpassed, in richness of language, in fertility of fancy, in majesty of sentiment, in grace of imagery, this Spenser of English prose ? "

The great crystal has begun to swing. He divagates ; he quotes, at a length which attests the possession of an astonishing memory, prose passages equal to " the sublimest poetry," adding : " How pleasant it would be to go on thus, if my memory would enable me, gathering choice specimens of sublimity, pathos, and picturesque truth ; collecting the precious stones of which his charms are strung ; for even his ornaments are never chosen for their lustre alone ; and in the most gorgeous festivals and riotous enjoyments of his imagination, a Hand is perceived writing on the wall. Never did a soldier of the Holy Cross issue forth in a more gorgeous equipment to fight for the Sepulchre of Christ. But the resplendent sword is of celestial temper, and that costly armour was mighty against the dart of the enemy as any coat of mail ; it protected while it shone." You must imagine the face of the speaker, rapt, radiant, moist— his eyes " sending out great signals." " I am glad," wrote that matter-of-fact Miss Martineau, " to have seen his weird face and heard his dreamy voice ; and my notion of possession, prophecy—of involuntary speech for involuntary brain-action has been clearer ever since." Thus Coleridge talked. To talk like that now would be like singing at dinner.

21

VI

Carlyle's talk, though utterly different from
that of Coleridge, must have been as remarkable.
He, too, was an oratorical talker, but he excelled
particularly in vehement denunciation, in fantastic
and vivid bluster. There were sardonic surprises
in it. I heard George Meredith imitate him once ;
it was a *crescendo* of picturesque curses which ended
in a shout of laughter, laughter which subsided
gradually into a wistful stillness, while Carlyle
would slowly rub his hands up and down his shins
and sigh, " Ah, weel, ah, weel." His chief
intellectual fault as a talker seems to have been
that, according to him, no one could be actively
interested in the progress of the species without
being off his balance and in need of tenderness
from his friends. He would speak of himself as
though he were all his life compelled to the dismal
necessity of ransacking the graves of the dead
in order to find some poor spangle, still untarnished,
of nobility in human nature. This must have been
tiresome in the long run. " You wondered at
last," Henry James, Senior, said of him, " how any
mere mortal got legitimately endowed with a com-
miseration so divine for the inferior race of man."
There was clearly more of the play-actor in his
talk than there was in Coleridge's. But what
a splendid performance it must have been ! And
how amusing ! What gibes he flung about him ;
now at the Quaker orator, Bright—" pugnacious,
cock-nosed John " ; now at Ruskin—" a beautiful
bottle of soda water " ; now at Mill, the Saint
of Rationalism—" saw-dust up to the mast-head."
A humorist, you see, in the guise of a Jeremiah !
There were often stirring scenes in the little sitting-
room in Cheyne Row ; perhaps a merciless mellay

if a belligerent with sturdy opinions of his own dropped in. At the bare mention of certain topics Mrs. Carlyle would nudge a sympathetic neighbour and whisper in dread, " Now for the deluge." Down sure enough it would come, hot and heavy, for an hour or more. But nothing exasperated Carlyle so much as the reverential readers who offered devout and grateful homage. Such adorers reminded him too intimately of the essentially histrionic and humoristic nature of his genius beneath its apocalyptic cloak : their simplicity was an insult. They were intolerable bores ; and, as a lighthouse-keeper finds lying after a storm, upon the platform round the lamp, birds which have dashed themselves against it, so, he used to say, did he expect to find every morning the bodies of several dead Americans on his doorstep. Even if his fame as a talker had not survived, even if his spoken phrases were not still flying from mouth to mouth, from his style alone, from its vehemence and its vividness, posterity would have guessed that Carlyle must have been a glorious converser. His talk must have been inferior only to his best prose.

VII

With regard to Wilde's talk, tradition is unanimous : it was more surprising than his writing. I have often interrogated those who heard him. Wilfred Blunt and Max Beerbohm both told me that, in their experience of talkers it was a case of " Oscar " first and the rest nowhere. The variety of his range, too, was astonishing. He excelled in nonsense, in repartee, in description, in narration, in sentiment ; and he excelled too in that general kind of talk, ranging over biography and history, in which for the most part men like Lord Morley, with well-stored minds and with experience in affairs, are easily first. Wilde was also an exceedingly amiable talker, uncompetitive, and immensely appreciative of other people's contributions. That remarkable biography, *The Life of Oscar Wilde*, by Frank Harris, is full of convincing records of his talk. You will find in a little book by Laurence Housman, *Echo de Paris, A Study from Life*, an account of a restaurant conversation which took place after Wilde's release from prison. Twenty-four years is a long time to carry talk in one's head, even Oscar Wilde's ; but it can be done, and probably Mr. Housman took notes at the time. The prelude to the luncheon is characteristic. Oscar Wilde is a little late ; he enters with deliberate ironical reference to his imprisonment. " But what are two minutes in three years of a disintegrated lifetime ? It is almost three years, is it not, since we missed seeing each other ? " There is a slightly uncomfortable pause, when, as it were a minstrel throwing back his cloak to pluck a few chords upon his instrument, the famous talker begins. What he says is not in substance very remarkable. It is the grace, finish, and flexibility of the performance that delights. The suggestion which he makes that Carlyle lost his chance of producing a permanent work of art greater than his *French Revolution* by choosing Frederick the Great instead of Napoleon is interesting ; also the suggestion that Carlyle did so because he worshipped success : " I have come to see that St. Helena is, for a world which follows Cæsar and not Christ, the greatest place on earth next to Calvary." Then the significance of failure (he is thinking of himself) becomes the main theme of his discourse ; but the charm and, I am sure, the verisimilitude lie in the skill with which the talker keeps modulating into a lighter key and out of it again, backwards and forwards. I feel sure

24

that it was this faculty which made Oscar Wilde's conversation such an astonishing performance. I know no living talkers who equal this, or who seem to take conversation seriously as an art. Good talkers nowadays are proud of taking no trouble. It is the fashion of sincerity.

The two talkers I have known in recent times whose sentences would probably read best if written down are Bernard Shaw and Sir Edmund Gosse. The only talker I have heard who in conversation will launch the high poetic phrase is Yeats. He will say that " the music of Heaven is full of the clashing of swords " without seeming conscious that others might conclude that he was talking for effect. I like that myself. And even if he were talking for effect, I should, for my part, only be the more grateful for a fine ambitious phrase. When I meet remarkable people whose company is coveted, I often wish that they would show off a little more.

CASTLES IN THE AIR

I

SINCE I mean to write upon Day-dreams, let me begin by indulging in one : I am ordained, and about to preach my first sermon. Of course it is most important that I should prove myself to my new flock a physician of souls, and no ordinary one. As I shake out the folds of my surplice, all eyes are fixed upon the interesting young preacher. What is my text ? I will not choose one which will offer an excuse for lashing poor humanity where the strokes of moralists have fallen so frequently that the place has become hard and cicatrized ; that will not serve the purpose. No, to establish my power I must discover a disquieting intimacy with weaknesses so shamefully silly that they are rarely spoken of, even among friends. I catch beneath the brims of glamorous hats earnest glances, in which curiosity and reverence are delightfully mingled. Ah ! young women, you will wince first, but before I have done, yonder grave church-warden, whose mind, to judge from his deportment, never strays from the matter in hand, whether practical or holy—he too, and others like him, shall feel my probe. My text is already given out : " Behold, this dreamer cometh."

Alas, the sermon itself is too long to report in these pages. Besides, I am not in Holy Orders, only a critic who must choose his text from secular books.

26

As a reader of novels, I have often been struck by the fact that modern novelists, even those who set out to display the secrets of the recesses in human nature, never seem to be aware of the extent to which men and women, sensible matter-of-fact men and women, indulge themselves in building castles-in-the-air—castles of such absurd, fantastically-improbable architecture that the Prince Regent's pavilion at Brighton is a sensible edifice compared with these. It is the commonest form of dram-drinking. And yet, if we were to believe these novelists, who pretend to hold up a glass to human nature, we should be persuaded that men's and women's thoughts and emotions habitually spring from rational expectations and actual events. Nothing of the kind. The average human being's imagination is employed almost perpetually in feeding a preposterous vanity upon food which, though airy and insubstantial, has apparently a certain nourishing quality. His or her interests and rational ambitions are only attended to in the interstices of a long wool-gathering process. When anything disagreeable occurs, if the remedy does not lie to hand, they proceed to nestle down in a little warm nest of dreams. The hygienic property of work and of society lies almost entirely in their being pre-ventatives of day-dreaming, for this habit, if it gets strong possession, reduces the mind to a condition in which anything that really happens hardly affects it ; to rouse such a person is like churning skimmed milk, you may stir and stir and stir without any result. If introspection fails to convince any reader of the truth of this charge (a wide shot which hits half the world), let him reflect upon these additional facts, which are symptoms of the fantastic prevalence of the castle-in-the-air habit. Think how many a contented

27

failure you have known, who yet, you are sure, has neither stoicism nor romance enough to be one of whom it could be prophesied : *cantabit vacuus.* What is the secret of their placid resignation ? Dreaming.

Look at the type of literature that is really widely and profoundly popular. Are not the novels which run like a prairie fire through continents, and against which the cold douche of criticism is an ineffectual hose—are they not made of the same stuff as castles in the air ? Are they not reflections of those idiotic, egotistic dreams of satisfied vanity, to which their voracious readers are ashamed to confess ? Our fiction is on the average so bad because its writers mistake for the genuine impulse to write, the desire (coupled, of course, with the honest hope of royalties) to fondle their own dreams of how splendid it would be to appear like their hero or heroine in such intensely gratifying circumstances. If by any chance you are snowed-up or rained-up at an inn, with a set of trashy novels as the only possible means of distraction, and you are not in a mood to let your mind flow with the author's current, some amusement may be derived from divining in his book the nature of his day-dreams.

When you meet the crowd stepping westward along the pavements, watch the faces of the solitary people hurrying by. Do not be deceived by portentous, magisterial appearances ; that wheezy old gentleman in a top-hat is really crowned with an all-England cricket-cap, and has hit to the boundary three times running in the most critical test match of the year ; that most improbable person has saved the life of a famous beauty under the most heroic circumstances. Watch his lips, he is talking to her now. That young clerk (England is invaded, her fleet is sunk) has invented a marvellous submarine, and at the last moment, when

CASTLES IN THE AIR

all seemed lost, he has saved his country and blown the enemy into smithereens. He is replying now to his own toast at a great banquet in the Mansion House. That little woman with a prayer-book in her hand, demurely hurrying as the church-bell rings more quickly on the hour of the afternoon service, has reared a still higher-towering aerial edifice. It is the day of the Last Judgment : proceedings are interrupted by a gratifying duologue between her and the Maker of the Universe: her landlady and friends who have neglected her had better take care—her magnanimity will on that day be overwhelming. Dreams, dreams, "we are such stuff as dreams are made on."

II

Of course, I build airy palaces myself, but those fantastic, pinnacled structures soon grow top-heavy, and are apt to crash. It often pleases me instead to day-dream on a modest scale; to build not palaces, but cottages in the air. How delightful it would be, if— that conditional particle is the foundation of day-dreaming—*if* half-a-crown were worth what it was before the war, and *if* my desires were much circumscribed, and *if* my obligations were much restricted, to spend my days in research at the Record Office. The fee for rummaging among old papers used to be (I think I am right) half-a-crown an hour. I like to imagine myself, inconspicuously but neatly dressed, oscillating between the Tudor-esque building in Chancery Lane and a small suburban home. But I stipulate, in addition to these humble earnings, for a modest private income, say a pre-war £300, safely invested. It would ease my mind, too, if my small residence, with one umbrageous tree in the back-garden, could be a freehold. Then—but, perhaps, you do not realize the charms of such an existence ?

29

I will not expatiate upon the blessedness of modest security—read Horace, Pope, Robinson Crusoe ; but upon the romance of my imaginary occupation. Dull and monotonous ? Yes, undoubtedly it would be so, but that is part of its romance. If looking through, deciphering, collating old papers were not a task scaring to the light-minded and trying to the impatient, where then would be the glory of its little triumphs ? I call them little, but they can be catastrophic. They can shake the foundations of history, humble biographers, and scuttle, with a few words, the most proudly-sailing generalizations afloat. When Herbert Spencer once confessed that he had secretly written a tragedy, Huxley immediately cried out, to his amazement, that he knew its theme : " It will be the story of a beautiful theory killed by a horrid ugly little fact." I know a famous art critic whose knowledge of old masters, little and great, is so thorough and minute that his ascription of a picture to such and such an artist is next best to a signature. I do not suppose that he is afraid of contradiction from any connoisseur alive, for his own reasons are, he knows, more likely to be cogent than those of others. But it is a chancy thing, this business of attribution. Though he need fear no other critic clad in shining learning, I think he goes in some fear of those indefatigable searchers and fumblers among old archives who any day may turn up a receipt, a bill, a letter, knocking the bottom out of the best-grounded attribution—and a couple of noughts off the value of a picture.

III

Rasselas is full of discourses and aphorisms which stick in the memory : " He who has nothing

external that can divert him, must find pleasure
in his own thoughts, and must conceive himself
what he is not ; for who is pleased with what he is ?"
—the sage Imlac is speaking, and he goes on to
expatiate on the danger of day-dreams, to which
the solitary are addicted and all men are inclined.
Of the day-dreamer he says :

> " He culls from all imaginable conditions that
> which for the present moment he should most
> desire, amuses his desires with impossible enjoy-
> ments, and confers upon his pride unattainable
> dominion. The mind ... unites all pleasures in all
> combinations, and riots in delights which nature
> and fortune, with all their bounty, cannot bestow.
> In time, some particular train of ideas fixes the
> attention, all other intellectual gratifications are
> rejected, the mind, in weariness or leisure,
> recurs constantly to the favourite conception,
> whenever she is offended with the bitterness of
> truth. By degrees the reign of fancy is confirmed ;
> she grows first imperious, and in time despotik."

At the close of Imlac's discourse the Favourite
resolves that she will no more imagine herself
Queen of Abyssinia, the Princess that she will no
more play the enchanting shepherdess in her
waking dreams, the Prince that he will no longer
construct ideal Utopias with himself as the founder
of them. Of course they never kept these resolutions.

In my day-dream sermon I thought my text,
" Behold, this dreamer cometh," would hit practically every other person, including the most unlikely
people. Was I wrong about this almost universal
addiction to the day-dream habit ? Perhaps there
are grown men and women who never imagine
themselves in circumstances gratifying to vanity,
soothing to care, or satisfying to the heart ? When

I meet exceptionally concentrated, busy, imposing, eminent, successful people—the sort in whom the childishness and wild extravagance of day-dreaming would be utterly incongruous—I should like to ask them how often they indulge in these solitary pleasures, and if their air castles, when they build them, are extraordinarily silly. I strongly suspect the answer would nearly always be, if they told the truth—which they never could—in the affirmative. But it is only a guess. I wish some correspondents who have the knack of asking really intrusive questions would collect a few statistics for me, and thus either corroborate or dispel this suspicion. Dr. Johnson himself, whom from his demeanour and his massive common sense no one would have suspected of such weaknesses, was by his own confession an inveterate day-dreamer. Indeed, he was terrified of this tendency in himself. It is not only in *Rasselas* that he inveighs against it. He often recurs to the subject ; he even valued company and business very largely as safeguards against indulging, perhaps to the point of delusion, this powerful propensity. His moral sense was shocked, too, at the quality of the delights which solitary reverie presented to him.

Samuel Butler told me that he was an inveterate day-dreamer. He used to pull himself up by murmuring, " Oh, Christina, Christina." The character of Christina, Ernest Pontifex's mother, in *The Way of All Flesh* was the first character, I think, to appear in fiction in whom the part that day-dreaming often plays in a life was accurately reflected. Her reveries are winding and long, but here is an inch of one of them :

" And if Ernest got into Parliament—so young too—there was nothing to hinder his being Prime Minister before he died, and if

32

so, of course, he would become a peer. Oh!
why did he not set about it all at once, so that
she might live to hear people call her son " my
Lord "—Lord Battersby she thought would do
very nicely, and if she was well enough to
sit he must certainly have her portrait painted
at full length for one end of his large dining-
hall. It should be exhibited at the Royal
Academy : " Portrait of Lord Battersby's
mother," she said to herself, and her heart
fluttered with all its wonted vivacity."

One of Butler's harshest strokes of irony was
the epitaph he allowed her husband to put on her
grave : " Blessed are the pure in heart, for they
shall see God."

My friend Whynot, with whom I can discuss
almost anything, tells me he has frequently slain,
in imagination, every one to whom he is, and has
been, most attached, simply as a necessary and
logical preliminary to the setting up of some scene,
or to the establishment of some condition of
circumstances, in which it gave him pleasure to
imagine himself playing a part.

"In my youth," he told me, " I used to recover
a sense of what I was doing with a stab of shame,
but long before I became the man you know, I had
ceased to reproach myself beyond the point of calling
myself a damned fool. Sometimes I could descry
a reason for my murders not so discreditable
to my heart. The death-bed was only a condition
of calling up a scene in which I could express the
affection that was in me ; to do myself justice,
it was often I, and not the loved one, whom the
dramatist of my day-dreams decided to place
in extremis. But," he added, raising his voice
almost to a shout, as he always does when owning
up to anything of which he is ashamed, " *but* many

EXPERIENCE

a time the motive has been merely mercenary, or
vanity—the desire to imagine myself the object of
sympathy or admiration." Yet Whynot has not
a bad heart, and he does not strike one as vain.

The cures for day-dreaming may be many ; I
know of three. One is Dr. Johnson's—constant
occupation and company. The second is to secure
a little *real* satisfaction of desire. It may be a petty
achievement, far too small to figure in the carnival
of a day-dream, but the glow it throws dims
glories imagined, as the dullest of dawns a
festal illumination. The third is to go on piling up
fictitious triumphs to such a fantastic height that
they crash from the weight of their own absurdity,
or, in other words, to make yourself rapidly sick
by eating the sweets of imagination by the handful.
Afterwards the tone of your stomach revives, and
your appetite for solid but meagre realities recovers.

SNOBBISHNESS

I

PERHAPS some of my readers also received a copy of the prospectus which I found enclosed in a large envelope of superfine quality on my breakfast table the other morning. The drift of it was unusual. In this document, Mr. Ponde, M.A., of Harley Street, announced that his consulting hours were 10 to 1 and 3 to 5, and that between those hours he was at the service of anyone who wished to consult him about whatever uneasiness they might feel with regard to their social position. " It is not uncommon," the prospectus goes on, " for those whose accomplishments, education, incomes and good sense might be expected to render them immune from such uneasiness, to suffer inter- mittently, or even chronically, from distressing doubts as to their own claims to gentility, especially in the company of people who set store by such distinctions. Their trouble has been, in most cases, much aggravated by reserve, such matters being regarded as too delicate and invidious to be touched upon in conversation. For although the claims of the absent to be lady or gentleman, as the case may be, are often brightly discussed among their friends, the person concerned derives little benefit from these discussions ; on his or her appearance the conversation is too often turned into other channels. On the other hand, free com- munication on the part of the patient of his own sufferings and symptoms—the open-mind cure—wide experience has convinced Mr. Ponde to be the first step towards healthy recovery. He therefore holds himself prepared to examine into and advise all upon such cases between the hours mentioned above. The strictest confidence is, of course, guaranteed."

Enclosed were a number of testimonials announcing complete recovery from fear of flunkeys, unintentional condescension, unwilling humility, chronic oblivion of unsuccessful relations, and cases of the most virulent compound snobbishness. One well-known novelist writes: " Since undergoing three weeks' treatment at the hands of Mr. Ponde, dining-out in fashionable houses has been an *unmixed* pleasure to me. . . . I no longer experience a painful acuity of delight on such occasions, nor on returning home to my wife and flat do I suffer from any wistful sense of depression. . . . The scenes of social life in my books have gained, too, in verisimilitude. Such phrases as 'undefinable charm,' 'easy breadth of manner,' ' gracious frankness ' no longer come with undue frequency from my pen ; nor have I lately let slip such sentences as ' Certainly,' he replied, ' wiping the duchess's cream from his moustache.' "

A business man of great resources and wide influence also writes : " Thanks to Mr. Ponde, I am a richer man than I should otherwise have been. I have not only refused a peerage, but I am much harder to get round. It is almost impossible now to persuade me to employ idle young men of good connections to the detriment of my own business. The bracing effect of the Ponde treatment upon my own deportment may be illustrated by an extract from a letter written by my youngest daughter to her brother at Oxford. ' Papa,' she writes, ' is changed. He no longer fusses about like

36

a little dog that has been scratched behind the ears when Lady X. drives over here in the afternoon.' "

Although Mr. Ponde's fee was high, two guineas for a first consultation, my curiosity was so strong that I felt that I must visit this interesting specialist. I flattered myself that I stood in no need of his professional advice; but half-an-hour later, on ringing his bell in Harley Street, I confess I felt the qualms of a patient. As the man-servant opened the door my nervousness was increased by having to step aside for an elegant lady hurrying out in a state of unmistakable agitation. She was adjusting her veil, on the meshes of which a tear trembled, and I noticed in the palm of her little gloved hand, squeezed into a tight ball, a tiny, damp, cobwebby handkerchief. I began to conceive a distinctly alarming idea of Mr. Ponde.

In the waiting-room, decorated with the usual massive bronze ornaments and large, inexpensive oil paintings, sat two other patients, one of whom lowered his paper for a moment to throw a penetrating glance at me as I entered. After a few minutes, this one—an elderly, grizzled man, with pince-nez, and perfectly dressed—was silently summoned from the door. He got up with prompt determination, crossed the room with a quick military step, and left me alone with a pair of legs and the broad sheet of the opened *Times* facing me in the chair opposite. The boots conveyed nothing; the trousers were black. Could he be a clergyman? I gave a barking cough, but the large clean hands only shifted their grasp upon the crackling paper, and raised it a little higher, displaying a well-filled waistcoat and a watch-chain. However, I thought, he must reveal himself presently, and I relapsed into wondering vaguely what could be the matter with him. At last the

37

front door shut again and the man-servant appeared ; but to my great disappointment my companion did not move. " I have a definite appointment at a definite hour," said a sonorous voice behind the paper. " I prefer to wait."

The consulting-room was large, with dark corners. Mr. Ponde, a pale, beardless man of forty, was standing before the fire with his coat-tails up. Without shaking hands, but with a re-assuring, almost humorous smile, he motioned me to a great chair, on which the full light from the long garden window fell, and he sat down himself at a large writing-table. Taking from a drawer a heavy indexed volume, he asked me my name and address, the amount of my income, my father's profession, my own, if I was married, who my grandfather was, my maternal grandfather, whether I was richer or poorer than my parents ; and while I was answering these questions he looked at me narrowly yet not unpleasantly. I was just explaining that my wife's father imported bananas when he said quickly : " You should be more careful about your dress ; but I will give a few practical hints presently." After having jotted down my replies in the ledger, he got up and stood again before the fire, this time warming his hands and with his back to me. " Well," he said heartily, " I have seen very little of you, but I can tell you one thing positively : you need not change your address. You can stand Pimlico. Now tell me your symptoms." Oddly enough, I was not prepared for this. Quite a long pause followed.

" I know," he began in a steady, kind voice, " these things are difficult to tell, but you must treat me with the same confidence as you would your medical man, or I can do nothing for you."

As I could not collect my wits and remained silent, he went on : " However strange and

delicately humiliating your own case may seem to
you, let me assure you it is not an exceptional one.
My experience enables me to tell you confidently
that others whom you would not suspect have felt
the same. Come, I will ask you some questions.
Do you, for instance, feel more embarrassed—
excited, shall we say—when actually in the company of your social superiors, or afterwards on the
way home ?   An important temperamental
difference is involved, and I must be quite clear
as to the category to which you belong, if I am to
diagnose your case and prescribe for you."

At this point, I could not help telling him that
it was no uneasiness whether I was, or was not,
a gentleman that had brought me to him, but
merely curiosity to hear what he would say. He
smiled. " Do you know thirty per cent of my
patients tell me that ? " This, I confess, staggered
me, and a dreadful misgiving crept into my mind.
" Could I all the time have felt unconsciously
that. . . ? " But his scepticism nettled me, and
I told him rather tartly that a man of my descent,
with a pedigree going back to a Giant Mog who
lived A.D. 202, could not possibly doubt his gentility
or suspect himself of being a snob.

" There you make a great mistake," he said
quickly. " Some of the most difficult cases of
diffident snobbishness that come under my notice are
precisely those in which a lively sense of lineage is
combined with either poverty or a position to
which no dignity is attached. Oh, in private,
such people think themselves as good as anybody,
and don't worry their heads about such matters,
but in the company of important personages
they are apt to be as uneasy about themselves
as the most conventional parvenu, and, on the
opposite sort of occasion, as insufferably
condescending. My usual method of treating such

39

patients is to make them fetch their pedigree and to point out that as a matter of creeping fact they are as much descended from women as from men. In forty-nine cases out of fifty pride of birth collapses under this test. I have had hundreds of letters from patients, thanking me in glowing terms for having removed secretly-nourished pretensions which prevented them from behaving to everybody in a natural straightforward sort of way. But, of course, when the descent is unimpeachable on both sides, the case requires more delicate handling. The most difficult case of diffident snobbishness I think I ever treated, was that of a great-nephew of a Duke who happened also to be a dentist ; he died. Indeed, the poor relations of great houses are, alas, almost incurable, and when they have inter-married, I usually say quite frankly, ' Dear Madam or Sir, you are wasting your money ; I can do nothing for you.' You know these folk, how rude and disagreeable they often are to the people they meet staying at the great house on their annual visit there, and how they work the head of the family for all he is worth the rest of the year, till his name becomes a perfect bugbear to their neighbours at home.

" Your case, however, is happily different, but your mention just now of Mog (do not wince at my flippancy) suggests that you might find it salutary to follow up some of the female branches of your pedigree. Anyhow, try it, try it by all means. But look here, I must give you a warning. It is, indeed, part of the prescription. Don't, in consequence of your investigations, pull yourself together like a man who looks facts in the face and proclaim yourself heartily ' middle-class.' If you catch yourself doing that, believe me, you are not cured. *Plus ça change, plus c'est la même chose.*

40

And a word of counsel with regard to criticizing other people. Don't think that snobbishness in all its forms is a disease peculiar to any one class ; it is sporadic. Let me disabuse you of the dangerous idea that it is a middle-class ailment. Only the other day a man of the people, as the phrase goes, a Labour leader, mark you, came to me literally pale with distress, having experienced a peculiar and delicious glow while driving with a Marchioness. He concluded that he was tainted with snobbishness, a thing he abhorred and despised ; and having marked it down in himself he now sees it sticking out not only of determined Radicals, but even of some of his colleagues. He has put himself entirely in my hands, and at the present stage of his ailment the principal mischief against which I am contending is the subtlety and persistence of his penetration. He goes about sniffing for the tainted breeze, damning and swearing with tears in his eyes, and whiffing it everywhere. When he comes here, I say to him, ' Old chap ' (he likes being called ' old chap '), ' old chap, you have missed your vocation, you're another Thackeray.' I am trying, you see, a little chaff-treatment.

" Again, at the other end of the scale, one of the saddest cases of snobbishness, taking the form of Chronic Condescension, is a young Countess, a sweet, charming creature with a heart of gold. She comes to me week after week, always with the same lamentable story : ' Oh, Mr. Ponde, it's too dreadful. I *can't* help feeling, whenever I do anything kind, even when it's a little ordinary thing, that it's quite specially kind as coming from *me*. It's too, too awful. I can't even hand a cup of tea to an author or an artist whom I admire *intensely*, without feeling somehow that he ought to respond as though it were a great favour. Dear, dear Mr. Ponde, tell me what I ought to do.'

Well, I always try to spare my patients all the pain I can, but this morning, in her case, I was driven to touch a nerve. I simply told her, ' My dear lady, they all notice it, and grin about it behind your back.' It quite broke her down, but I think it may do her good."

Mr. Ponde paused, and smiled at me : " I have talked to you chiefly about my other patients, but that is part of my method. In one sense, you are an unsatisfactory patient. I mean," he added kindly, seeing a look of consternation on my face, " from my point of view. For I am conscientiously compelled to prescribe for you that for the present you do not visit me again. On these topics you must give your mind a good rest. You have told me you are a journalist, and it will do you no harm, nor me either, to give a certain publicity to our interview, but after that let the subject drop." We parted, and I never found it so little embarrassing to give a professional man his fee. On leaving the house, owing no doubt to some miscalculation on his part, I found myself confronted with the person who had sat behind *The Times* in the waiting-room. I recognized his imposing features in a moment, having myself heard him lash Society from the pulpit. I sat under him last Sunday ; the congregation was thinner. His denunciations lacked something of their old romantic gusto. " The Ponde treatment is working," I thought ; " I really believe he is better, but he will lose his congregation."

II

In spite of Mr. Ponde's injunctions to give this subject a rest, I find, on looking through my articles, that I did return some years later to the study of this curious and humiliating passion called snobbishness. I will end my reflections by retelling a story, a tragic story, of an arch-snob—more harrowing even than Max's perfect little study on the same subject, *Maltby and Braxton.*

An old gentleman, who had a finger in my education and occasionally expressed himself in aphorisms, bade me " Snub snobs." I have failed to carry out his injunction with the severity he would have approved ; I have met too many amiable snobs. Indeed, inverted snobbery depresses me far more than the frank, eager kind ; there is a childishness about the latter which is disarming. Soon after I first came to stay in London I got to know an elderly artist who worked among the poor, and took his pleasure in the grandest society, which in Victorian days was much more exclusive. He seemed to specialize in duchesses. I think I can remember seeing on one occasion as many as three, after one of his small dinner-parties, holding with rather alarmed expressions little, fizzling Japanese fireworks in front of their faces.

There were usually drawing-room fireworks at these entertainments, to which, having met him in misleading circumstances, I was sometimes invited. In the intervals of Philanthropy he used to paint weak, but excessively noble, portraits of distinguished ladies, and very rich sketches of park-vistas or of corners in their gardens. In front of his windows hung shattered fragments of a glass chandelier, and the last rays of the sun, shining through them on late summer evenings, used to scatter about the room and over his guests prismatic patches of colour. His delight in titles and great possessions, in glass prisms and Japanese fireworks, struck me as all of a piece ; and I never could echo the moral contempt with which he was sometimes

43

mentioned by other artists and social workers. He was exceedingly kind.

Yes, the person who takes social distinctions very seriously may be a fool for doing so, but I cannot get up much indignation against that particular form of foolishness, especially when it has its roots in natural aesthetic preferences and sensibilities. It does not seem to me base to be attracted by historic names, fine houses, prestige, or the agreeable qualities which are the product of ancient riches. Though, of course, it is childish to think a glittering chandelier is the most beautiful object in the house of life, still, it is not less foolish to think that the coal-scuttle must be. What is detestable in snobbishness is the obverse side of it : the incapacity or refusal to see what is lovable or interesting in people who do not exhibit certain social characteristics. It is not the foolishly looking-up that offends me, but the foolishly looking-down ; not the belief in the existence of " the right " kind of people, but the belief that there are " wrong " kinds of people.

Hasty readers of Proust have sometimes exclaimed, " Surely Proust is the most gigantic snob ever endowed with genius." I shouldn't put it like that. If they said, " Proust is the subtlest observer who made the study of Society, the study of social shades and special types, an important part of his work," they would be nearer the mark.

I admit that most of those who figure in *À la Recherche du Temps Perdu* appear as ferocious and impassioned snobs ; but Proust, though he responds to every quiver of emotion in them, is himself detached. His temperament was extremely worldly, and yet he was also a born solitary. The world attracted and repelled him. It gave him exquisite gratifications, and yet gratifications of a kind which he knew would destroy the experiences that he valued even more. It was this duality in his nature which made him such a superb chronicler of manners and social passions.

The snobbishness objected to in Proust was not only of the " looking-up " kind, but of an unusually poetic sort ; and you cannot have read far if you have not discovered that the drama of the hero's experiences in the grand world is a process of slow and absolute disillusionment. The people who seemed wonderful to him when they were inaccessible, prove on closer and closer acquaintance more and more ordinary—and sometimes even vulgar. This is part of the whole " moral " of Proust's view of life : the world, like love and everything else in it, is only enjoyed in memory and imagination.

III

Now for the pathetic story of the unfortunate arch-snob. I have condensed it from the pages of Lenôtre's enchanting book of historical research, *Histoires Étranges qui Sont Arrivées*. To make the fantastic story of poor Bouret a little more credible, I will first repeat an anecdote of the times when he lived and Louis XV was on the throne.

When the young duc de Fronsac, then at school, informed his magnificent grandfather, M. le maréchal de Richelieu, that he did not want the purse of a hundred louis which the latter had brought him, because he had economized from his last allowance, that perfect eighteenth-century model of manners for the great, immediately opened the window and flung the purse to a beggar below : " *Voilà ce que M. le duc de Fronsac te donne, pour se former aux bonnes façons !* " Then he turned indignantly on his grandson. " Economized ! What does that wretched word mean ? A young man of your rank has no right to think of anything so sordid ! " This anecdote is characteristic of the epoch. French society despised money with an ostentation which, if rather mad, was not without a certain grace and magnanimity. To be a millionaire in those days was to be downright despicable ; and bankers, whom lucky speculations had turned into Crœsuses, pathetically did their best to squander their fortunes at once. M. Lenôtre gives instances of the insults which were heaped upon financiers who had been successful, and the eager humility with which they promptly proceeded, in obedience to good form, to ruin themselves and win a little respect.

Bouret was the son of a valet and a lady's maid. In 1747 there was a famine in Provence, owing to several speculators having made a corner in wheat, and Bouret, who had made a little money, broke the ring in eight days, by sending down sacks three-quarters-filled with sand with a covering of corn on the top, at the same time announcing that they were sent by the Government to stop the famine. The speculators at once released their corn and sold their stores at any price. The crisis passed, and Provence hailed Bouret as its saviour. He was nominated treasurer-general of the King's household, and then *fermier-général* ; ten years after being a drayman, he found himself the possessor of a fortune estimated at a hundred million francs, a figure then fabulously great. He gave dinners at which the guests were presented with the carriages and horses which he had sent to bring them to the feast ; the ladies were given diamond aigrettes, and the gentlemen, on unfolding their napkins, found orders upon the numerous banks which Bouret controlled. A suggestion reached him that Louis XV would be willing to accept an advance of five or six millions. " Ten,

twenty millions, all he would deign to accept,"
was Bouret's answer, " without interest if—the
condition would cost the King nothing—if M.
Bouret were granted the favour of presentation
at Court." Alas, *that* was impossible ! But the
King wanted money badly, and if M. Bouret would
walk in the gardens of Marly, the King, by accident,
might meet him. During the next few weeks, in
the hope of this encounter, M. Bouret, daily dressed
in diamonds, feathers, and his finest clothes,
never left the park, and at last, one day, he saw a
little group of people approaching of whom only
one was wearing a hat. He recognized the bearers
of dazzling names to whom he had lent money,
but in whose presence he felt ridiculously small ;
they were chatting easily to the King, who wore
a hunting coat. The poor man felt faint ; the
blood drummed in his ears ; had emotion not
paralysed him he would probably have fled.
Louis XV, his attention apparently fixed upon
the swans in a piece of ornamental water, was
approaching him. " *Monsieur Bouret !* Ah,
Monsieur Bouret, this gives me pleasure. . . . When
I go to Fontainebleau, Monsieur Bouret, I shall
stop at your country house and eat a peach. . . . "
When the financier recovered his senses, the King
and his companions had passed into the distance.

So the King would stop on his way to
Fontainebleau and eat a peach from the garden
of a poor millionaire ! What exquisite condescension ! Bouret's first step was to acquire
a magnificent property on the banks of the Seine.
In a few days hundreds of gardeners, masons,
and waggoners were at work ; terraces covered
with peach trees transported bodily from all parts
of France were constructed in a few days ; an
exquisite pavilion rose like an exhalation from the
ground. And when fountains, statues, lakes,

groves of peach trees, avenues of peach trees, new walls on which old peach trees were spread, pergolas over which they were trained, were all complete, the master of this Eden waited, first for days, then for weeks, then for months, perfecting or embellishing a paradise in which the King would deign to spend a few minutes. At last, he timidly contrived to remind the King of his promise. " Yes, yes," said Louis XV when the message reached him, " M. Bouret, of course. . . . Tell him I'll come for a day's hunting one of these days." When these words were repeated to the financier they threw him into dismay. There was no hunting to be had at Croix Fontaine ! He bought at once a forest neighbouring the royal forest of Sénart, stocked it with herds of deer, pheasants, stags, and roebuck. He learnt to ride and to bow from horseback ; he recruited a battalion of huntsmen, a band of trumpeters and several packs of hounds, and then he began again to haunt the paths of Marly park—finally not in vain. One day the King with a winning smile came up to him. " Ah ! M. Bouret. . . . So faithful M. Bouret is still attending me on my little walks. I have not forgotten my promise to breakfast with you. You can count upon me ! " Breakfast ! So the King was coming to breakfast ! Such a favour was only granted to his most intimate friends : either to those whose ancestry could be traced to remote antiquity, or to those who had performed great services to the State. And, more wonderful still, it was a certainty—the King had said " Count on me ! " How little time there was to prepare ! Stables would have to be built for seven or eight hundred horses, coachhouses for the carriages, since the whole Court would accompany the King. There would have to be at least forty or sixty tables ; refrigerators for the champagne, huge kitchens for roasting, an army of

footmen would be required ; and then, the food ! ...
Messengers would have to be sent to England for
lace napkins, to Strasbourg for *pâtés*, to Geneva
for trout, to La Rochelle for oysters. How much
plate would be required, too, in addition to Venetian
glasses and Chinese porcelain ! Bouret felt that
if necessary he must ruin himself. The insolence
of his enormous fortune could only be palliated
if he were prepared to squander it on the King's
caprice. When everything was at last ready,
he once more betook himself to Marly to fix the
date on which he should give the order to put his
army of cooks and scullions in action. Louis XV
seemed ill and old that day. He complained of his
health ; the journey to Fontainebleau tired him
now, he said ; he would like to break the journey :
" If it does not give you too much trouble, M.
Bouret, will you put me up for a night ? "

Bouret withdrew in a very grave state of
mind. He knew that wherever the King slept,
he was *chez soi* ; there would be nothing for it
but to leave his own house if the King deigned to
pass a night under his roof. At a little distance
from Croix Fontaine, Bouret built a castle for the
King and his Court. He made a bridge over the
Seine, and a paved avenue leading from it to this
fairy palace. In the library of sandal-wood were
forty huge magnificently-bound volumes, entitled
Le Vrai Bonheur, each marked with a date ranging
from 1774 to 1814. Each volume contained
365 pages, and on each page in illuminated letters
were written the words, *Le Roi est venu chez
Bouret*. The first volume reposed on a platinum
and onyx desk ready for the King to sign on the
day of his arrival. A statue of Louis XV with an
inscription by Voltaire stood in the courtyard.
At the last moment a humorist suggested that
one thing was lacking, a hostess to receive the

King. Bouret rushed to Paris and married a wife. The morning the King was expected, Bouret and his wife, servants, and musicians were waiting in a silk tent at the bridgehead, when a courier was seen to approach, galloping at full speed, and he would have passed had not the frantic shouting of Bouret arrested him : " You are from the King ? The carriages are on their way ? " " The carriages ? Why, the King died this morning ! I am bearing the news to Fontainebleau." There was an awful silence. Bouret, whose legs had failed him, sat down. Then he lay down. Presently he began to clutch the air with both hands. He died on the carpet he had spread for a man who would never set foot upon it. Near Cesson on the banks of the Seine, there are still two *châteaux*, M. Lenôtre tells us, one called the *Pavillon Bouret*, the other the *Pavillon Royal*.

IV

We cannot wander back a hundred years in imagination without being struck by the rigid reality of social distinctions in the past ; and eighteenth-century memoirs often suggest that these barriers were sometimes quite impervious to natural sympathies. We come across odd streaks of apparent callousness in sensitive people where their social inferiors are concerned. Of course only at moments ; for however strong convention may be, consciousness of a common humanity is always there at the back of people's minds ; sometimes, especially in earlier days, producing the queerest contrasts in behaviour. I do not suppose that the courtiers who ragged with " Old Rowley " felt it at all odd that the next moment they should be offering him a dish on their knees, and when I have peeped into the court of the Great Eliza, the rapidity with which she was wont to pass from the grossest familiarity into hieratic aloofness has seemed startling. In the Middle Ages, when the divinity of Kings, the sacredness of the persons of Bishops and Cardinals, the venerability of Lords and Princes, were more instinctively accepted, these chops and changes must have been still more violent. What an immense surprise reverberates through old literature that the great are also human, and " come to dust " ; what portentous and we may fairly say, what humourless humility, similar thoughts seem to have inspired in the great themselves ! The mortal King prostrated himself before the Invisible King, and when he turned round, lo ! while still remaining man he was also a golden image ; the great in turn knelt before the idol, and upon them too some mystic shimmer was shed, a gleam faintly transmissible to those immediately beneath them ; they, too, were splashed with a few drops of gold from the fount of honour. This hierarchic system does not exactly collapse ; but generally it engages more and more constantly, except in war and danger, only men's frivolous moods—their snobbishness if you will, until it fades away into a potent system of social make-believe which intimidates without convincing. Literature, as usual, lingers behind change. Far into the eighteenth century tragedy is still the property of nobles and princes, nor are other men allowed to feel sorrows sufficiently august ; their sufferings being conceived as more trivial, and fitter for the Comic Muse.

51

SOCIETY AND SOLITUDE, OR HIS FIRST DISCIPLE

DEAREST LADY,—I shall have the pleasure of kissing your hand on Thursday week at the very latest, if—oh ! how I hate that exceptious particle ! —if the delectable little tyrant of Dunstable does not *insist*. You know how very peremptory she can be in her favours, and how impossible it is to cope, dear creature, with her innocent oblivion of other people's feelings and arrangements. Between you and me, the Noble Lord in the Blue Ribbon is beginning to find that out—and other things besides ! Sticky moons about the gallery and terraces at Hodleston with a decidedly chastened and watchful air, so Tishy Cardoyle tells me. Well, in case, *unberufen, unberufen,* I miss my crack with you, I will write my news now, though writing is a poor substitute for pouring out to you who understand everything, and never did I stand more in need of the sympathy of a delicate, humorous penetration. How we might have laughed over my story together ! But, seriously, dear Lady of undoing smiles, there was something rather pathetic about him too. You were right : there is certainly a ray of moonshine mixed with his brains. It was waste of time and money, both scarce things with me, going all the way to Badheim to see him—at least I am tempted to think so, whenever I forget that my ludicrous adventure will amuse *you.*

Never did I rise from a posture of worship, dusting my knees, and feel more foolish. What comforted me afterwards was the remembrance of

52

your once saying that what you admired most of all in me was my worship of genius. Certainly, if my own " Grapes of Proserpine " does not live, I shall be at least able to reflect on my death-bed that I have paid ungrudging homage where it was due, and bestowed sympathy where it was needed. Yes, and who knows ? Perhaps one or two of the lusty young heirs to fame, to whom I gave their first sweet sip at the cup of success, may some day remember and immortalize even poor little me ! You see, dear friend, it is little I ask at the hands of Destiny, who has seen fit to dower others with her greatest gifts, and pass over the one who would have appreciated them perhaps most of all. I hear you protest. It is sweet of you, but on this point I will not listen to the arguments even of my dearest friends.

Talking of *les jeunes*, that reminds me of the first surprise of my visit to Badheim. You remember how positive we were from his writing, from his *saugrenu* audacities, and the sonorous aberrations of his style, that he was young—you added, broad-shouldered, with a beautiful plangent voice and an excited eye just a millimetre too wide open. Well, he *is* a short, grizzled, yes, almost *old* man, with a walrus moustache, spectacles, and one shoulder higher than the other. And he wears a made-up tie. My second surprise was that *Lucid Intervals*, so far from being his first book, is his sixth ! He has written two others since ! So you see it was not interesting, after all. We were had, dear Lady, we were had. He has been before the world nearly thirty years, and *all* his books—he admitted as much himself—have been wretched draggle-tailed failures. Once or twice he has only sold about twenty copies, and he never, or hardly ever, gets reviewed. My third surprise—but I must begin at the beginning of my story, or you

53

will never mount to the comic climax of my humiliation.

I believe the good little cherub who sits up aloft and looks after the life of poor Jack was wanting to warn me that night I parted from you, after we settled that we had discovered a new philosophic genius who must be written to. Never before had I found a letter of that kind so hard to write. I supposed then it was his personality which was embarrassing me ; for we had divined it—hadn't we ?—as decidedly *farouche*. I believe now my good angel was trying to save me ! I must have torn up at least three sheets of paper, and when I did get started, of course, I wrote much more excitedly and enthusiastically than I felt— in fact, I was, I know now, quite ridiculous. No answer came for nearly a week ; but at last a letter with a foreign stamp arrived. It was very long, written in a queer hieroglyphic hand, and, with our preconceived notions of the writer in my mind, it pleased me very much. I thought it rather grand. It read, too, as though behind its guarded gravity (oh, it must have taken him hours to write —it was most elaborate !) lay pent-up a longing for sympathy which suggested thrilling conversations. And when I learnt from the postscript that he was at Badheim for his heart (probably incurable), I wrote back at once still more enthusiastically, I am afraid, about his philosophizings, adding that I was longing to see him. Should I come out ? I got back a letter, quite different from the first—I had written purposely myself with more intimate effusiveness the second time. My letter had drawn him with a vengeance. It was exactly like lifting up a weir-hatch ; he simply poured. (I must show you the letter ; there really are some striking things in it.) It was the sort of letter one might write if one had not seen a soul to speak to for weeks. It began : " My friend." I wired back : " *Cor ad cor loquitur*, I am coming." Three weeks later I was in the train. By the by, just before my departure I received a third letter from him—most touching— suggesting I should postpone my visit since, partly from physical causes, partly from excitement at the prospect of meeting me, he had lately got only snatches of sleep and was far from his best. I started at once. You know how delightful it is to feel that one can *help*.

On arriving, I found at my hotel an excited dithyrambic little note : " O long-awaited friend ! " it ran, " the feast of feasts is set " ; and after continuing as though we were going to breakfast at dawn on the top of the Matterhorn, he ended—I need not say, without a glimmer of humour—by inviting me to *Mittagessen* at his pension. How- ever, before the time came round I heard from him again : no, it was not thus, apparently, two half- blind, battered Titans, labouring in different hemi- spheres, should meet at last ; he would expect me at four. You know how strongly I hold that men and women destroy the interest of life by not expressing what they feel, and by being ashamed of their great emotions, and how convinced I am that reserve is the death of friendship and all we mean by society, in the best sense of the term ; yet I confess something in this last missive blew a little cold draught across my enthusiasm for him. It is not good manners to take for granted that anyone, before you have seen him, is like yourself, however sympathetic he may have shown himself by letter. The note pointed to a stupidity and an ignorance of the world which slightly alarmed me. I thought I would find out a little more about our Berserk philosopher before I approached his den ; so immediately after luncheon I went round to his *pen- sion*, and introduced myself to the occupants of the

salon. The *Frau Haushälterin* was most com-
municative. I made her laugh by describing my
trepidation, after having travelled from England to
see our flaming prophet in the flesh. I do not know
whether she was more astonished at my pilgrimage
(you see, dearest Lady, she did not know *you*) or at
my preconception of him. For it appeared that he
had no belongings and hardly ever received letters,
that he was a polished, quiet little man, always
elaborately polite, even when suffering and in pain,
and that he made himself agreeable sometimes by
taking ladies of the *pension* out for botanizing
expeditions. I was relieved, but even more disappointed. Everybody has heard of the labouring
mountain producing the mouse, but you and I, who
know the world of letters, have oftener met with the
more amazing, illusion-shattering phenomenon of a
mountain issuing from a *ridiculus mus*! "Is this
going to prove yet another instance of it?" I
thought, as I ascended the stairs. I heard him
walking in his room, tapped, and opened. He
stared at me in astonishment, an emotion, by the
by, which his features are peculiarly adapted to
express. Then he asked me stiffly to what he was
indebted. . . . I was nearly an hour before my
time, and I saw that he had not put two and two
together. I smiled. " I am the long-awaited and,
I am afraid, now over-punctual—friend," I said,
as soon as I had partly recovered from the shock
of his appearance. I thought the moment before
that his face had reflected the last limit of blankness
of which the human countenance is capable, but
at this reply it dropped to an even profounder gape
of stupefaction. I moved forward, saying gently :
" May I sit down ? " when suddenly he pounced at
me—it is the only word—and, gripping my
shoulders with his hands, almost dragged me into
the room. " You! I must look at you first."

You know how silly one feels when a doctor takes
one's head in his hands and turns one's face to the
window to look at one's throat ? Think of your
feelings if a stranger did it without a moment's
warning ! It is true he didn't hold my tongue
down with a spoon and make me quack : " Ah !
ah ! ah ! ", but under the stare of his sunken eyes,
which were near enough to mine to look enormous
behind their spectacles, I was as helpless as a patient,
and when his hands slid from my shoulders, I
assure you, I felt positively *weak*. Then, without a
word, he turned his back and looked out of the
window, while I stood there literally unable to
frame a single sentence. Presently an odd sound
came from him, something like a gulp and a chuckle,
and he turned to me, grinning queerly : " Take a
chair. I'll ring for coffee." When we were settled
he asked me why I had called him " Master " in
my letters. (Had I ? Heaven knows what I had
written !) I said I hoped my letters explained what
I felt. " Nobody has called me that before " ; and
then—the vanity of these cranks !—he proceeded,
if you please, to put me through a sort of catechism :
which of his books had I read ? What had I
written myself, etc., etc. ? I have conveyed
nothing if you cannot believe that I had entirely
lost grip of the situation. It came out that I had
only dipped into *Lucid Intervals*—appropriate title
that !—and that I had often written before to
authors I did not know. Indeed, he made me go
through the list of them, and he laughed every now
and then when I mentioned a name. Really, the
childish jealousy of authors ! Do you remember
Meredith's story of the erudite professor who
objected to his visitor going out for a walk with
another distinguished professor, and who, after a
short prelude of gloom and obscure explosions,
" behaved to his faithless admirer (if we exclude

the dagger) with the vindictive jealousy of an injured Spanish beauty "? Our friend's laughter gave him away, and to salve his wounded vanity on discovering he was not the *sole* object of my admiration, though I doubt if he valued it, I told him that he had another admirer in a charming and distinguished lady, who was most anxious he should visit her. (Don't chide me ; we could have wriggled out of it somehow.) This provoked a bitter but really quite amusing harangue on " modern simony," which no longer, he said, consisted " in buying promotion in the Church, but in rich society people fancying they can purchase the Holy Ghost by dabbling in Literature and the Arts," and getting artists and philosophers to dance attendance on them. It really hit some of our friends rather hard. He then had the impertinence to ask if I was your lover, and when I snubbed him, he laughed very much. Naturally I got up to go, and he suddenly became grave. We were both standing. " I shall keep your letters by me always," he said, for a moment, I thought, rather kindly, certainly most solemnly, " and read them sometimes. When I feel lonely it will refresh me to recall " (he bowed to me with insulting formality) " my first disciple ! " He watched me go down the stairs, and then I heard him blow off a great sigh and slam the door. Love to the chicks, etc. . . . etc. . . . Your devoted POPPLES.

THE PADDED MAN

SOMETIMES the critic sees himself, or rather reads himself, as others read him. He does this when he reads other critics. For instance, the other day I read a review of the *Life of Bulwer-Lytton*, which struck me as unfair to him both as a man and as an author. The critic wrote as though the most significant thing about him was that he was an "idol of Belgravian drawing-rooms," a "pet of Lady Blessington," who had no right to call any man, let alone Tennyson, "effeminate." Now if there is one fact which this grandson's biography brings out, it is that Bulwer-Lytton was a prodigious worker, a novelist who toiled at fiction with something of the furious, hurried concentration of Balzac, a reviewer as indefatigable as Jeffreys, a forcible and prompt pamphleteer, a speaker of set orations among the best of his day, at once elaborate and voluble, a satirist in verse, a producer of epic poems, a Cabinet Minister, and a man of fashion who took his recreation in shining as a wit and conversationalist. And what remains now of this prodigious activity ? Little of much value, I admit, but something. Lytton cashed his cheque on fame for ready money. But the significant fact about him was that he was *not* the pampered author of society, but a writer who appealed, and aimed at appealing, to "the great heart of the people." The people were his audience, and the extraordinary thing is that, in spite of competitors, he has held that audience for eighty years. His popularity may be at last on the wane, but still in

59

little back-parlours, in lodgings, in wayside inns, on the shelf which serves for a library you will probably find among the latest best-sellers one of Bulwer-Lytton's ancient novels The critic will exclaim that I am giving him all—more than he asked for ; but wait. I urge him to reflect that it needed an extraordinary dose of that power, whatever it is, which captivates and satisfies the imaginations of a million, thus to have kept his place so long

What is this power, and what is its value ? Like myself, the writer of that review has probably paid, at the age of fourteen, his tribute of tears to *The Bondman* and *The Deemster* ; at the age of fifteen, soared perhaps into the empyrean on the wings of Marie Corelli ; and at a still tenderer age been led beneath the humble roof by the gentle hand of Mrs. Henry Wood. We have thrilled at the horror of Gagool and rejoiced in the valour of Umslopogaas ; we have—it is surely not taking too much for granted ?—bathed with immortal tenors at Trouville, and envied the splendours of Strathmore. If, now, to read *The Last Days of Pompeii* were to us a penance exactable only for the gravest excesses of literary fastidiousness, yet once we were under its spell, or the spell of books like it ; we have no right ourselves to dismiss such authors as men with no power in them.

The power which underlies a great and prolonged popular reputation in fiction, and sways the imaginations of those who, either from youthfulness or heedlessness, instinctively take books on trust, is a kind of " go." It is usually inseparable from an unfaltering good faith on the part of the author in the scenes he creates, and is a gift so precious that when it is absent it can only be made up for by most exquisite economy and artistic precision ; and even then generations will always recur who place a Dostoievsky far above a Turgenev, a Zola above an Anatole France. The vitality which made Lytton's or Ouida's fame is akin to that which roars down the crowded thoroughfares of the *Comédie Humaine* and packs the pages of Meredith, contriving somehow to hold together for the delight of even exacting readers a world as glittering and incoherent as a smashed chandelier. It is because Arnold Bennett could also write *The Grand Babylon Hotel* that he riveted our attention when he described Mr. Povey's shop in *The Old Wives' Tale*. By itself this power makes no man an artist, but it certainly gives him a right to call any man "effeminate," if he thinks him so. Bulwer-Lytton had it to an eminent degree. What justification he had for abusing Tennyson I will not examine here. Personally, I would rather have written one phrase like " the music of the moon sleeps in the plain eggs of the nightingale " than (remuneration apart) any two of Lytton's novels. I am on that side. But I understand the impatience of the writer who sends his leaves flying daily to the press, with the craftsman in words, who spends a delicious hour wondering if " the mellow ousel fluted from the elms " is a line which could be possibly improved. There was a note of somewhat peevish and passive lamentation in some of Tennyson's poems concerned with lovers' woes which may well have irritated a man whose love was not only as a mill-stone, but as a bag of ferrets round his neck ; and one whose reputation was an open raw, buzzed about by flies, might be pardoned for thinking he detected in the poet's too-nervous dread of gossip an over-pampered sensitiveness. " The padded man who wears the stays "—Tennyson's rejoinder in *Punch* —was formidable, but the phrase does certainly not sum Bulwer-Lytton up. There is a story of

his saying to a friend after that poem had appeared :
" I don't know what to do about these fellows in
Punch. Do you know what they are saying now ?
They say I wear stays ! " " Well, my dear fellow,"
replied his friend, " what does it matter if you
don't ? " "Oh, but I *do !* " Does not that story
make you like Bulwer better ?

It starts me wondering which of the two was
really " the padded man," the poet or the man of
the world. I do not grudge Tennyson an inch of the
thick, soft, warm cocoon which devotion and admiration spun round him through life He wrote too
beautifully—how beautifully our grandchildren will
understand better than we who are in reaction
against him. But if ever a man enjoyed the
advantages (such as they are) of quilt and screen
and padding, it was Tennyson. Why, Lytton
lived on the decks of the world compared with
him ! " Pet of Lady Blessington," indeed ! True,
he took his pleasures in society, but that is a
strenuous form of recreation, demanding a light
stoicism not to be despised.

I declare my heart warms to the flashy, vivid,
laborious dandy burning midnight oil (and morning
sunshine for the matter of that), keeping as many
balls in the air at once as a juggler, including
philandering and politics. A great man ? No, no,
no. But do not let those stays deceive you. The
first step in an English schoolboy's subsequent
education is to dissociate the idea of virtue from
the morning bath, the second (I forget the second),
the third is perhaps to perceive that a valorous
temperament is not incompatible with stays.

One who wrote of Bulwer-Lytton complained
that in relation to his troublesome wife he did not
behave like a gentleman. The standard applied
must have been severe. I know what happened.
The critic was comparing Lytton's behaviour with

that of men who would never have got in such a predicament with their wives at all. Biographers, critics and moralists are always doing that. Has a man got into debt ? His behaviour in that trying circumstance is compared with the hypothetical behaviour of, say, a man like Franklin, who would never have got into debt. Does a passion make hay of a man's life ? His struggles are dubbed feeble by his biographer because Cromwell would have got his impulses under. Does another write a play on a theme which Ibsen would never have chosen ? He is hauled over the coals for not conducting his plot with Ibsen's consistency. If we take Bulwer-Lytton on his own line, so to speak, the story of his private life, which his grandson has told with admirable impartiality, is by no means to his discredit. *Pelham*, *My Novel*, *The Caxtons* may not often be read now ; but try them, enterprising reader, try them. You will find *Pelham* quite as witty as *Vivian Grey* or *The Young Duke*, and the others far better than you expected.

VERSAILLES

THE fountains of Versailles play, I believe, during the summer on the first Sunday of every month, but only for an hour, for the expense of refilling the reservoir is considerable. The gardens are, of course, crowded on those days. The long vista from the palace terrace is then black with sauntering people, and the grand flights of steps which lead down from one stone-framed mirror of water to another are as packed as seats in a theatre. Then, at four o'clock, every gesticulating triton, nymph and river-god begins to spout at once, throwing jets this way and that, and white refreshing columns are sent up into the sky. And it is not only in that stately vista itself, which reaches far beyond the middle-distance, that these graceful forms suddenly appear, diminishing to the eye from the height of tallest poplar to the size of an aigrette; but wherever, to the right and left of it, avenues converge upon some mossy marble basin, there, too, a fountain tosses up above the trees its clustered foam and tattered crystal, and bubbling balustrades are hung with water-curtains. If you chance to visit Versailles on one of those Sundays, do not fail to explore the beeches on the left of the famous *Perspective*, and to find the less famous but most elegant *Cirque*. Built by the king for music on hot summer nights, it lies like a crown of stone in the dark wood—a crown which lacks its jewels, till, between each pair of slender pillars and beneath each light arch, a little fountain stands and glitters.

I am often entertained by commonplace

reflections, provided they are my own ; an idea which, imparted by another, might possibly provoke from me a somewhat hasty assent, can, fortunately, beguile my solitude. Thus, watching the crowds moving about the domain of the Grand Monarch, the approximately happy families squatting on the grass, the listless processions of quiet drab people loitering along the alleys and past the statues of this royal garden, where once it had been the privilege of few to walk, I reflected upon the Triumphs of Democracy. Clearly, the value of delightful scenes and objects was enhanced by their being enjoyed by many. True, those who were now enjoying these scenes, myself included, were not themselves delightful objects ; indeed, we detracted from the beauty of what we had come to admire; but the increase in diffused pleasure was so enormously greater than the loss, that no sane man could regret the turn the world had taken. What, after all, did I as one of a crowd chiefly miss while visiting such places ? Only the swelling joy of a special privilege which, in other days, might conceivably have been mine. And, pleased to find myself thus approving the age in which I had been born, for

> Qui n'a pas l'esprit de son âge
> De son âge a tout le malheur,

I was about to rest upon this commonplace, when I was conscious of a dim misgiving. A name, once a bugbear to all decent people, occurred to me— Mandeville. Why had I thought of Mandeville ? What semi-conscious train of reflection had reminded me of *The Fable of the Bees*, or rather, of his own prose commentary upon that work, so much the most important part of it ? I had thought of him once before, I remembered, when floating past the gorgeous palaces of Venice.

The theme of that reckless but ingenious thinker (you can tell from his style that his aim was to be as upsettingly clever as possible and to give pain) was that men's vices and their selfishness had been the creative factors in civilization. Judged as the comprehensive generalization it claimed to be, the theory did not stand ; vice had not built the cathedrals and temples ; those poems and those works of thought which attested most clearly the dignity of man and the value of life had not sprung from greedy and selfish impulses ; scientific discovery had been the result of disinterested curiosity. Yet how much truth still remained in Mandeville's contention ! Man was a competitive and ostentatious animal, and in every land, what, I asked myself, was, apart from its natural beauties, most worth a visit, if not its traces of the free sway of those ungenerous passions ? I asked myself what made the English country-side delightful : its soft green parks, stately houses and carefully preserved, most uneconomic woods. What did we now rush about in trains and charabancs to enjoy, if not the pride of palaces and castles ? What did we gaze at longest in museums ? The remnants of splendour intended to abash and over-awe. In every town the street or square through which it was exhilarating to walk was stamped with the spirit of exclusion. In Venice—the whole of Venice, it had been obvious at once to me, was one vast explosion of cut-throat competition in luxury and swagger ; that was why Ruskin had gone about it cursing and lamenting, and inventing strange theories to excuse himself for yielding to its charm. And now, as I looked about me, I asked myself what was the scene which the crowd was enjoying before they went back to their flats and tenements, but the creation and the shell of a ruthless and selfish pride ? Democracy had found the pin with which to kill and pick out animals which made such shells; but could it make such shells itself ?

Its spokesmen, looking into the future, prophesied pinnacled cities and bright-robed populations. (I had read Mr. Wells, and sometimes been uplifted.) A million moderately rich men of to-day were richer in spare cash than Louis XIV, but had they begun to decree their stately pleasure-domes ? If Democracy came to an end now—in a hundred years (it might)—what traces for which posterity would be grateful would it have left behind ? I thought of the inky and ill-proportioned town halls of the north ; with slight relief of the huge new building by the side of Westminster Bridge (" tax not the County Council with vain expense ") ; of public parks which had not merely been taken over, but created. It was a bad business. Future historians would say that, though in imagination Democracy had dreamt of splendid common efforts, the real urge behind it had been towards securing for individuals a monotonous equality in mediocre and uninspiring safety and comfort. Well, and whose fault was that ? I asked the future historian with some indignation. Did I not myself ask for a little box of a house, a bath, perhaps a scrap of garden, before anything else ? It was so, but that only went to show that Democracy was probably uncreative.

Then I turned for relief to considering the life that had been lived among such splendid surroundings as Versailles. How petty, monotonous and stiflingly dull it had been after all ! In the *Mémoires* of Saint-Simon we have a picture of it which for vividness and exact truth is without a rival. What backbiting, boredom, squalor, baseness ! It was immensely entertaining to read about ; never had there been a better chance of observing human nature at close quarters, and never had an observer

67

taken better advantage of such an opportunity. But what a life! I have derived much comfort since my visit to Versailles from the *Mémoires* of Saint-Simon.

THE CHINESE IDEAL

ON hot afternoons I find the high room at the British Museum, where the Oriental pictures hang, a very pleasant place to wander about in. Its dark floor, on which footsteps make no sound, gleams like a sheet of water ; the light is tempered ; the air is cool. And there is a Chinese picture on one of its walls which I find as soothing to the spirit as the great, quiet room itself is to the senses. It is called *The Earthly Paradise*, and, while I look at it, I am not inclined to prefer fifty years of Europe to a cycle of Cathay. As often in Chinese pictures, everything in this one seems to hang enskied. The cunning disposition of the figures, of the blossoming trees (happy the country which has no perspective!), of the little boat upon the lake, in which ethereal yet courtly beings sit amicably together, seems to lift a scene of earthly beauty into the atmosphere of a soft enchantment. The gestures of this courteous company are those of boon-companions, entirely at ease with one another. But to what a delicate feast have friendship and the graces led them ! Calm and composed they sit in timeless intimacy, participating at once in the pleasures of humanity and the immunities of disembodied souls ; enjoying, it seems, with condescension, the wine, the little dishes, and the shower of blossom which an exquisite lady—or is she a goddess ?—shakes down into the water from a bough. No doubt they are conscious of the passage of the hours and the fragility of happiness, which the falling blossom recalls ; but with what inward sweet security, with

69

what bland acquiescent irony they remember! Surely they would laugh, if laughter, too, had not been left behind in this region, where they have been gently weaned from all mortal concerns— except the most refined of simple pleasures, and unending intimacy.

The ideal world this picture represents is typically Chinese. It is quite unlike a Christian paradise, since ecstasy and worship are absent from it. There is no circle, such as Fra Angelico portrayed, of saints embracing on their knees. This is a communion of friends. And it is still more unlike that later Christian heaven, Protestant and energetic, which cannot be painted, that heaven of " adventures brave and new," of more splendid activities and more triumphant struggles, to which Browning looked forward. Nor is it an Oriental mystic's heaven, nor such a paradise of pleasure as the followers of the Prophet hope for. This Paradise is more human than the Buddhist's ideal, more spiritual than the Mohammedan's. It is the paradise of an affectionate people, who feel that it is not through the passions, but through a kind of detachment—philosophic, religious, æsthetic ?—I do not know which to call it—that men draw closest to each other. Epicurus would have understood it.

Travellers returning from China tell us tales not always to its credit ; the latest news from China hardly stirs our envy. But neither travellers' tales nor the newspapers can influence those who, through poetry and art, have learnt to delight in the subtle equipoise of the Chinese mind. That Chinese mind is a quaint marriage-flower of two opposite ways of taking the world ; an Oriental indifference, to which the chances of life are of little significance, and a doctrine of conduct whose most marked characteristic is an intense apprehension

70

of the importance of human dignity and tradition. To understand the sentiment of Chinese art and poetry, it is a help to have some knowledge of their two great rival, theoretically incompatible, philosophies: Confucianism and Taoism.

Confucius is the prophet of social life, of the life of citizenship. He is the least mystical of sages. His religion is a religion of conduct. In the ordering of man's relations to man, in the observance of dignity and comeliness in all those relations, of a ritual of duty, lay, according to him, the secret of the best kind of life. Many wise and humane saws are attributed to him: "Do not unto others what you would they should not do unto you," "Render good for good, and unto the evil justice." (It is also recorded of him that he would not sit on a mat which was not laid perfectly straight.)

Taoism, on the other hand, which is the name for all the literature which has clustered round the doctrine of "Tao," or "The Way," is antagonistic to this teaching. Unfortunately, I cannot tell you what "Tao" is. According to the great Lao-Tsze, "Those who know do not tell; those who tell do not know." But, though you must not conclude that I am among the former because I do not tell you, the Occidental need not despair of gathering some notions about it. The utterances of Lao-Tsze himself and of his followers show that the spirit of "Tao" is one which is common to all Eastern quietism. The end of "Tao" is a state of mind which is a communion with a divine reality. "By no thoughts, by no cogitations, 'Tao' may be known. By resting in nothing, by according with nothing, 'Tao' may be approached. By following nothing, by passing nothing, 'Tao' may be attained." To the believer in "Tao" our life is really a dream. "Once upon a time, I Chuan

71

Tzu," wrote a famous Taoist, " dreamt I was a butterfly, fluttering hither and thither, to all intents and purposes a butterfly, and unconscious of my individuality as a man. Suddenly, I awoke, and there I lay, myself again. Now I do not know whether I was then a man dreaming I was a butterfly, or whether I am now a butterfly dreaming I am a man." To us the philosopher's perplexity is comic ; to the Chinese that question, if a joke at all, is one of delicious seriousness.

Quietism turns readily in practice to the pursuit of easy pleasure. The same Chuan Tzu was once fishing in a river, when the Prince of Chu sent two high officials to ask him to take charge of the administration of the Chu State—for the Chinese have ever had a Platonic faith in the practical wisdom of philosophers. The sage went on fishing without turning his head. At last he said : " I have heard that in Chu there is a sacred tortoise which has been dead now some 3,000 years, and that the Prince keeps this tortoise carefully enclosed in a chest on the altar of his ancestral temple. Now, would the tortoise rather be dead and have its remains venerated, or alive and wagging its tail in the mud ? "

" It would rather be alive," replied the two officials, " and wagging its tail in the mud."

" Begone," cried Chuan Tzu, " I, too, will wag my tail in the mud."

Thirty-four years ago, Professor Giles, from whose *History of Chinese Literature* this story comes, published an anthology of Chinese poems. In this delightful book there are many in praise of the wine-cup, of " drunkland," as the Chinese call it. They are not rollicking bumper-songs. They celebrate the release of the spirit from oppressive surroundings and painful reflections, and describe the detachment of a delicate and fantastic intoxication. But what is most striking about these poets, even in their more Anacreontic and pleasure-hunting moods, is the restraint of their appreciation, and their capacity to find poetry in modest actualities. Life may be empty, yet the beauty of a flower may fill it : sad, but there is consolation in a memory or a thought. In Mr. Arthur Waley's *One Hundred and Seventy Chinese Poems* (his translations from Chinese poets have made many familiar with them, and influenced our own poets not a little), you will find poems which illustrate this fine economy of emotion, this gentle stoicism in grief. " If life has not a garden and an old tree I see not," says one of the Chinese sages, " whence the everyday joys of life are to come." Ah ! but if only it has ! After all, man's capacity for happiness is a little cup, which does not need a waterfall to brim it. The poet, so common in the West, who gathers beauty by the handful, like a child wading among bluebells in a wood, wrenching them from their roots with a kind of covetous love, and running back, arms full, at once excited and unsatisfied by the glorious too-muchness of life (is not this an emblem of the romantic spirit in literature ?), cannot draw breath in the lucid atmosphere of Cathay. The Chinese have a proverb taken from their painters' art : " One touch—and it is spring " ; it might have been drawn from their literature, which resembles their painting in economy of means.

> Car nous voulons la nuance encore,
> Pas la couleur, rien que la nuance

—Verlaine's words, which became the watchword of Mallarmé and his school, might be taken as the definition of the principle of Chinese literary tradition. Only, whereas the symbolists used that method to express ambiguous and tenuous emotions, the themes of Chinese poets are old, certain, and familiar. Though the dates of the poems in Professor Giles's anthology range from 550 B.C. to the eighteenth century, yet in choice of subject, in treatment, in their subtlety and simplicity, in their ingenious naïvety, they resemble each other so closely that one might suppose them the work of a single poet. The shortness of life, of youth, the frailty of pleasure, the wisdom of living in the present, the pangs of absence, the joys of retirement, the sorrow of parting, the poignancy of happiness remembered—and love, love as it is reflected in the still waters of memory—these are their ever-recurrent themes. Out of passion and its agitations they make no poems. There are no urgent addresses to mistresses or lovers, no cries of despair, of rapturous expectation, of jealousy: rather a golden patience, which, notwithstanding, has never ceased to yearn. "The poets who wrote them seem to have come to an end of experience, to have passed long ago through the wonders and tumults of existence, to have arrived at last in some mysterious haven where they could find repose among memories that were for ever living, and among discoveries that were for ever old": so Lytton Strachey wrote in an essay on this book. It is not a haven of philosophic or religious contemplation : human things are still the things which are most important. Indeed, it is the poignancy of some detail, some trivial circumstance remembered with the intensity of the homesick, which is the very means by which the poet evokes the mood.

After separation, and in memory, the poet of Cathay sees in his passions the beauty which moves him most. The wrinkles left in the sand when the waves retire are what interests him. Without a certain stillness, he would say, there can be no beauty ; the shadows of things are more consonant with contemplation than things themselves ; shadows which are the substance of this painted Paradise of the East.

CATS

WHEN anyone tells you he (or she) likes cats better than dogs, he (or she) confesses to more than was perhaps intended.

I once quoted a bad poem about a cat by Swinburne. No sooner had my copy gone to press than other poems about cats floated into my memory. On the whole, it was clear that so far as poetry was concerned (prose is another matter) the cat had cut a better figure in literature than the dog. There are touching poems about dogs, but they are all sentimental and celebrate a personal relationship. True, it was a story about a dog watching beside its dead master (on the side of Helvellyn) which inspired, according to Coleridge, the only perfect line of poetry Scott ever wrote :

> When the wind moved his garment how
> oft did'st thou start ?

But compare Matthew Arnold's poem on his dachshund, with the delightful one on his cat, of which the climax is,

> Thus Tiberius might have sat,
> Had Tiberius been a cat.

No doubt Matthew Arnold would if necessary have made soup of his cat to feed his dog ; but that is only another proof that true affection is not necessarily a source of inspiration.

The first poem which occurred to me was Gray's

Ode on the death of a favourite cat. (A "favourite"
cat! How exactly that defines the limits of the
relation possible with a member of the feline race!)

> 'Twas on a lofty vase's side,
> Where China's gayest art had dy'd
>   The azure flowers, that blow ;
> Demurest of the tabby kind,
> The pensive Selima reclin'd,
>   Gazed on the lake below.
>
> Her conscious tail her joy declar'd ;
> The fair round face, the snowy beard,
>   The velvet of her paws,
> Her coat, that with the tortoise vies,
> Her ears of jet, and emerald eyes,
>   She saw ; and purr'd applause. . . .

It is tempting to go on writing out the whole poem,
especially nowadays, when a neat felicity is the
last quality held in estimation by poets, but it
would not be to my purpose. Every detail is
perfect : " conscious tail," " ears of jet," " emerald
eyes," " round face,"—the poet is certainly keeping
his eye on the object. I am not so sure, however,
of " snowy beard "—perhaps because in childhood
I supposed that all cats were females and all dogs
males. Consequently, the faintest suggestion of
masculinity in describing a cat is still to me a false
note—anyhow, for good or bad reasons, I protest
against " beard." Although Gray does not take the
cat as seriously as other poets have done, I think
his poem the best.

Pierre Loti and Anatole France have both written
beautifully about cats. " Hamilcar," who is so at
home in " the city of books " with her master,
Sylvestre Bonnard, is a delicious animal. Her
creator was right to give a cat as a companion to
Sylvestre Bonnard and a dog to M. Bergeret. It is,

perhaps, a trait which more than any other helps
the reader to keep those two characters apart in his
mind. But the French writer who has taken cats
most seriously is Baudelaire. "*Je vois ma femme en
esprit*," he exclaims, gazing at his cat. Of course,
Baudelaire loved cats ; we might have guessed it
had he never written about them. Every dandy
loves them—every one who dreads or despises the
slovenly, warm, homely intimacy of natural
relations.

Towards the middle of the eighteenth century
there lived in Paris an author who is by this time
almost entirely forgotten.

M. Paradis de Moncrif composed innumerable
ballets ; and that Rameau wrote music for some
of them was probably a matter of indifference to
him compared with the opportunities they gave
him of making love to the daughters of the opera.
He was to be met in all worlds ; he purred about
the skirts of Madame du Barry when she was a
grisette, and contributed Pastorals to the whirl of
fêtes spinning for ever round the Royal melancholy,
fêtes in which Madame de Pompadour figured as
Ragonde, Ismène, or Almazis ; he has left traces in
the records of the well-known houses of debauch
in the capital. He was a man of letters, a func-
tionary, a parasite, a cynical wit, a famous fencer,
an Academician, an *amant du cœur* of as many
demoiselles as possible—and he adored cats.
Well, there is not much left of him now, nor (let me
hasten to remind myself) is there of others once as
lively and now as old as he. He published a little
pamphlet " On the Necessity and on the Methods
of Pleasing," and lived adroitly with an oblivious-
ness of principle which disarms the moralist. I cull
one of his maxims : " One advantage of having a
mind is that it is a means to procuring an agreeable
life." He used his mind as recklessly as some

78

women use their bodies ; and by all means call his
recklessness prostitution if it makes you less hard
on them by comparison.

His *History of the Cat* is an odd little book ;
I suspect it of being a kind of cryptic, indirect auto-
biography. I think I know why Monsieur Paradis
de Moncrif adored cats : he envied them. He must
have admired the way those silent, subservient,
egotistic little creatures, with solemn eyes which
seem to look disdainfully upon human frivolities,
had established themselves in the drawing-rooms
he frequented. He, too, was on the look-out for a
cushion beside a fire and a lap to lie in. How, then,
could he justify his own life better than by cele-
brating the excellence of *ses chères amies*, the cats,
whose own lives also were at the mercy of caprice,
and yet free to the point of intoxication in the
gutter ?

I notice he praises the voice of the cat. It is
indeed an organ of marvellous range and expressive-
ness. Often, when I lie awake, I listen to it with
astonishment. Hark, what a wail was that, torn
from the bowels of despair ! Another, another ;
and as they follow in crescendo, the rising voice
seems to grow bright with anger (or is it triumph ?),
till it sinks at last through sobs to a croon of gentlest
pity. It is no wonder that our violins are strung
with cat-gut, or that sound from them can draw the
soul from us like a spider's thread ! Naturalists
have, I know, an explanation of these midnight
cries which I should be embarrassed to expound
here. Aristotle is of the opinion that the temperament of the male cat is so lethargic that the
female must attract him by violence and abuse. To
this, however, I prefer a mediæval explanation that
he is particularly liable to distraction, so that if
suddenly a mouse were to appear he might forget
the purpose of the *rendezvous ;* and therefore that

it is from prudence and a knowledge of this weakness in him, that his consort utters cries which are certainly calculated to keep all mice far from the spot. Women ought to be grateful that in similar situations such expedients are unnecessary.

CHESS

IN Messrs. Bell's excellent Chess Library is to be found *Modern Ideas in Chess* by Richard Réti. In this book the well-known Czecho-Slovakian master traces the development of the game through a study of the methods of famous players from Morphy to Capablanca ; " showing," says the wrapper, " the road along which chess has travelled —from the classicism of Anderssen, by way of the naturalism of the Steinitz school, to the individualistic ideas of the most modern masters."

Classicism, Naturalism, Individualism—it does me good to see these ancient jewels of literary jargon in this new context ; used doubtless with no less, though probably with hardly more, precision. It does me good to recognize a familiar note of defiance in Maître Réti's preface : " The artists who, in spite of derision and enmities, follow their own ideas, instead of imitating nature, may in times of doubt, from which no creative man is free, know, and cherish hope therefrom, that in the narrow domain of chess these new ideas in a struggle with old ones are proving victorious." The passage calls up a picture of Bogoljubow storming along under a night sky racked with doubts about Alekhin's variation of the French game, but winning through at last to peace and confidence. Though it may be difficult for those who are not chess-critics to understand how in playing chess it is possible " to imitate nature " too closely— unless you kick over the board—the same sort of intellectual difficulty must be frequently

81   C

encountered by readers of other kinds of criticism; when, for instance, a cornice is described as " sincere," or the colour of Lopokova's dancing as " pyramidal." Such are the regrettable subtleties of expert enthusiasm.

I am told that in the abstract world of mathematics, the methods of one man will reveal his individuality to fellow-mathematicians as clearly as a writer's style reveals him to literary men. It is the same in chess. True, you and I, reader, are unlikely, when playing over a match between, say, Lasker and Rubinstein, to detect in the moves of the former a magnificently deep vascular temperament, or in those of his adversary the refined tranquillity of an ascetic artist, diffident but of great integrity. But let us not be too much surprised if in the Q-Kt3, QR-B1, etc., etc., of Schlechter's game with John, Réti sees " a love of Nature " and " the grace and airiness of Viennese music." Upon Schlechter he grows lyrical. " His games," he says, " stand out through their breadth of scheme—just as in the forest the trunks of trees and their branches stretch themselves out on all sides wherever there are open spaces : thus did Schlechter develop his forces ; forcibly and, like nature, as it were, objectlessly. No hidden places and traps were there, but only sound development. With him was no undue haste and no pinning himself down to one idea, but one harmonious evolution. And, indeed, combinations by Schlechter are not artificially-reared roses which amaze everyone with their beauty and which, to the true nature-lover, soon savour of excess ; nay, they are rather the humble and hidden forest flowers that have to be looked for, and the love of which increases with their gathering." To the genius of Capablanca, Réti bows with grave, profound recognition—but it is a *moriturus te salutat* gesture. There is little

82

life in his admiration. Capablanca is not æsthe-
tically delightful to him. The ex-champion's
" technique incorporates the spirit of modern
times "; it is imposing, but everything is sacrificed
to efficiency. " Behind the old works of art we
could always trace the artist and recognize the
human countenance of their creators " : γνῶσις
without ἀγάπη—that is the sum of his criticism
of the ex-world's champion. " O for ' the joyful
dance ' of Schlechter," we seem to hear Réti sigh,
the plodding, searching depth of Steinitz, the wild
freshness of Charousek, even the extravagant
iconoclasm of Breyer, who declared that " after
the first move P.-K4, White's game is in the last
throes."

I recently read, with some interest, in the
Harleian Miscellany, a small pamphlet on the
Evils of Chess, this game which I prefer before
all others. I did not think that the writer of this
broadsheet, which appeared in London in 1680,
made out a very strong case against the game. He
shares the opinion of the Reverend Mr. Baxter,
" that the student that needeth chess or cards to
please his mind I doubt hath a carnal empty
mind." His first argument against chess is that
it is a great time-waster, which does not seem to
me a reason for condemning any occupation when
all day long we do many worse things with time
than wasting it. The broadsheet writer was
evidently a natural chess-player, for he confesses
that the game " hath had with me a fascinating
property ; I have been bewitched by it : when
I have begun I have not had the power to give
over." He appears to have been a clergyman.
" It has followed me," he adds, " into my study,
into my pulpit ; when I have been praying or
preaching I have in my thoughts been playing at
chess ; then I have had, as it were, a chess-board

before my eyes ; then I have been thinking how I might have obtained the stratagem of my antagonist, or made such and such motions to his disadvantage ; nay, I have heard of one who was playing at chess in his thoughts as appeared by his words when he lay dying." (This last argument seems to me to cut both ways.) And when he goes on to add that it has caused him to break many solemn resolutions and vows, because he has sometimes promised to play with people and not kept his word, surely it is rather far-fetched to lay the blame upon the game ? He reports that John Huss was an enthusiastic chess-player, but " that he was greatly troubled with the using of this game a little before his death."

Chess is the best sedentary game in the world. It is a complete distraction. Why take to drink in a world full of potent but harmless alleviations ? You cannot remember your sorrows while bathing, or worry over your worries while playing chess. It has appealed to Chinamen, Persians, Indians, Icelanders (who, like the Chinese, have a chess of their own) and to Europeans of all times. Men as different as Tamerlane, Charlemagne, Haroun al-Raschid, Canute, William the Conqueror, Rousseau, Voltaire, Napoleon, Mr. Bonar Law, have all enjoyed it, and even Ferdinand and Miranda soon sat down to a game upon their enchanted island, though it was full of voices and sweet sounds.

EATING

DO you remember the description of the meals prepared for poor Mr. Polly by his wife, and Mr. Wells's comment on them ? I reckon it among the soundest of his generalizations upon the life of man. It runs as follows :

" Drink, indeed, our teachers will criticize nowadays both as regards quantity and quality, but neither Church nor State nor school will raise a warning finger between a man and his hunger and his wife's catering. So on nearly every day in his life Mr. Polly fell into a violent rage and hatred against the outer world in the afternoon, and never suspected that it was this inner world to which I am with such masterly delicacy alluding, that was thus reflecting its sinister disorder upon the things without. It is a pity that some human beings are not more transparent. If Mr. Polly, for example, had been transparent, or even passably translucent, then perhaps he might have realized, from the Laocoön struggle he would have glimpsed, that indeed he was not so much a human being as a civil war.

"Wonderful things must have been going on inside Mr. Polly. Oh ! wonderful things. It must have been like a badly-managed industrial city during a period of depression ; agitators, acts of violence, strikes, the forces of law and order doing their best, rushings to and fro, upheavals, the *Marseillaise*, tumbrils, the rumble and the thunder of the tumbrils. . . ."

Mr. Polly is one of the best stories Mr. Wells ever wrote. I think of Mr. Polly from time to time, though it is years since I read about him. The above passage came into my mind through association by contraries. I had been reading Lady Jekyll's moving *Kitchen Essays*, and feeling as I read, for the first time, the kind of pleasure musical people must derive from reading a score. Her chapter on " Christmas Cheer," for instance, dispelled for me, as I read, recollections of the gloom of the festal season. After a paragraph or two about decorations, and after reminding us that we set plum puddings and mincepies on fire, not, as we suppose, to increase their wholesomeness, but to invoke the blessing of the Sun, she proceeds : " Let us, then, keep Christmas with all time-honoured usages of high festival, and again welcome the *turkey* with abundant accompaniments of bread sauce and gravy. Let an additional brown fire-proof or white metal dish follow it with ample supplies of chestnuts darkly braised with good stock, or creamed to a delicious purée with milk and butter. Then there will be room also for the midget sausages and tiny, crisp curls of bacon, for browned or new potatoes (bottled by the prudent), for grilled mushrooms and little balls of stuffing or precious truffles. These can never all be swiftly or adequately distributed from one dish."

You catch the thrill ? Of course you do ! But, as a literary man, let me point out, not the practical good sense of the advice, but the power of the adverbs, " swiftly or adequately." They bring before us the tension of the expectant guests.

I have never read Dumas' *Cookery Book*, but this book of Lady Jekyll's has the gusto one fancies his must possess. The merit of these *Kitchen*

Essays is not merely practical ; they convince the reader that good cooking is thoroughly worth achieving. And there is another point about them. To a certain extent we are all psychologists about food—we do not offer our friends *crème brûlée* at breakfast, for example ; but Lady Jekyll carries such discretions further. She has separate chapters, on a little dinner before a play, on supper after the play, on luncheons for motor excursions in winter, on food for travellers, on food for musicians, speakers and singers before their ordeals, on food for the punctual or the unpunctual, on bachelors' dinners, and on holiday hampers. In each case she shows a subtle sense of what is likely to give most pleasure. The motto of her book is a modest one from Montaigne, " Here I have but gathered a nosegay of strange flowers, and have put nothing of mine into it but the thread to bind them." I cannot criticize her recipes, but the quality of that thread I can judge of : it was woven by an enthusiast who knew what she was doing.

* * * *

During the War food acquired a romantic importance. The most emaciate or most complicated sage would in France have recaptured the forgotten gusto of a smuggled dormitory feast. Other familiar things, too, acquired a profound significance ; a smooth pillow and a turned-down sheet, for example, meant peace and rest unfathomable. My own war experience was comparatively mild, yet a bird of mountainous grandeur, eaten at Christmas at Ypres, stands out against the sky of memory. In dessert we were well off—we had figs, raisins, chocolates, gingerbreads ; but till a ham in a tin box like a musical instrument arrived—and that bird, it seemed likely that our dinner would lack in staple dishes. How was the

87

turkey to be cooked ? Oil lamps with a blowpipe attached were not adequate, and to drop it in the porridge-pot and boil it soft would have been desecration. Now there were nuns still left in Ypres in 1914, and it was decided that I should take the turkey round to their kitchen.

Christmas Day had begun for ambulance-men like any other ; there might be a truce along the line that morning, but there had not been a truce the day before. Still, work was over by ten o'clock, and the rest of the day was spent in nailing up holly, fixing a chandelier of motor lamps, beating up and borrowing things of every description from spoons to trestle tables—and in constant visits to see how the turkey was browning. Our feast, like all good feasts, began in portentous solemnity and ended in song. The nuns came to listen to the songs and pull crackers with us ; and when the Mother Superior was crowned with a paper cap they laughed, flung up their hands and clapped them down on their knees like true Flemings. It was all over by nine o'clock ; but we felt we had eaten and drunk like Belshazzar.

*   *   *   *

Meredith seemed in *Richard Feverel* to poke fun at " the wise youth " for giving Lucy after her marriage a cookery-book to read ; but he projected a cookery-book of his own to be written in collaboration with his wife. I do not know if it has ever been published.[1] When I was told that Mrs.

[1] When this essay was first published in the *New States-man*, a correspondent, Mr. R. B. Beckett, I.C.S., wrote from Lahore to tell me that Meredith's Cookery-Book, in manuscript, was on sale with one of the London booksellers just before the War, at a moderate price. It was stated to be a work of collaboration with his first father-in-law, Thomas Love Peacock, not as I supposed of Meredith and his wife.

Conrad had such a book in preparation, I immediately thought of the august adjectives that Conrad could have contributed to it. But there are many authors whose cookery-books I would not trust. I do not want to read one by Mr. Bernard Shaw, nor I think by Mr. Hardy, nor one by Mrs. Meynell, though I am not quite sure in her case; and it would only be from intellectual curiosity that I would buy one by Ibsen.

*　　*　　*　　*

The art of cooking is regarded in England as an inferior art, and those who proclaim their pleasure in good fare fall under the suspicion of being sensualists of the poorest kind, whose foible has no touch of poetry about it. Thackeray and Disraeli have each introduced accomplished cooks into one of their famous stories, but what a contrast in their respective attitudes towards the pretensions of professors !

Monsieur Alcide Mirobolant in *Pendennis* is a ridiculous figure, with his richly-flowing ringlets, his crimson velvet waistcoat, and his passion for Blanche Amory. " I declared myself to her," said Alcide, laying his hand on his heart, " in a manner which was as novel as I am charmed to think it was agreeable " ; and he proceeds to describe the dinner he sent up one night when Miss Blanche was entertaining some of her school friends : " a little *potage à la Reine—à la Reine Blanche* I called it—as white as her own tint—

My correspondent continued : " I suppose you have noticed how often the germs of Meredith's work can be found in Peacock's, particularly the condensing of what there is to be said into dinner-table conversations, and the *succulence* of any description of comestibles : the importance of port, and the introduction of characters with a chief interest in their interiors."

89

and confectioned with the most fragrant cream and almonds. . . . I followed with two little *entrées* of sweet-bread and chicken ; and the only brown thing which I permitted myself in the entertainment was a little roast lamb, which I laid in a meadow of spinaches, surrounded with croustillons, representing sheep, and ornamented with daisies and other savage flowers." The climax, after a dish of opal-coloured plover's eggs and a little *gâteau* of apricots, was an ice of *plombière* and cherries. " How do you think I had shaped them, Madame Frisbi ? In the form of two hearts united with an arrow, on which I laid, before it entered, a bridal veil in cut-paper, surmounted by a wreath of virginal orange-flowers." This is delightful mockery. But now turn to Disraeli. There are many passages in which he takes banquets and the art of cooking with a gravity so grave as to be indistinguishable from irony. Disraeli's sympathy was always divided between common-sense and the wildest romantic pretensions—his irony springs from the conflict between these sympathies. Thackeray, on the other hand, cannot stand any nonsense. Though at first he is indulgent towards poor Mirobolant's claim to be an artist, he cannot put up with such absurdities for long, and the only way in which he can preserve his patience is by making Mirobolant a little crazy.

At the beginning of *Tancred* Disraeli introduces us to the *chef*, Mr. Leander, who has just been summoned to celebrate the coming-of-age of the Duke of Bellamont's son. It is to be a business of the Thousand-and-one-Nights, and the duke's cook is not equal to the occasion. When the story opens we see Mr. Leander making his way down one of the by-streets of Mayfair to call on " Papa Prevost," to ask his advice. The great man, who is sitting in a nightcap reading a French newspaper, with a glass of sugared water by his side, receives him most warmly. " What do they say ? That Abreu rivals you in flavour, and that Gaillard has not less invention. But who can combine goût with new combinations ? it is yourself, Leander ; and there is no question, though you have only twenty-five years, that you are the chef of the age." To which Leander replies, bending his head with great respect, " You are always very good to me, sir, and I will not deny, that to be famous when you are young is the fortune of the gods." Disraeli has as much sympathy with the fame of a cook as with the fame of an author or a duke.

*   *   *   *

In Paris every summer a culinary exhibition is held, and on these occasions the President of the Republic, who opens it, addresses a few words to the assembled Vatels in this vein : " France is celebrated throughout the world for her literature and her arts, and above all for her cookery. No-where—it is universally agreed—can one dine so well as in France. You, gentlemen, contribute therefore most potently to your country's reputation and prosperity. You are conscious of the importance of the part you play : Persevere therefore, etc., etc."

The boast that the cookery of France rules the tables of the world is no vain one. From a gastronomical point of view the language of man-kind is French, and France exports accomplished cooks to all countries. There they develop their art on the lines laid down by the famous masters of their own country, Carême, Vatel, Berchoux. But there is unfortunately no doubt that the esteem which their art has enjoyed is waning. Most of those who consider carefully to-day what they shall eat, approach the question from the dismal angle of hygiene. They are concerned not with flavours, but with ingredients. Already one restaurant in London recommends items on its *menu* as " body-building," or " very body-building." If this is carried further we shall find ourselves masticating hygienic concoctions to the rhythm of a metronome.

" MAX " once wrote a delightful essay called "Dulcedo Judiciorum," in which he owned to finding the drama provided by the Law Courts superior to that provided by the theatres. At the same time, he said, he much preferred listening to civil cases :

> " I cannot but follow in my heart the English law and assume (pending proof, which cannot be forthcoming) that the prisoner in the dock has a character, at any rate, as fine as my own. The war that this assumption wages in my breast against the fact that the man will, perhaps, be sentenced is too violent a war not to discommode me. Let justice be done. Or, rather, let our rough and ready, well-meant endeavours towards justice go on being made. But I won't be there to see, thank you very much."

I understand what he means, but I confess my curiosity is usually stronger than such qualms. I have only attended two sensational cases in my life, but if opportunity offered I should, no doubt, attend another.

The first was the trial of a woman for the murder of her child, a poor little creature about eight years old and subject to fits. The child was illegitimate, and a great burden on its mother. She was living with a man whom she hoped to marry, and he had consented to pay a few shillings a week to some home for such unwanted waifs, because no landlady would keep a child with fits. Perhaps

93

the woman had discovered that more money was required for this than he would be likely to give ; anyhow, she determined to spare his pocket by leaving the child with her parents, while telling him she was taking it to the home. With that end she went by train to Reading and set out to walk. It was a wet, windy day. She had twelve miles to go. Witnesses came forward who had passed her on the road, and according to them, she was sometimes carrying the child and sometimes pulling it along ; one witness reported that the child was crying. They were all going in a direction contrary to hers—perhaps if she had been able to get a lift that crime would have never been committed. She became exasperated and tired ; and when she approached her home it seems suddenly to have struck her that, after all, her plan could not work. She had already deposited another little misbegot with her parents, and about that child she had not owned up to her man. If she left both children there, sooner or later, he would find out about the first, and then—would he marry her ? So she turned back, lugging the crying child. What happened on the walk back we never learnt, but the child was afterwards found, strangled, in a wayside pool.

I did not pick out this painful case. I happened to be staying with the Sheriff, and so accompanied him to the Assizes. In Court that war of sympathies within the breast of which " Max " speaks was considerably mitigated in mine by one little incident. The accused woman betrayed no emotion during the trial until the Judge asked the witness who had found the body to show the jury how the lace collar had been wound round the child's neck. The witness did so by putting the collar round his own. The prisoner then bent her head to hide a smile—the gentleman looked so funny !

This seemed to betoken a degree of insensibility in the criminal type which relieves one from too acute a fellow-feeling.

* * * *

The only historic trial I ever attended was that of Sir Roger Casement, and the impressions it left in me are as fresh as they were that day.

To me, when I attended the High Court on the last day of this trial, the prisoner was not a symbolic figure of Ireland's wrongs, nor was the court an embodiment of England's rights. He was a man, and I—one who looked on and listened. We all of us have a characterless percipient in us, though he is rarely active; indeed, it is only in the small sleepless hours of the morning that most of us are aware of him. Come with me, at any rate, in the spirit of those small hours. I cannot take you excitedly by the arm, as some reporters might do, and point to this or that; characterless percipients have no arms, and there can be no good-fellowship between us.

Imagine, however, that we have successfully " seen," as the police call it, the policeman who keeps back the crowd, a crowd which lingers in the dark passage with the wistfulness of hungry urchins outside an eating-shop—resigned to not going in, but unable to tear themselves away—and that we have pushed together through these swing-doors.

So this is an historic trial! One day some future Carlyle or Macaulay may describe it in phrases which will make it vibrant with passion and life. How convincing his description will be, and yet how false! He will mention that the venerable ex-ambassador and historian, Lord Bryce, was there, looking down an interested spectator from the gallery; he will sketch the career of the young Lord Chief Justice, Lord Reading, destined to be an Indian Viceroy, and who was also once a ship's boy ; and, perhaps, if he is a very learned historian, he will touch in lightly the careers of the two judges who sit on either side of the Lord Chief Justice. He will certainly paint the portrait of the Attorney-General, whose political career had been deeply implicated with Irish affairs, and who, as Lord Birkenhead, was destined to take a most important part in the creation of the Irish Free State. Yes, distinguished personages are there, careers and all ; but such accessories, out of which historians create an atmosphere, seem at the moment of precious little importance. The air of sleepy unreality which haunts the Courts of Law broods over even this trial, too. Ramparted behind desks, and raised above everybody, sit the judges in scarlet ; their dress denotes that it is impossible to speak to them as a man to men. They have ceased, in a way, to be human. They are embodiments of impersonal forces. When they speak of each other they call each other " brother," and the word excludes the rest of mankind. Do they make a joke or pay a compliment to counsel ? The remark has a peculiar savour, as though it were a kind of *lusus naturæ.* And there is the usual contrast between the leisurely matter-of-factness of the proceedings and the excruciatingly vital issue at stake.

A long man in a black gown, with wig tilted off his forehead, like a straw hat on a hot day, and an oddly undergraduate air, is talking ; talking as emphatically as his preoccupation with what he is going to say next allows. It is the Attorney-General. He is saying that it is not necessary to go into old, unpleasant controversies, for an event has happened which has altered the whole face of Irish politics : he means the war with Germany.

For a moment, my mood changes ; I cease to be a detached observer. I feel inclined to interject, " But it didn't alter them—that's the whole tragedy. And why ' old,' as though these controversies were dead and buried long ago ? " Then I slip back into being a characterless percipient. The Attorney-General goes on. His passion comes in irregular gusts, like the noise of talking through a swing-door which is constantly opening and shutting. There seems no particular reason why he should be so moved one moment or so casual the next. His moral indignation appears something he can turn on and off with a tap. These contemptuous gestures of abhorrence directed towards the prisoner—at whom he never looks—what kind of emotion do they represent ? Is the speaker's heart really aflame ? If so, how account for these sudden drops into the conciliatory casual tone of a sensible man addressing all sensible men ?

The argument is sound enough and well arranged. It is clear as a pikestaff that Sir Roger Casement has committed treason ; that he tried to land arms in Ireland, and to persuade Irish prisoners in Germany to fight against England. The verdict is a foregone conclusion. I keep wondering why the accused does not jump up and cry, " Enough of this ; I deny nothing ; sentence me to be hanged and have done." For the first time I look at him steadily and try to read him. He sits, fidgeting a little now and then, in a lassitude of composed impatience. I guess that he is suffering from an internal, churning sensation of anguish. He looks at his watch ; occasionally he yawns a little. It is not a yawn of indifference—I saw that half-yawn on the faces of men in France, just before they were going into action, or when shells were beginning to arrive. But the prisoner does not jump up ; he allows the Attorney-General to

go on telling a perfectly clear story, which, nevertheless, as a human story, is quite incomprehensible.
There are no motives in it ! And he ends by telling
the jury that they have a duty to perform as
painful as that which is being performed by others,
elsewhere, in these bloody and critical days, in
the service of the Empire. Here, it strikes me that
the Attorney-General is speaking as a civilian. I
wonder if the Lord Chief Justice is really going to
find charging the jury as painful as he would find
charging the Germans at La Boisselle.

The Lord Chief Justice turns in his chair
towards the jury with an almost confidential
movement, which says as plainly as speech, " Now
I am going to make everything clear ; you can't
go wrong if you listen to my words, and they will
be nearly all of one syllable." He takes out his
eyeglass and looks at them, while they crane forward as though fairly hypnotized. He begins by
telling them that they must not think the counsel
for the defence a wicked or disloyal man for having
said what he did on behalf of the prisoner ; that
it is, on the contrary, the pride of the English
Bar that the prisoner should be defended whatever
the crime of which he may be accused ; that it was
a courageous, admirable speech. He then goes on
to say that he has always felt anxiety in a Court
of Justice when there was any possibility of political
passions being introduced : " Justice was ever in
jeopardy when passion was aroused." " Yes,
my lord," a voice cried out within me (perhaps an
Irish voice), " that is true ; but justice of the
finer sort may be also in jeopardy when the existence
of political passion is ignored." He goes on explaining what is meant by " aiding and comforting
the King's enemies," the clause under which the
prisoner stands indicted. It covered (no one felt
surprise) seducing the King's soldiers with a view

to making them fight against England, also import-
ing arms for the use of rebellious subjects from
a country with which the King of England is at
war.

"Put a coronet on a man's head, and the blood
in his brain will start circulating in different
fashion, flooding new channels, and changing in
important respects his outward demeanour." It
is the same with a judge's wig. I hardly recognized
in the Lord Chief Justice the advocate I remembered. His clear, ringing voice had become
a minatory mumble; his delivery so weighty
as to be almost indistinct. He seemed to have
aged thirty years. The stand-firm, prompt-pounc-
ing manner of the advocate had changed into the
ominous formality of immemorial authority. I
hastily remind myself that it is unfair to charge
a man with insincerity for adopting a manner, not
natural perhaps to him, but appropriate to his
function. Yet sometimes circumstances arise which
sharpen our contempt for acting of all kinds, and
then. . . . Well, it was precisely this that was to
happen after the luncheon interval.

Of course, during the morning I had looked
from time to time at the accused. I noticed two
things about him : First, he was obviously a
foreigner. He might have been, for all one could
tell, with his sallow face, black beard, and that
peculiar lift—did it betoken vanity or pride ?—
of the eye-brow, a Spanish hidalgo. I decided he
was very vain. Secondly, he was a type of man
whose "spiritual home," to use a phrase then
famous, was certainly not a Court of Justice.
Doubtless he would have been a better man, a more
reliable one, had he had something of the final
matter-of-fact sense of right and wrong which
reigns there. He looked the sort of man who
might put devotion to a purpose or an ideal so

high that, when that emotion possessed him, nothing else, no virtues, consistencies, or loyalties, would seem to him of much consequence. There were, I knew then, grave inconsistencies in his career, and I learnt afterwards there was also a grotesquely morbid streak in his temperament. Somewhere, in some legal or political archives, his private diary is still kept, and the publication of extracts from it would effectively prevent the canonization of his memory. It would be itself a dirtier action than any private shame recorded in that diary, but it would be effective.

Looking at him, I realized how inevitable it was that, as he had accepted a knighthood from the King, he should have done so in a graceful letter. Such a man could no more be curmudgeonly than he could be raspingly rude. As for his living on a pension from a Government he was betraying, I said to myself he would regret he had done so, yet he would feel he had earned every penny of it in the past—and anyhow, loyalty to his cause came first. It was a miserable, irretrievable fact that " his honour rooted in dishonour stood," but there was no helping it. Thus I explained him to myself. What those whom he had betrayed had a right to think of his conduct was another question. He himself would not expect mercy where he had betrayed confidence.

The jury were away about an hour. What they were hesitating about I could not conceive. When the hush of Court was disturbed by the jury's return and the curtain shook and the usher came in, we stirred uneasily. The prisoner smiled ; he seemed happier now.

After the verdict the Lord Chief Justice asked him if he had anything to say. He was, of course, standing up between the warders at that moment, and he stepped to the rail with a manuscript in his

100

hand : " My Lords, as I wish my words to reach a much wider audience than this, I intend to read all I propose to say." The new voice was very agreeable—a little uncertain and agitated ; and the papers shook in his hand. It was the first perfectly natural voice we had heard in Court all day, and at the sound of it something very strange occurred : the dream-like formalism of the proceedings vanished ; the tension relaxed ; his judges turned to look at him for the first time, and with a kind of friendly curiosity, leaning on their elbows to listen.

What a different point of view, what a fantastically different point of view, was presented to us ! " If true religion rests on love, it is equally true that loyalty rests on love. . . . Loyalty is a sentiment, not a law. It rests on love, not restraint. The Government of Ireland by England rests on restraint and not on law ; and since it demands no love it can evoke no loyalty." Good heavens ! either this was the most arrant rubbish, or Sir Frederick Smith and Lord Reading had left out a great deal. I felt that at bottom it was my view, too, but the difference between me and the rebel in the dock was that I loved England, and I could never have wished him success at the cost of England's downfall. Yet I could understand him. For, if instead of being a hyphenated Irishman, owing everything that makes life worth living to Englishmen and to living in England, I had been brought up in Ireland, could I have helped putting Ireland first ? Would the legal aspect of my position as a subject of King George have seemed the absolutely final word on what my attitude ought to be during the War ? I do not think so. But presently I was wondering far more at the strange world of romantic legality into which the condemned man seemed to be drifting. He was reading to us about Edward III, and the claim of the English Crown upon French subjects ! It seemed fantastic, till I grasped that, to him, it was an obvious fact that England had no more claim over Ireland than she had over modern France. The Press afterwards commented on his impenitent and smiling departure from the Court. But, if this was what he believed, what reason had he for repentance ? To me the relations of these two countries did not seem so simple that they could be summed up by saying that they had nothing to do with each other ; but what I felt was that England had so ruled Ireland that she had forfeited her right to expect loyalty as a matter of course from all Irishmen.

He finished his speech ; and as if by magic (one had not noticed the attendants behind the chairs) three black squares of cloth appeared on the wigs of the judges. The Lord Chief Justice read out the death-sentence in low, even tones, while the other two kept their eyes upon their papers.

The memory which will stay with me is that of a sincerity in the prisoner at once more human and more idealistic than the sincerity of the men who were sitting in judgment upon him, and of its strange effect on the proceedings. At its touch, the trial, even the solemnity of the death-sentence, seemed to lose their significance—their power, at least, to brand as well as to kill.

THE WONDER ZOO

IT was Saturday afternoon. Each train disgorged two or three hundred people, and a number of children of different ages and sizes. I, too, passed into the entrance lobby of Olympia. The turnstiles were worked by large men in tall, white coaching-hats and drab ulsters. The next moment I was in *The Wonder Zoo.* The first impression is a complex one. You walk up a slight incline and find yourself in a place which reminds you of a vast railway station, a huge terminus which has been touched by the wand of a somewhat theatrical Bacchus. Extravagant pale green vines have covered the glass roof, shutting out the light of day, and the familiar, glaring electric balls, which depend from it, are half shrouded in clustering creepers. Fix your eyes on the tobacco or sweets kiosk at your elbow, and you might still believe yourself at Paddington or Charing Cross ; but raise them, and you are astonished to find yourself at the foot of a towering cliff, on the stony ledges of which are huddled in squalid sociability dozens of brown pink-behinded apes. A little to the left, on a less precipitous slope, lies an Abyssinian bear, frowning majestically and trying to doze. A flight of steps leads you to a kind of platform grooved in the rock, and then you perceive that a deep trench, some twenty-five or thirty feet wide, separates you from these animals. This is the best spot for getting a general view of your surroundings. Below lies a rocky landscape with flat-bottomed hollows in it, and here and there a pool of water. One of them is full

103

of birds.   In it all sorts of cranes are preening their feathers and stretching their necks, and beside it ostriches are launching themselves about with that jaunty, springy gait, at once so elegant and so ridiculous.   There are geese and pelicans, too, round the water-hole, and a lovely zebra, looking as smart as a new carriage in a coach-builder's window, and a number of meek-eyed, brittle-legged antelopes. To the left again there is a dark pool, with two pairs of eyes and nostrils just apparent above its surface. The young hippopotami are enjoying that euthan-asia which is the aim of their existence.   True, they have never known the joys of mud-wallowing or of reaping sheaves of succulent reeds by the mouthful; still, they are free from one of the principal worries of hippopotamic existence, being washed down river in their sleep.   On the whole, next to the crocodile, of all captive animals I am inclined to commiserate them least.   Yet they are particularly difficult to keep in captivity, which suggests, as is the case with some poets, that a somewhat stolid appearance betrays an inward deep capacity for sentiment.   Not far off is a two-horned rhinoceros or rhinaster, a native of East Africa.   He lives in a depression in the rocks with a sandy floor.   He has a choleric and saurian eye.   The skin of this animal does not fall in heavy folds like that of the Asiatic species ; of it no poet could write, " Rhinoceros, your hide is all undone." Naturalists describe it as a " truly fearful opponent," though all are agreed that it is not so formidable as the keitloa, which is bigger, and, size apart, can easily be distinguished from it by the shape of its second horn.   This is equal in length to the first, while the rhinaster's second horn is short and conical. It is an animal difficult to please.   The Asiatic rhinoceros can be placated (so they say) by anyone who has the nerve to lift up one of the heavy flaps of hide and remove the parasites collected there ; but I do not see how one is to please the smooth African rhinoceros.

In another of these depressions in the rock lives what is called a " happy family " ; that is to say, a number of animals which would naturally fly at each other's throats, if they did not share bed and board. In this case " the happy family " consists of young bears, Eskimo dogs, young hyenas, young lions, and a young Himalayan bear. I do not care for " happy families " myself. In them, as in human homes where deep incongruities of temperament exist, the individuals by living together seem to lose in spirit what they gain in wariness. Think what your own feelings would be if you were born with the traditions of a young lion, and had to put up with a beastly hyena snuffling round you all day ! Of course they get used to it, but I do not believe in total eradication of racial prejudices, however difficult they may be to justify in the court of reason; and Pliny says that the lion hates the hyena so intensely that " if both their skins be hanged together, the hair of the lion's skin shall fall away." Lastly, immediately in front of you as you stand on the platform, rises an immense round object, like the socket of a gigantic night-light. This is one end of the arena. The spectators are hidden, but out of it issue shouts of laughter and sudden crepitations of applause. There was not a seat to be got last Saturday, not even for ten shillings. Looking through the various passages leading into the arena, I could see for a second a racy individual twinkle by in a light buggy, or a deft and spangled lady poised on a bare-backed steed. I felt like one of those little louts who lie on their bellies at travelling shows and peep under the tents—" Hi ! Bill, here ; I can see the 'oofs of the 'orses." No, not quite like one of them, for

105

I do not care for performing animals. To see an elephant make a fool of himself does not amuse me in the least, and I had much rather watch seals catching fish than catching balls. I saw the seals in their tank between their performances. There was a constant flow of water in and out of it, and the liveliness of the slippery creatures was more delightful to me than any of their acquired antics could possibly have been. The seal is one of the most intelligent and affectionate animals, and it is very painful to think of what goes on at the seal fisheries every year. It has, as my first natural history book taught me, " a disposition to become familiar " ; and my next instructor, the Rev. Wood, added that seals taken young " have been strongly domesticated with their captors, considering themselves to belong of right to the household, and taking their share of the fireside with the other members of the family." Dear old Wood ! If modern naturalists write with more knowledge and terseness than you, none tell us so many things we should like to believe about animals. I cannot now quite believe in a seal on anybody's hearthrug, gazing with melting eyes upon the glowing coals, though at one time, had I been fortunate enough to possess one, I should no doubt have tried to domesticate it " strongly."

Near the tank was a row of young Indian elephants, each tethered by one hind and one foreleg and standing shoulder to shoulder. They were presumably performers, waiting for their " turn." They were shuffling and swaying up and down uneasily, and in spite of the notice PLEASE DON'T FEED US above their heads, they kept lifting their trunks and showing the inside of their moist, pink mouths. Many of them were so young that the sparse black hair on their weighty foreheads was not yet rubbed off. It is extraordinary how this

thin-set growth adds to the majestic thoughtfulness
of their appearance. No man was ever as wise as
a young elephant looks. The story of elephantine
sagacity which pleases me most is that of the
painter, who wished to paint an elephant with its
trunk erect and its mouth open, and therefore
engaged a man to throw fruit to it during the sitting.
The supply of fruit running rather low, the man
began to feign, instead of throwing an apple every
time. After a series of disappointments, the
elephant turned to the artist, and directing his
trunk at the canvas, obliterated it completely with
one wet blast.

At the other end of the arena are two cages :
one large semicircular one with a tank, containing
" Tilli Bébé's " polar bears ; the other, a long
narrow travelling cage, containing Mr. Richard
Sawade's ten Bengal tigers. The bears were
trained for Captain Amundsen as draught animals
for Arctic exploration, but it was decided that they
would want too much watching when off work.
Besides, however docile at their job they may appear
in the arena, once they got upon their native snows
and felt the fierce delicious cold, I am sure they
would prove a difficult team to drive. Although
the cage is small for twenty bears, they appear to
be in prime condition. I do not think I have seen
such fine specimens anywhere before. I watched
them for a long time ; some, after the manner of
their race, swinging doggedly back and forth,
as though doing some exercise prescribed by an
ursine Sandow ; others rolling each other over like
great snowballs, or standing on their hind legs and
playfully cuffing each other with their paws.

The tigers are young, but they are very large
for their age, and remarkably sleek. It must
be remembered that in the case of lions, bears,
or tigers which, like these tigers, have been

practically reared in a Zoo (the oldest of them is only sixteen months old, and they have all been exhibited and trained for eight months) their natural ferocity is much less, and consequently the process of cowing them much less drastic. They may even require a flick of the whip to kindle that sudden flare of temper which the public expect, if they are to believe in the danger to the tamer his exhibition nevertheless always entails. I watched Mr. Sawade get his tigers out of their cage. Most of them went like lambs; only one glared and snarled when he touched the bars of the cage with his whip, and then drew off with a sullen slink of lovely treachery, licking its stiff whiskers as though it longed to fasten its jaws on him. They are superb beasts. The beauty of the tiger is so impressive that I wonder anybody wants to see it play tricks, but on the other hand so terrifying that I am not surprised people like to see man dominating it. The tiger is at one moment the very incarnation of the beauty of anger, and yet " how politic his grace in moods morose ! " How thrilling to see him sharply shorten his body for a spring ! He took his name from his swiftness, for the Parsees call an arrow " Tigris." And then " the royal cruelty of that face ! "

It is not the tamer but the big-game sportsman the lover of animals loathes. Though tricks may bore him and even depress him, though the sight of caged animals makes him sorry : yet without the one he would miss opportunities of seeing many of their movements, and if there were no Zoos he would probably not see the animals at all. When we alarm ourselves with the idea that training implies punishment, it is reassuring to remember that most of the men who train animals have a passion for them, and to recall that teaching one's own cat or dog has implied keeping their confidence

and winning their affection. Personally, I wish
all tricks were given up, but it is not the showman
but the sportsman who rouses my wrath. I hate
him as some hate those who destroy old buildings,
with his " bags," explosive bullets, and tree platforms, well stocked with powder and refreshments.
Look at him as he is photographed in his sun
helmet, his sandwich-box slung round him, posing
for us in the public prints as an Horatius Cocles,
arms crossed, his foot upon the neck of one of
a row of glorious beasts, each possessing a hundred
times more beauty every hour of the day than he
could create in a life-time. Who can walk up the
stairs of one of our big clubs, past the hundreds of
horns of lovely and harmless creatures, now being
exterminated in every quarter of the earth merely
to give young men healthy exercise and distraction,
without whispering a wish to the propitious heavens
that every married man among them may be horned
himself before he dies ?

The Hagenbecks have a good tradition. Their
father, Carl Hagenbeck, introduced the system of
substituting for cages plots of variegated ground in
Zoos. At Olympia many of the animals are
necessarily kept in their travelling quarters, which
are, of course, narrow ; but they have every
appearance of being admirably tended, and the
only smell which reaches the nostril (even the vul-
ture's cage is odourless) is a human one. It is, of
course, a trying experience for a wild animal, a
show like this ; the glaring electric light, the
shindy and ceaseless shuffling of feet. Many of
them struck me as looking like passengers in a night
train, woken up to show their tickets. But let the
tender reader comfort himself or herself—the nerves
of the Bactrian camel or the dwarf hippo are
probably firmer than either his or even hers.

THE DUKE OF YORK

THE Duke of York's Steps is the finest site in
London for a statue. It struck me particularly
the other day, for I had heard a rumour that a pro-
posal was on foot to remove that royal personage
from his exalted position and replace him by the
effigy of a worthier man. Few people know how
he came to be perched there. The best account of
his character and career is to be found in that delightful book of historical gossip, *Glimpses of the
Twenties*, by Mr. William Toynbee. Mr. William
Toynbee is one of the few English writers who
handle historical subjects of the personal kind
with the wit and neatness of French memoir-writers.
He writes from a full mind, and he knows the
beginning of the nineteenth century as well as
Mr. Austin Dobson knew parts of the eighteenth
century. I cannot think why his two books, the
one I have just mentioned and *Vignettes of the
Regency*, are not better known; they are delightful
reading.

The Duke of York was George III's favourite
son. He came next in age to the Regent, and he
was called " the Hope of the Family," not on
account of his brains—of these he had a scanty
share—but because, one of a bad bunch of brothers,
he was the most amiable, courageous and genial.
His life was spent in raking, drinking, gambling,
and sinking ever more deeply into debt, but
" Tommy Atkins " liked him. There was a kind
of boisterous bonhomie about him for which the
English have a weakness. He got into some ex-

110

THE DUKE OF YORK

traordinarily disreputable scrapes, for all his life
he was at the mercy of venal adventuresses; but he
behaved once very well in a duel, and he was always
excessively good-natured. On two occasions he
was entrusted with the command of the British
Army in the field ; an appointment which resulted
in the gravest discredit, if not disgrace, to our
troops. He was an inveterate toper, and about
the worst strategist whose name has been handed
down in history. After the disaster of the Helder
expedition he was retired to the Horse Guards,
where he did fairly well, thanks chiefly to his
personal popularity, which was based on a reputation for never refusing an interview to a private
soldier. There he remained until "his career
was temporarily checked," says Mr. William Toynbee, "by an unfortunate attempt to reconcile
the worship of Mars with that of Venus, the repre-
sentative of the latter divinity being the incon-
stant spouse of a bankrupt stonemason named
Clarke, whom the Duke 'protected' in a sump-
tuous establishment in Gloucester Place." Mrs.
Clarke was fond of having everything handsome
about her ; and to the Duke extremely good and
large dinners were as essential as cigarettes are to
most journalists ; moreover making presents (on
long credit) of costly diamonds had become second
nature to him. But as a "protector" he had one
great drawback : not only had he seldom any
ready-money, but even when he had he was not
willing to part with it. Mrs. Clarke took the situation into her own hands. The house in Gloucester
Place became the business resort of officers in quest
of promotion and of clergymen with a desire for
preferment. She drove a very brisk trade, sometimes touching four figures at a bargain. Then
the Duke quarrelled with her over an accom-
modation bill, and left her with but £400 a year.

111

She promptly threatened to publish her " Recollections," " embellished with over fifty effusions from his impulsive pen." Publication was for a time averted by promises, but the promises failing to mature, Mrs. Clarke took the step of coaching a Whig M.P., and a public inquiry was instituted. Though the Duke was exonerated from actual participation in the proceeds of her traffic," it is difficult to resist the conclusion that he was cognisant of it, indeed, welcomed her corrupt transactions as contributing to raise the supplies which he failed to provide." So he wisely resigned, and a year or two afterwards he was reinstated as Commander-in-Chief by his affectionate brother, George IV.

This is a human, all-too-human story ; but how on earth did he get to the top of that column, next to Nelson's the most towering monument in England ?

The story is one which might teach the most ambitious the vanity of fame ; for if not only fame, but popular adulation, is so easily won, what is it but an empty breath ? One morning in 1825 he awoke to find himself famous. I do not suppose the night he went down to the House of Lords, purple with indignation and with wine, he had the smallest notion that a confused philippic would cause him to be hailed as the saviour of the Church, let alone exalt him in the eyes of all men high above the chimney-pots for at least a hundred years. The Lords had shown signs of weakening on the subject of Catholic Emancipation, and in a hobble-gobble fury down rushed the Royal Duke. The combed and depleted record of his speech, afterwards printed in gold, probably ill reflects its spontaneous character. It ended with the words, " So help me God " ; and the next day he " was acclaimed as the heaven-anointed champion of religion. Bishops fawned upon him ; anti-Catholic associations canonized him. He could not have awakened greater enthusiasm if he had been a reincarnated John the Baptist."

Fortunately he lived but two years more. Dropsy saved the situation. Although Newmarket and cards would probably, it is true, have kept him from doing the utmost harm, still, with such a figure-head for the Church and State party, it is not impossible that the row over Catholic Emancipation might have developed into something like civil war. Well, Catholics have votes and the Duke of York has his statue.

What do you think of that, my cat ? What do you think of that, my dog ? Shall we pull him off his pedestal, or shall we leave his pillar as a monument to human folly ?

Statues which have become invisible to the public owing to their complete indifference to the person commemorated, or are disgusting to taste, would be better removed. They only cheapen glory. But I would have it done tenderly, and with regard to the pathos of the occasion. Let us fake an appropriate ancient ceremonial. As I imagine it, the ceremony of veiling statues would be accompanied by music. The choir would be divided antiphonally ; one section asking the question anthem-fashion, *Usque adeone mori miserum est* ? (Is it then so hard a thing to die ?) and the other replying for the subject of the statue, *Liberavi animum meum* (I have delivered my soul) ; thus confessing through their voices that whatever he did for mankind had ceased at last to be operative, and that there was therefore no excuse for his bodily presence in the streets of the living, since his stone ghost could no longer remind them of anything. Then an official (His Majesty's Reputation Remover) would step forward and make a short

I

valedictory speech from the plinth, and the Cap of Oblivion would slowly descend. For this extinguisher I can think of no better inscription than the words *Mortuo Morituri*. What could be more appropriate, at the moment of consigning a fellow-mortal to oblivion, than to admit it was our destiny also? Lastly, to the cheerful strains of a good march we, the respectful crowd, would disperse and go our ways. If in the course of the next thirty days no British subject over fifteen years of age should observe and report that the statue or monument had been " veiled," the Authorities would be entitled to remove it.

CROWD PSYCHOLOGY

THE *Psychology of Crowds*, by Gustave Le Bon : it is years since I read it, but as clear as though I had written the words in the margin yesterday, the verdict stands in my memory : a good subject, a second-rate book. M. Gustave Le Bon is a slap-dash writer. Here was a subject worthy of subtlety, and M. Le Bon told us little beyond what we all knew, that assertion convinces a crowd better than argument, that a crowd regarded as an entity is a simple emotional creature with poor brains, that the feelings of its components get rubbed down to a common emotional denominator. M. Le Bon is a sort of usher or major-domo to the Courts of Science ; he is willing to show round large parties for (so to speak) a very low intellectual fee. It is a useful function, and if he did not seem to asseverate continually that we are being shown everything, when clearly we are not, I should feel nothing but gratitude to him. If anyone wishes to learn more about group-consciousness, and see the curious way the study of it links on to that of the religious consciousness, he had better read the works of M. Durkheim.

During the War Mr. Trotter published a very interesting book on *The Herd Instinct*, which was scientific enough until near the end, when his own herd-instinct ran away with him, and made him try to prove that that of a race called " Germans " was intrinsically different from others. I remember at the beginning of the War getting a pungent whiff of the herd-instinct while sitting at dinner next an eminent man of science. "I can assure you," he said, "that if a man of science refers to a German book in a footnote, it is sheer vanity. He does it to show he knows the language ; the Germans have contributed nothing "; for a minute or two I could not meet his eye again for shame. Good gracious, I thought, would he kick a stray dachshund if he met one on his way home ? Dachshunds were kicked in London and bulldogs (no doubt) in Berlin. This would not be so very depressing if one were not sure that it will be completely forgotten when, in the next war . . .

* * * *

Last Monday [1] I was in the crowd in Parliament Square ; it was this experience which reminded me of books about crowds and crowd emotions. I did not go for copy, nor did I at the time observe my feelings, which are best observed, not as they rush in, but, as I have said before, in the wrinkles they afterwards leave in the sand. I went to welcome back a statesman who for some years had been shamefully mishandled in the Press. The whole length of Whitehall was braided with people ; a crowd swirled and eddied round the wide open gates of Palace Yard. Immediately in front of me stood the bareheaded statue of Palmerston with his coat over his arm ; a little further off, bronze Disraeli, with his ironically courteous stoop, was waiting patiently for his annual tribute of primroses. Hitherto the figure of Palmerston had always reminded me of a man at a cloak-room barrier, who, having received his coat from the attendant, still holds out his hand for his hat ; but the moment the distant cheering rose to a solid roar, and Mr. Asquith's battered war-chariot (why

[1] March 1, 1920.

not simplify progression on these occasions by
reviving Boadicea's device of scythes on the
axles ?) turned at last into the yard of the House
of Commons, Palmerston seemed to express by
his gesture—(one hand outstretched, palm upwards)—as distinctly as if he had shouted it, the
words, "There! I told you so!" He was a good
judge of popular feeling, and what was I at that
moment but a thermometer under the tongue
of the public ? I felt glad, uncommonly glad.
No Prime Minister or Ex-Premier for many years
had had such a reception in the streets of London.

* * * *

Few, perhaps, have seen the medal designed and
struck by Captain Freddie Guest and Sir William
Sutherland which was presented to the successful
coupon-candidates in the Mad Election. "It
is put safely away among my more cherished
possessions," is the sort of evasive reply one receives from coupon-candidates on asking to look
at it. I have been more fortunate, for strolling
into the dressing-room of an M.P. while he was
changing for dinner, I happened to notice a bright
object lying in a small whatnot box containing
a few odd links, toothpicks, black pins, old watch
keys, and dusty tabloids. "A man has so few
receptacles," he said apologetically when I fished
it out, for it was the medal in question. It is
a gilt disc about the size of a sovereign, perhaps
a little larger ; on one side is engraved a gallows
with the Kaiser dangling from it, on the other,
a map of Germany with the words *Ex victis fiat
pecunia.* Their Latinity is perhaps open to criticism;
but the meaning conveyed is clear. Above it hangs
a star with fourteen points, and below a rather
prettily designed Welsh harp or liar. There was a
small ring attached to the edge so that the object

117

could be worn on the watch chain ; but few members of the Coalition had, I was given to understand, taken advantage of this convenience.

* * * *

Of all sounds reputed sad, none equals the sound of far-off cheering.

Dieu ! que le son du cor est triste au fond des bois ! To the sense of that famous line perhaps nothing in you responds ; perhaps because it recalls first to most Englishmen a huntsman's horn, while the poet was thinking of the death of Roland, when he tried, too late, to call back Charlemagne to Roncesvaux. The sound of small waves collapsing one after the other on a beach, when it is growing dark, has seemed to most poets a sad one. And so it is ; like all sounds which measure gravely the passage of time. But to my mind it does not equal in melancholy the sound of distant, intermittent cheers, a sound which, though excited and exciting, carries to one who sits alone a sense of the transitoriness of emotion. Those who are used to being cheered, and whose appearance is the signal for a demonstration, become very sensitive to shades of quality in cheers, independent of the volume of the sound. The ears of Royalty are quick to distinguish them, and, I imagine, the quality of their " receptions " on various occasions is a frequent subject of their discussions. What a curious, vague, histrionic emotion it is, which seizes the person on the kerb-stone when at last the procession appears ! It is a moment of complete self-forgetfulness, in which there may or may not be enthusiasm. I believe it is a desire for this momentary euthanasia which keeps people waiting so long and so patiently in the streets, a longing to lose themselves for

118

a second in a thousandfold exhalation of vague emotion.

The art of receiving cheers is a difficult one, and is by no means common. The flustered bow which implies " You are really, really too kind," is better, say, than Sir Thomas Beecham's bow at the close of a performance, which is distinctly distrustful, as much as to say, " Oh, this enthusiasm is all very well, but why then don't you come to the Opera more often?" and far better than Parnell's: " The sooner this damned noise stops the better." But the perfect enthusiastic-reception manner is a compound of gratitude, and collected sympathetic attention. The public man should throw quick glances about him, responding as though to individuals in the crowd ; for a crowd is a composite animal, and each member of it will feel (though no such thing has happened) as if his own eye had been caught.

KALOPROSŎPY

IT is easy to scrape odd acquaintances in London, about the parks or in the streets. But, of course, you must be properly dressed for that pursuit, as indeed for any other. There must be nothing about your get-up which entitles you to particular respect, certainly nothing that extorts deference, for that puts your relations to others all wrong from the very start. You must indeed be dressed badly enough to be embarrassed if you encounter your tailor, or an old prosperous friend whom you have not met for years ; for the personal appearance most favourable to easy talk with strangers is a cheerful shabbiness. Cheerfulness must peep through the shabbiness, since people do not fall into ready talk with glum, embittered, down-in-the-world strangers, especially if they have good reason to know those moods themselves. They do not expect any extraordinary sympathy from a casual acquaintance, nor any help from him if he does not look prosperous ; but those who lead lonely, haphazard lives (unlike people who live in society) are quite ready to believe a little pleasant intercourse is possible with a casual stranger, and the stranger who encourages that belief is one who wears an air of not having made a very good thing of life himself, but yet remains content.

One summer evening, during a long sunset, I was sitting on a bench in the Marble Arch quarter of Hyde Park, just out of earshot of the orators. I had gone the round of the platforms, and was now feeling glad to be out of the babel—glad to be

away from the secularist whose speech had broken
down into a dialogue (the conduct of the Creator
was under discussion), and who kept on repeating
with calm annoyance, " That's not my question.
I ask you, is it behaving like a *gentleman* ? "—away
from the frantic, hunted-looking young man who,
his moist pale face working in the twilight, kept
declaring, with the emphasis of despair, that he was
the happiest man in the world since his salvation ;
away from the woman who was grappling with the
decline of the birth-rate in Australia ; away even
from a large, shiny, radiant negro, who, having just
read a text-book on astronomy, had rushed out to
explain the heavens to the world, shouting to us,
"and de earth goes round and round de sun, and
de moon goes round and round de earth," whirling
an arm in an ecstasy of explanatory enthusiasm.
He certainly had (as the phrase goes) something to
say, but I was glad I had got away from him too.
The Park is the University of the People ; but it is a
University in such a hubble-bubble ferment of con-
viction and curiosity that those brought up at one
of the quieter seats of learning cannot attend it
long without feeling worried and alarmed.

In front of the platforms, and some distance
from them, I had noticed several times an elderly
man in a cloak and a soft hat with a high crown,
standing almost stock still. He had a soft bushy
beard and a noble hooked nose. Every now and
then someone on his way to sample another speaker
would linger as he passed him, as though expecting
to be addressed. Indeed, in the old man's passivity
there was something arresting, something that at
first incited approach, and then repelled it. I had
not sat long on the bench, when I observed him
coming down the path. He looked so aloof, I did
not like to speak to him, but as he was about to
pass, I moved significantly to one end of the bench :

it was a suggestion he could accept or ignore with perfect politeness. He stopped without looking at me, and sat down. We remained silent.

It is a mistake to start immediately talking hard to anybody you do not know. People with " social gifts " invariably do it, but it is a mistake all the same. You have a better chance of getting to know each other if you get used to silence together first, and after an odd, long pause you are not nearly so likely to fall into futile, mechanical converse. " It is a fine evening," I said at last, " but I think we shall have some rain." This was not a penetrative conversational opening, you will think, but remember we had been sitting quite five minutes together, thinking not about each other, but of anything under the sun. We had learnt in that short time that our companionship was compatible with the internal freedom of each, and after that the fear of embarrassing and being embarrassed is much soothed. The weather did very well as a topic, and while we were still speaking about it, I was wondering of whom he reminded me. His large white hand caressed a beard as soft and grey as woodland smoke ; his dark eyes, which seemed both opaque and bright, were fixed beyond the round tops of the elms. Those eager features, grand, yet delicate as porcelain—where had I seen them, or when had I imagined them before ? Suddenly I remembered. There is no evidence for the transmigration of the soul, but of the reappearance of the *body* Samuel Butler furnished startling instances. I myself have dined at the same restaurant table with Henri IV, and my family doctor is no less a person than John Bright. And does not London already contain statues and busts of Joseph Chamberlain from which the name of William Pitt need only be deleted ? Here upon the bench with me sat—Leonardo da Vinci. Yes,

122

somewhat shrunken, dusty, harassed, it was surely
no other than the great Archimage of Florence.
I knew his restless, distinguished face—brooding,
eager, worn by the attrition of thought.

" If this world were as it ought to be, it's a
delightful place you'd be living in," I exclaimed.

" Ah, well," said he, and his eyes turned towards
heaven's emblazonries in the west, " p'r'aps you'd
like to know what I am." I nodded, expecting
anything.

" I'm a professor," he said.

I must confess I was disappointed. I had expected a stranger claim, a preposterously romantic
revelation.

"My science, or rather the art which I profess,"
he continued, in a sweet discouraged tone, " is one
men stand in need of, but do not know they need.
Possibly you have not heard of it. It is called
Kaloprosōpy. It is a lost art. καλός is a Greek
word meaning beautiful, πρόσωπον was their word
for the person, a man's person. By kaloprosōpy,
I mean the art not merely of embellishing the body,
of graceful movements, but of expressing and
bringing into relief the individual nature through
gesture and demeanour."

" I should like to read your book—or books,"
said I.

" I talk, I do not write," he replied. " I am
well known about here." He added, " They call
me Old Soapy."

Feeling I should do him wrong, " being so
majestical," if I condoled with him, or even
expressed disapproval of his mockers, I made no
comment.

" You seem interested," he continued after a
pause. " Politeness is, I need not say, a branch of
this science, and it is the easiest one to master.
For politeness is simply the charity applicable to

persons whom we cannot help at the moment, either in body or soul. We must do what we can, and circumstances seldom allow us to be more than polite. The rest is more difficult to learn."

He stopped, and I asked him when in history men had most cultivated the art of kaloprosōpy.

"Never less than now. Yet never was there greater opportunity. The man of leisure should consider himself as an actor impersonating his own character. We cannot all be creative artists, we cannot make ; but what material, what marvellous material, has not each one in himself! The living person has an advantage over the most beautiful statue in the world : he is capable of an indefinite series of movements, and a series of poses, gestures, charming, expressive . . ."

Here I could not help interrupting. "But many of us are not the right shape."

"Then," he continued, ignoring my interruption, "the beauty of the eye! Art can never translate it, for it is made of changing dreams, of vision, of desire. Think, too, of the human voice. In modulation it is capable of indefinite melodies more tantalizing and satisfying than Wagner himself has written. The voice is the spirit, the soul of movement, movement which the subtlest curves of an artist's pencil or sculptor's chisel can but catch to petrify : music itself is only the movement of a perfect voice. And yet with such resources in themselves, men and women of leisure will turn to paint or clay or the piano, thinking indifferently-acquired accomplishments in these directions can —O lamentable, scandalous neglect ! Think, think, too, when a man has so trained his instrument, his body, that every gesture, every intonation is expressive, what a part he has to play ! Whoever he is, it is one more intricate and unique than genius ever wrote for an actor on the stage. Now

124

the student of kaloprosōpy begins his inner task : he must decide what he is, and behave accordingly. Society, institutions, traditions, all come to his aid. What figure is less æsthetically-expressive than a country rector or a Member of Parliament ? Yet I never see a specimen of these familiar types without being overwhelmed with a sense of their opportunities. What is a rector ?—an Ambassador from Heaven. He should be absent and remote. His silence should be full of unction, and his speech of enthusiasm. He should never laugh, and never joke. He should not read the papers in public, nor by word or deed convey that he is part of the civil order. And the Member of Parliament, what is he ?—the Physician of the Body Politic. *He* may smile ; but he, too, is better grave and silent. The power he wields over liberty and life should weigh upon him like a sorrow. Nor can he show a personal sentiment without avowing himself unworthy of his abstract role of justice and utility."

At this point a question rose to my lips : " But would not kaloprosōpy, if widely and conscientiously practised, lead to a good deal of posing and humbug—not to speak of loss of happiness and amusement ? "

" On the contrary it would destroy hypocrisy. Life would cease to be tolerable if what was within a man did not correspond to his outward expression. Besides, remember what St. Ignatius said : ' Perform the acts of faith, and faith will come.' "

I was not prepared to argue with a saint, and thinking that a tentative course of kaloprosōpy might do me no harm, I proposed myself as a pupil.

" I shall be happy ; you will be my first."

During the last ten minutes of his discourse, had I not been listening intently, I should have been distracted by an intermittent shower of small missiles, twigs, and pebbles, which kept coming from behind. Finally, quite a large clump of earth caught me on the back of the neck, and another knocked the philosopher's hat over his eyes. There was a juvenile squawk of " Old Soapy," and looking angrily round, I saw two urchins making off among the trees. I turned to my master : " Would it be a very bad beginning if I ran after those brats ? " I am not sure I was right, but I interpreted a movement of his head, which may have merely expressed contempt, as assent, and started in pursuit. After an exhausting chase I caught one of them, and administered punishment with what will probably prove to have been the last ungainly gesture of my life.

UGLINESS

HE was leaning with his elbow on the mantel-piece, gazing into the looking-glass, with his head cocked a little to one side. I heard him murmur : " Ugly ? Yes, but there's something attractive about the face ! " The next moment he caught sight of my reflection behind his own, and spun round with an expression which any Macbeth confronted with the ghost of Banquo might have envied.

What, kind-hearted reader, would you have done in my place ? Laughed ? I hope not. I made a friend, or rather a devotee, for life. I went straight up to him and said : " Perhaps you feel foolish, but what you said is *perfectly true*." I have treated him, I fear, inconsiderately many times since then (he is an awful bore), but he is devoted to me still, and seldom meets me without delicately hinting that he will " cut up " much better than people expect. The moral is . . . but it is not with worldly morals I am concerned ; I want to talk about being ugly.

It is not the ugly we handsome fellows com-miserate ; it is the plain ; the people who provoke in those they accost an impulse to say : " I remember your name, but I cannot remember your face." Most men are sensitive about their appearance, though few to the extent of the Roman Senator Fidus Cornelius, who, as every school-boy knows, burst into tears (*circ.* A.D. 60) when Corbulo declared that he resembled a plucked ostrich. It is possible to be magnificently ugly, but you cannot be magnificently plain. And yet I can imagine circumstances in which it would be gratifying to overhear a comment upon the insignificance of your personal appearance.

Imagine a crowded railway station, and yourself an author whose fame is just beginning to sprout. The platform is lined three deep ; there will evidently be a rush for seats, and all faces are turned towards the in-coming train. Suddenly, at this absorbing moment, you hear someone behind you say :

" Look, look ! Quick, there's X."

"Who ? Where ? " replies another, unmistakably eager voice : " Not the man who wrote . . ."

" Yes, there, on your left—behind you."

And if the second voice were then to exclaim : " What ! *That* little man ! " the very depth of disappointment expressed in its tone would be a proof of your literary talent. You would know you had written well.

Of course, if whiffs of fame kept coming your way in this form, it would, in the end, be depressing ; but the first time I am sure you would tingle with pleasure.

But if the circumstances in which a plain appearance can be a source of gratification are rare, ugliness, on the other hand, real crushing ugliness, is a sort of distinction. You remember Lamb's discussion in his *Popular Fallacies* of the saying : " that handsome is as handsome does " ? Anyone who uses this proverb, he says, can never have seen Mrs. Conrady without pronouncing her to be the ugliest woman that he ever met with in the course of his life. " The first time that you are indulged with a sight of her face, is an era in your existence ever after. You are glad to have seen it—like Stonehenge. Lockets are for remembrance ; and it would be clearly superfluous to hang an image

128

at your heart, which, once seen, can never be out of it."

The essay makes one envy the lady, and Lamb's conclusion, to which the reader inevitably assents, is that true ugliness, like true beauty, is the result of harmony. Lamb defies " the minutest connoisseur to cavil at any part or parcel of the countenance " of the lady in question. Mrs. Conrady convinced him that, if one must be ugly, it is better to be ugly all over, " than, amidst a tolerable residue of features, to hang out one that shall be exceptionable " ; in short, far better to be down-right hideous. And I would add a gloss to this. Ugliness is not only a distinction ; it may also serve as a palladium to its possessor, or as a weapon in the struggle of life.

In the terrible battle of Camlan, that fatal field where King Arthur fell with all his chivalry, only three Christian Knights survived : Sandde Bryd, who was so lovely to look upon that not one of the victorious heathen had the heart to strike him ; Glewlwyd Gavaelvawr (or Great Grasp), the porter to King Arthur, whose prodigious thews made all unwilling to attack him ; and Morvan ab Teged, who was so overwhelmingly hideous that the foe fled from him as from a demon out of hell. These three stalked through the battlefield, unscathed as gods.

The ugly should take this piece of history to heart. Let not, therefore, those dowered with an eye-searing ugliness reproach Nature, or throw away their singular endowment by attempting to mitigate their striking features. In dominating our fellows, the heavy lids and deliberate movements which suggest a saurian monster of the extinct world, the jaw which rivals the maxillary equipment of the larger apes, the complexion which in a savage tribe would render war-paint superfluous, these may prove important assets. To be as "ugly as a mud fence," as they used to say "Out West," is nothing ; but to vie in appearance with the inauspicious monsters of the deep may be of incalculable advantage. Would Mirabeau, do you think, have dominated the beginning of the French Revolution if he had been a pleasant-featured man ?

I am no nasologist, but who was not impressed by "the perpetual triumph, the everlasting bonfirelight"—to use Shakespeare' phrase—which accompanied the late Mr. Pierpont Morgan's victorious career ? And even those among the ugly whose longings are more amorous than ambitious, what need have they to be diffident ? The obviously presentable among the male sex may shrug their shoulders at women's whimsies, but experience shows that the man " with some architecture about him," however Gothic, is in wooing more than the match of the comely suitor. Wilkes, who was considered easily the ugliest man of his day, and whose portraits bear this out, boasted that he could give the handsomest man in England half an hour's start in the race for favours, and beat him. " Doesn't Mr. Wilkes squint abominably ? " someone asked a lady, who had met him. " Yes, he does," she replied thoughtfully, " but not more than a gentleman ought to." Review for a moment in your own mind the most successful "ladies' men" you have known. What facial types predominate ? The empty barber's block, the clean monkey, and the hairy gorilla. Fellows with pleasant, handsome human countenances stand no chance.

EPITAPH-WRITING

AS a frequent visitor to churchyards, I have come to the conclusion that the art of epitaph-writing is dying or nearly extinct. Someone once described a cemetery as a garden in which the labels had come up instead of the flowers. On the more recent labels I have seldom found anything worth reading : a name, a date, a text, or verse of a hymn—that is all. But our forefathers differed from us in this ; the art of memorial inscription was a recognized one. Its canons have been discussed by many, notably in England by two great writers, Wordsworth and Dr. Johnson. Wordsworth's essay is so good that I dare not re-read it for fear of submitting slavishly to his criteria. To Johnson's *Essay on Epitaphs* I will come presently ; but first I want to put this question : Why have we given up writing epitaphs ?

I think the answer is that we are both too self-conscious and too unconventional. We know that the laudatory generalities and lists of attributes which our fathers inscribed above their dead could not describe, except very vaguely and partially, any human being ; the convention has been destroyed by lack of faith and a growing sense of the complexity of human-nature. On the other hand, we are too self-conscious to express our grief. Epitaph-writing, we feel, is an exception to the rule that " what is worth doing at all is worth doing badly." Our predecessors did not, however, feel that it was. We content ourselves by saying : " Here lies the beloved wife or husband,

son, daughter," as the case may be, of " so-and-so,
who died, etc. etc. : Text." Not that our forefathers' epitaphs were always entirely laudatory ;
here is a striking example of the contrary which
can be read in Horsley-Down Church, Cumber-
land :

Here lie the bodies
of THOMAS BOND and MARY his wife.

She was temperate, chaste and charitable ;
But
She was proud, peevish and passionate.
She was an affectionate wife, and a tender mother ;
But
Her husband and child, whom she loved,
Seldom saw her countenance without a disgusting
frown,
While she received visitors whom she despised
with an
Endearing smile.
Her behaviour was discreet towards strangers ;
But
Independent in her family.
Abroad, her conduct was influenced by good
breeding ;
But
At home, by ill temper.
She was a professed enemy to flattery,
And was seldom known to praise or commend ;
But
The talents in which she principally excelled,
Were difference of opinion and discovering flaws
and imperfections.
She was an admirable economist,
And, without prodigality,
Dispensed plenty to every person in her family ;
But
Would sacrifice their eyes to a farthing candle.
132

She sometimes made her husband happy with her
good qualities ;
But
Much more frequently miserable with her many
failings :
In-so-much that in thirty years cohabitation he
often lamented
That maugre all her virtues,
He had not, in the whole, enjoyed two years of
matrimonial comfort.
AT LENGTH,
Finding that she had lost the affections of her
husband
As well as the regard of her neighbours,
Family disputes having been divulged by servants,
She died of vexation, July 20, 1768,
Aged 48 years.
Her worn-out husband survived her four months
and two days,
And departed this life, Nov. 28, 1768,
In the 54th year of his age.
WILLIAM BOND, brother to the deceased, erected
this stone,
As a *weekly monitor*, to the surviving wives of this
parish,
That they may avoid the infamy
Of having their memories handed to posterity
With a PATCHWORK character.

The first principle that Johnson lays down is
that those epitaphs are the best, which set virtue
in the strongest light, and are best adapted to
exalt the reader's ideas and rouse his emulation.
As usual, he judges as a practical moralist. In
the case of the truly eminent it is not necessary
to recount their achievements : the bare name of
such men answers the purpose of a long inscription.
But none but the first names can stand unassisted

against the attacks of time; the rest require an interpreter. It is in the composition of such epitaphs that art is required. Epitaphs, says Johnson, do not admit of "the lighter or gayer ornaments" permissible in Elegies, for due regard must be observed to the solemnity of the place, and nothing trifling or ludicrous must be allowed. Praise must not be general, "because the mind is lost in the extent of any indefinite idea, and cannot be affected by what it cannot comprehend." The inscriber need not consider himself bound to historical impartiality. "On the tomb of Mæcenas his luxury is not to be mentioned with his munificence, nor is the proscription to find a place on the monument of Augustus." In short, Dr. Johnson is against the "patchwork" epitaph, and as he said to Boswell, "in lapidary inscriptions a man is not on his oath." "The best subject for epitaphs," he continues, "is private virtue; virtue exerted in the same circumstances in which the bulk of mankind are placed, and which, therefore, may admit of many imitators." He quotes two Greek inscriptions, one of a woman whose memory is preserved only in her epitaph, the other of a famous writer; both were slaves, "the most calamitous estate in human life." The first reads in translation thus:

"Zosima who in her life could only have her body enslaved, now finds her body likewise set at liberty."

"It is impossible," says Johnson, "to read this epitaph without being animated to bear the evils of life with constancy, and to support the dignity of human nature under the most pressing afflictions." The other is upon Epictetus:

"Epictetus, who lies here, was a slave and

a cripple, poor as the beggar in the proverb, and the favourite of heaven."

A noble panegyric which should also comprise instruction was Johnson's idea of the perfect epitaph.

Thus he would probably have had little praise for the touching inscription over the unknown Roman dancer, *Saltavit et Placuit*; nor would this Greek one, I think, have satisfied him, yet it is one of my favourites :

" Sit beneath the poplars, here, traveller, when thou art weary, and drawing nigh drink of our spring ; and even far away remember the fountain that Simus sets by the side of Gillus his dead child."

Dr. Johnson believed too firmly in the impressiveness of direct exhortation. To me, the mood of tenderness that inscription conveys, the sense of a personal sorrow which has diffused itself as a friendliness towards the whole world, including the passing stranger, is worth any list of virtues and accomplishments which we should, no doubt, do well to emulate.

When people write their own epitaphs they frequently betray themselves. Here is such a one, which makes me know and dislike the man whom it commemorates :

WILLIAM HUNTINGDON S. S. ob. 1813.
Here lies the Coalheaver,
Belov'd of his God but abhorred of Men.
The Omniscient Judge at the Grand Assize
Shall ratify and confirm this
To the confusion of many thousands :
For England and its Metropolis shall know
That there hath been a Prophet among them.

W.H.S.S. Sinner Saved.

THE CROWDS AT BURLINGTON HOUSE

THE tremendous crowd which gathers every day from all parts of England to see the Exhibition at Burlington House is a most curious phenomenon. It is a tribute to the prestige of art, not of course a sign of love for it, or understanding of it. The National Gallery remains empty. What then makes all these people rush to get a peep between each other's shoulders at these pictures? Curiosity—they like to glance at famous and very valuable objects. Social obligation—owing to the dearth of conversational openings they find themselves incessantly asked, " Have you seen the Italian Exhibition ? " or, " Are you going to the Exhibition ? " Vanity and uplift—a reluctance to admit indifference to art, and a faint hope that it may be overcome. Lastly—sheep-in-a-gap, follow-m'-leader instinct. The majority of those streaming out (read their faces) have experienced a " something-attempted, something-done " satisfaction; the majority streaming in, feel " I am doing what an educated person ought to do." Few of them, however, stop opposite any picture for a quarter of the time they do in front of something for sale at Selfridge's. They loiter round and round in a mazed condition of vaguely elevated depression ; and no mood can be less propitious for art, since depression is a non-conductor, and vague longing to be impressed destructive of discrimination. Of pairs doing the Exhibition together, the one who reads in a low halting gabble from the catalogue usually appears the happier ; but there comes a moment when he, or she, also, must gaze at the picture described before passing on. Oh, that moment of blank effort to respond ; the muttered misery of his or her ineptitudes ! " That's . . . don't you think ? . . . I like. . . . Yes, yes, a distinct look of Aunt Mary, and aren't the baby's legs wonderful ? "

The few but crowded benches display the unostentatious stoicism of the railway waiting-room. There the old who have won the game of musical chairs enjoy a mild sense of triumph, but no view. They are to be commiserated least. The exhausted sweetly-sour atmosphere has devitalized them, but they are seated. Nor must we pity the children, who from a peep at the pictures between thighs lift their faces to catch from their parents appreciation of their artistic zest : they are buoyed up by the pride of extreme youth in sharing what they suppose their elders enjoy.

It was the great moving, muddled, middle-aged mass that touched me. Why were they there ! What had they come for ? In a fashion I have already answered those questions, and in the study the answers satisfy. But in the presence of the Phenomenon they seemed inadequate : there was no pushing or thrusting ; the public washed up gently against the walls like driftwood sluggishly circulating in a current ; their mutual consideration was perfect, and reminded me of journeys in the Tube during the War when all were sobered down to even kindliness by common calamity. Oh, Culture, what cruelties are committed in thy name !

It is inevitable that the dogged pursuit of culture should implant in the human heart a deep unconscious hostility to art ; and what is worse, arrogance. Art is a living force ever taking new forms, and its transmigrations are least likely to be recognized by those who have painfully approached

137

it in the hope of self-improvement and not in pursuit of pleasure.

At this point I can imagine my reader interrupting me. " Ah, I know you. You're one of those superior persons who, believing they understand art themselves, are anxious, with dog-in-the-manger vanity, to suggest that the perceptions they enjoy are beyond the reach of ordinary humanity." Acute, but hypercritical reader, you are mistaken. Pictures have meant very little to me compared with the beauty which is transmitted through the written word. All I have obtained from them is a mild but constant pleasure. In the mildness of that response I resemble the crowd. For such as me, it is the constancy and reliability of the pleasures of the eye which constitute the chief part of its value. It is more detached from mood and circumstance than the satisfactions which literature can give, though it is far less strong. I have met in my life some half-a-dozen people of whom this was not true, who lived through the eye with an intensity which I can just imagine but can never experience. It is therefore as one of the crowd that I address those who resemble me.

Firstly, there is nothing disgraceful in being unable to appreciate painting ; the disability is too common to be distressing. The important thing is to get rid of the idea that in such matters one's opinion and taste are of consequence. This at least will restrain one from tarring and feathering, either in conversation or in fact, anything new which has not yet prestige behind it. It has also a further advantage. Once rid of a sense of responsibility, one is free to enjoy what one can ; and this freedom brings one nearer in spirit, though not necessarily in taste, to those to whom painting is really important. People seldom lie more flatly than when they utter with exasperating modesty

138

the familiar formula, " I know nothing about art, but I know what I like." If they spoke the truth they would say, " I have some idea what others think I *ought* to like, but I have not the smallest notion what I do."

The safest approach to the art of painting is not through the gate of aspiration or self-improvement, but through the humble door of pleasure, and the first step to culture is to learn to *enjoy*, not to know what is best. It is not true that we needs must love the highest when we see it, only vanity ever convinced anyone that it was. Those who do not deceive themselves need no enlightenment on that point.

OBSCENITY AND THE LAW

IN 1928 and 1929 two novels were successfully prosecuted, *The Well of Loneliness* and *Sleeveless Errand*. *The Well of Loneliness* has been sufficiently discussed, and even those who sympathized with its suppression now see that it was a mistake to have given it prominence by instituting proceedings. It is said that 60,000 copies have been sold in Paris alone as a result of its " destruction " ; scarcely a thousand would have been bought unless the Home Secretary had moved in the matter. In *The Well of Loneliness* there was not an obscene word nor one passage of alluring description, but the story asked sympathy from the reader on behalf of women who are so constituted that they fall in love with their own sex; though not obscene, it might, therefore, be held to be immoral. The case of *Sleeveless Errand* is an exact converse, except that in it, too, there are no alluring descriptions. *Sleeveless Errand* is a novel which contains gross and vulgar expressions, though it is an austerely moral indictment of sordid sensuality and lack of decent human standards. In the case of *The Well of Loneliness* the reserve and decency of the author's treatment of her theme was held to be no defence against the charge of immorality ; in that of *Sleeveless Errand*, though every incident described was deterrent to sympathy, this was not regarded as excusing the realism of the " talk " reported in it. In my own opinion it was a novel which every youth and girl tempted to join a tippling, promiscuous set such as the author

140

describes, might well read with profit; I know several sensible parents who have borrowed it for their children.

The conclusion that many people have drawn from these two decisions is that the law should be altered. But, speaking as a layman, after reading the Act of 1857 and the leading case under it, namely Regina *v.* Hicklin, 1868, I am inclined to think that pending a better definition of obscenity —certainly needed—what is required and should be obtainable at once is a more precise application of the actual law.

* * * *

All proceedings against books are taken under Lord Campbell's Act " for more effectually preventing the sale of obscene books, pictures, prints and other articles." When introduced in 1857 this Act was regarded as a mere police measure. It roused little interest among men of letters ; Disraeli, Macaulay and Bulwer-Lytton, the leading men of letters in politics, were silent. Monckton-Milnes was, I think, the only literary man who took part in the debates, and he supported it ; the *Athenæum* did not think it worth mentioning. Its prime object was the suppression of a trade in obscene books and pictures which flourished particularly in Holywell Street. Lord Campbell, in his autobiography, notes that it was instantly successful there, and that this traffic was stopped ; also that in Paris the police had begun in consequence to " purify " the shops in the Palais Royal which catered for British tourists.

The vital clause in that Act runs as follows : " If upon complaint there is any reason to believe that any obscene books, etc., are kept in any house or other place, for the purpose of sale or distribution, and upon proof that one or more such articles

141

has been sold or distributed in connexion with such a place, justices may, upon being satisfied that such articles *are of such a character and description that the publication of them would be a misdemeanour and proper to be prosecuted as such*, order by special warrant that such articles shall be seized, and after summoning the occupier of the house, the same or other justices may, if they are satisfied that the articles seized are of the character stated in the warrant, and have been kept for the purpose aforesaid, order them to be destroyed." The words I have italicized have an importance which has been overlooked. It is clear from them that it is *not* sufficient to prove that a book is " obscene " (whatever the legal definition of that word may be) in order to justify its destruction. The magistrate must also be satisfied (*a*) that it is " of such a character and description that the publication of it would be a misdemeanour "—that is to say, that its publisher could be convicted before a common jury for issuing an " obscene libel " ; and (*b*) that the book is " proper to be prosecuted as such." Condition (*a*) is a clear direction to the magistrate not to condemn a book because he is shocked by it himself, but to ask himself what conclusion a jury would probably reach after hearing all that could be urged in the publishers' defence. The meaning of condition (*b*) is brought out—and it is vitally important—by the comments of the judges in the case of Regina *v.* Hicklin, the case which also furnishes Chief Justice Cockburn's definition of obscenity, now applied by magistrates to all books brought before them, namely, " I think the test of obscenity is this, whether the tendency of the matter charged as obscenity is to deprave and corrupt those whose minds are open to such immoral influences, and in whose hands a publication of this sort may fall."

142

Now, when a book has been shown to contain passages capable of corrupting minds capable of being corrupted, it is to-day taken for granted by magistrates that the book is condemned under Lord Campbell's Act. I speak as a layman, but the comments of Lord Blackburn and Mr. Justice Mellor, who were Chief Justice Cockburn's co-judges in this case, strongly suggest that this is *not* the proper interpretation of the law.

The Chief Justice himself quoted the additional and necessary conditions, but it was Mr. Justice Blackburn (as he then was) and Mr. Justice Mellor whose comments explained their importance —Mr. Justice Lush acquiescing. What do the words " proper to be prosecuted as such " mean ? Lord Blackburn, who is regarded as one of the greatest English judges, after reading the section of the Act quoted above, said : "I think with regard to the last clause, that the object of the legislation was to guard against the vexatious prosecutions of publishers of old and recognized standard works, in which there may be some obscene or mischievous matter. In the case of Reg. *v.* Moxon and in many of the instances cited by Mr. Kydd (Counsel for the defence in the Hicklin case), a book had been published which, in its nature, was such as to be called obscene or mischievous, and it might be held a misdemeanour to publish it ; and on account of that an indictable offence. In Moxon's case the publication of *Queen Mab* was found by the jury to be an indictable offence ; I hope I may not be understood to agree with what the jury found, that the publication of *Queen Mab* was sufficient to make it an indictable offence. I believe, as everybody knows, that it was a prosecution instituted merely for the purpose of vexation and annoyance. So, whether the publication of the whole of the works of Dryden is or is not a misdemeanour, it would not

143

be a case in which a prosecution would be 'proper';
and I think the legislature put in that provision in
order to prevent proceedings in such cases." It is
clear, then, that in Lord Blackburn's opinion the
words " proper to be prosecuted as such " are not a
necessary presumption of law from the finding that
the work in question contains " obscene " matter,
but a separate and essential condition, inserted to
safeguard from prosecution works which would
otherwise come under Lord Campbell's Act. They
are, in fact, a provision for the protection of
" recognized standard works," *i.e.* works whose
literary merit has been recognized. Mr. Justice
Mellor's comment goes, I think, further, but to
make its bearing clear it is necessary to say a few
words about the actual case which was before the
court at that time.

In 1868, Henry Scott appealed against an
order made by two justices under Lord Campbell's
Act whereby a book entitled *The Confessional
Unmasked* had been condemned to be destroyed.
The argument for the defence was that the obscene
matter contained in it (extracts from the works of
certain theologians on the practice of auricular
confession) were justified as a means to exposing
evils, and that the book was a controversial one
and written with the object of doing good. Mr.
Justice Mellor's comment was as follows : " I confess I have with some difficulty, and with some
hesitation, arrived very much at the conclusion at
which my Lord and my learned Brother have
arrived. . . . The nature of the subject itself, if it
may be discussed at all (and I think it undoubtedly
may), is such that it cannot be discussed without
to a certain extent producing authorities for the
assertion that the confessional would be a mischievous thing to be introduced into this kingdom ;
and therefore it appears to me very much a question

of degree, and if the matter were left to the jury it
would depend very much on the opinion the jury
might form of that *degree* in such a publication as
the present. . . . It does appear to me that there is
a great deal here for which there cannot be any
necessity in any legitimate argument on the confessional and the like, and agreeing in that view,
I certainly am not in a condition to dissent from
my Lord and my Brother Blackburn, and I know
my Brother Lush agrees entirely with their opinion.
Therefore, with the expression of hesitation I have
mentioned, I agree in the result at which they have
arrived."

Now, if we put together the *obiter dicta* of these
two eminent judges, we arrive at an interpretation
of Lord Campbell's Act which is, firstly, much more
in harmony with the spirit of its preamble, "whereas
it is expedient to give additional powers of suppression of the trade of obscene books," and
secondly, an interpretation which obviously does
not carry due weight with magistrates to-day.
Lord Blackburn says that the words " proper to
be prosecuted as such " were intended to exempt
from prosecution, on the ground of containing mischievous or obscene matter, " old and recognized
standard works " ; and Mr. Justice Mellor (also a
judge of high repute) adds the gloss that, in the case
of other books, the question whether any obscene
matter in them brings them under the Act *is one
of degree*, the object with which such matter is
introduced being taken into consideration in deter-
mining that degree.

It is not an uncommon belief among elderly
men in whose lives literature plays a subordinate
part, that only " old " masterpieces are of any
importance to mankind. Lord Blackburn, in interpreting the words " proper to be prosecuted as
such," as a provision deliberately inserted in the

Act to protect literature, forgot for the moment that it is still possible to add to the world's store of " standard works " ; and, with all respect to so eminent a lawyer, those words he was interpreting afford no support for refusing to extend the same protection to all works of genuine literary value which do not aim at obviously pornographic effects. Mr. Justice Mellor, I think, saw this. At any rate, such a criticism is implied in his *obiter dictum* that the degree of obscenity permissible depends upon the nature of the work : a principle which is, by the by, entirely destructive of Lord Cockburn's definition of indictable obscenity as anything which might corrupt anyone. Yet how far these considerations are from influencing the magistracy to-day, I myself had proof when I, along with many literary men more distinguished than myself, attended as a would-be witness the *Well of Loneliness* case. Sir Chartres Biron then ruled that the question of literary merit was entirely beside the point. Mr. Birkett was not only not allowed to produce his witnesses, but he was not allowed to read the critical judgments upon the book which had appeared in the most reputable papers and journals. I could not help reflecting how much less fortunate he was than " Biron for the defence " in the case of Regina *v.* Thompson, who secured the acquittal of Thompson for publishing the *Heptameron* by relying on the *dictum* of Lord Blackburn and by reading, without objection from the Court, extracts from the *Encyclopœdia Britannica* and the *Edinburgh Review* to prove that the book in question had literary merit. Logically, in the case of a recent book, the equivalent of reading a critic's opinion from the pages of the *Encyclopœdia* must be to read criticisms from reputable contemporary reviews. If Lord Blackburn's interpretation of the words " proper to be prose-

146

cuted as such " is correct, and they were intended
to protect works of " recognized merit," there is no
reason why contemporary recognition of merit
should not entitle a book to protection.

*   *   *   *

Lord Blackburn says that the Act contains a
special provision for the protection of " recognized
standard works," and he instances those of Dryden;
Mr. Justice Mellor that the question whether a
passage is obscene or not is dependent upon the
nature of the work in which it occurs. Lord
Blackburn expressed disapproval of the prosecution
of *Queen Mab*, apparently because by his time it
had become a standard work and enjoyed the
protection which the legislature had given to
standard works. He regretted the prosecution was
successful. But how can any book become a
" standard work," even should it deserve to
become one, if it is destroyed on publication,
and if those who order its destruction refuse to
consider whether or not it possesses literary merit,
or to hear evidence on the point ?
    I do not say that *Sleeveless Errand* would have
been destined to become a classic, but it was clear
to me—and after all I am something of an expert
in such matters, having spent my life in the study
of literary methods—that the degree of obscenity
in it was very slightly, if at all, in excess of what
was necessary to effect the author's legitimate
purpose, that of exposing the ugly, dismally
dilapidated condition of a group of young people,
who certainly exist, whose lives even have a sort of
glamour for others who have not seen them close,
and whose " speech bewrayeth them." That the
purport of *Sleeveless Errand* was moral was not
disputed, but ignored. It was condemned on the
ground that it contained coarse expressions, and

147

because much of the talk suggested in the speakers an ignoble and irresponsible attitude towards sex, society, and religion ; that is to say, because the book infected the reader with precisely the kind of aversion from them which the author intended him to feel. It might very well have been defended successfully before a jury.

And what is the upshot ? It is this : that if the Home Office, when they cause a warrant to be applied for, and the magistrates when they hear the case, would consider, what in Law they are bound to consider, not only whether the book in question is obscene, but also whether the publication of it would properly lead to the prosecution of the publisher, and if they would give full weight to the *dicta* of the eminent judges who have interpreted Lord Campbell's Act, we might then keep that Act as the salutary check it was intended to be upon traffic in pornography. It might be kept without any damage to literature, and without interfering with that perpetual pooling of knowledge and experience on which civilization depends. But if they do not do this, then the law will inevitably fall into complete disrepute with reasonable people, and how bad that is for the moral sense of a community everyone with an inkling of statesmanship knows.

ETON

BOOKS that I have read are like old diaries to me. I find my old self in their pages. Do I want to be back in my School Library ?[1] I have only to open some book I first read there and as I allow my mind to wander, I see again the long book-lined room ; the busts, the model of the Acropolis, the large diamond-paned windows, the leather-topped tables, and the attitudes of the boys sitting at them. I hear the whispers and suppressed giggles. Again I see the look of well-simulated amazement on the face of the precise, tiny Librarian, when someone brings a Greek Lexicon down on the bowed head of a fellow-student. Do I wish to recall those twenty minutes of peaceful solitude (tea-time in my own room) between cooking for my fag-master and carrying up three flights of leaded stairs cans of hot water for his bath, and then running through dark streets to pupil-room ? Well, I need only open some novel like *The Deemster* and dream upon its pages. Instantly I am in the past again. Back it comes to me : the look and smell of my indigestible new loaf, whose doughy centre, well-squeezed, made such an excellent missile ; its crust, which was a mere pretext for huge dollops of jam ; my printed red-flannelette table-cloth, and even that after-football

[1] Before the South African War Memorial was built the School Library used to be on the upper storey of the New Schools.

feeling in my legs—if I had played well, such a delicious tingle !

Eton is very great, very big, very old and very rich ; certainly far more reminiscences of Eton are published than of any other school. This is not astonishing, for Eton stands near the main thoroughfare of the world, and often catches the eye ; while her own public is the largest for which books of this special kind are written. Nevertheless I, who was at Eton, am sometimes made uneasy by the tone of these books. Many seem to take for granted that the greater public, if it does not share the Eton sense of proportion, will at any rate try hard to do so, and that they will all be glad to pretend for a while to be old Etonians. This does not appear to be unnatural, but experience has taught me that it is not always the case. I have been sometimes embarrassed by such books, as we are sometimes embarrassed abroad by the confident yet very proper sentiments of a fellow-countryman. Could I read a book describing the appearance and analysing the temperament of old " Biped Brown " of Marlborough, or " Pinker Dickson " of Winchester ? Frankly, no. My inability is shown by the fact that I have actually had to invent these striking personalities ; for, with the exception of " Bowen of Harrow," I do not know even the name, let alone the nickname, of one bygone master at any school but my own. I feel sure such ignorance is reciprocated by old boys of other schools.

I have just been reading Mr. Percy Lubbock's *Shades of Eton*. Some of the figures, which do not require even a touch from his elegant pen to live for me, which need only be named to rise as vividly before my eyes as Nelson or Mr. Micawber, must surely appear empty of significance to any but Etonians. How, then, are these unfortunates to know when Mr. Lubbock has deftly hit off some characteristic ? What interest would there be to the public were I to venture to correct his drawing, say, of a nose ? These rhetorical questions answer themselves, or will be answered by my silence about those parts of the book which could not fail to be interesting to Etonians, but to them alone. *Shades of Eton* is, however, much more than a gallery of such portraits. It is, from one aspect, a self-effacing man's story of his own education, and raises questions of wider interest. It can be read as a book about Eton, or as a chapter of auto-biography, or as a subtle discussion of public-school and classical education. Fortunate is the reader who can read it from these three points of view at once.

Mr. Lubbock is one of the comparatively few contemporary prose-writers of whom it can be said that he has thoroughly mastered his craft. He writes with a beautiful precision. The suavity and the subtlety at which he aims he attains ; though the kind of perceptions which he wishes to record are by no means always easy to convey. He can express his own sense of the beauty of outward things ; and where character is concerned he has learnt the art of insinuating without being treacher-ous, of being even very kind without being very vague. His imagination in retrospect is deeply tinged with " piety " in the Roman sense of the word. Close contact with Henry James may well have deepened in him this mode of feeling—Henry James who was so horrified at the offhand wasteful callousness of the world, and whose imagination often liked to rest beside considerate, scrupulous people in the quiet garden of tradition. I seldom notice in Mr. Lubbock's use of words the imprint of that influence, but I detect it in his distrust of bare statements. In Henry James, revulsion from such

151

statements, when they might hurt, led him into periphrastic and metaphorical hesitations which by delaying a perhaps fatal verdict often made it in the end more crushing. Thus in conversation when he had done speaking one was sometimes reminded of that comment upon Renan : " *le plus doux des hommes cruels.*" And yet Henry James was not cruel. He had a merciless eye and a tender heart, and in a style of delicate and prolonged ingenuity he strove to combine the reports of the one with the promptings of the other.

Mr. Lubbock, also, is a writer of complex sensibility, but he attains unity by refraining rather than by combining. His charming book *Earlham* suffered in a measure from a too uniform diffusion of " piety " and sweetness, and the *Shades of Eton* are bathed, to my understanding, in too still and golden an air. I suspect him of having explored his past only where he could bless and praise. A writer so sensitive, so responsive to whatever in our precarious muddled state of being is gracious, ordered, gentle and safe, must have been frequently excruciated at a public school; and a boy so precociously alert must have seen many shortcomings in those who educated him. But of such excruciations and such defects there are few traces in the story of Mr. Lubbock's education, only a hint or two that he was often far from happy during it. It may seem odd, at first, that one who like myself enjoyed wildly every day of his school life—except, of course, those black intermittent days on which carelessly-provoked calamities trod him down— should complain of such omissions. Yet, after all, it is not strange. Whatever has given us massive satisfaction we can afford to criticize with ungracious freedom.

Mr. Lubbock says that he who tells us he was happy at Eton tells us much about himself but

152

nothing about the school. This is not so true as he thinks. If different kinds of boys are happy at a school, it tells us something most important about it. He and I were, I think, contemporaries, and yet in a sense we were not at the same school. His Eton is composed entirely of masters and traditions, mine of boys and places. He was educated by masters, I by boys.

This difference is a typical one, and one which confuses the whole discussion about public-school education. The boy-educated—and they are the majority—cannot understand these pedagogic heart-searchings. Mr. Lubbock reports Arthur Benson as saying sadly, " But we don't educate these boys." " I should think not," the boy-educated is inclined to reply, rather impatiently. " How can a handful of masters educate in any intense manner a thousand boys or more ? " One young mind out of ten they can affect, certainly not more. Masters must, of course—and they can—prevent the community from degenerating into squalor, and drum some elementary information into those thousand heads ; but what more can they do ? And, after all, would more be generally desirable ? There are grave deficiencies in the education of boys by boys, but the adultly-educated often suffer from a drawback : they cannot henceforth get on with, or get anything out of, anyone as young as themselves. There is something so restful and gratifying in the companionship and approval of a mature mind that they cannot afterwards stand the sharp illuminating crudity of their own generation. This, too, may be a disadvantage.

When I talk to a dog I am sometimes reminded of myself and my masters. Nothing could be seemingly more responsive than the dog ; but at the sound of a distant bark its whole being is suddenly possessed by the quiver of a very different

attention ; I am forgotten. I, too, could once only
attend to barks. I could be made for a few seconds
to sit up with pendent paws for a biscuit, and if
scratched behind the ears I capered and ran in
circles with delight ; when my masters talked to
me I heard them, but I only listened to barks.
Reviewing my contemporaries, this seems to have
been the case with most of them. The yapping and
baying and growling and belling, to me the most
exquisite of concerts, is a pandemonium against
even the memory of which Mr. Lubbock stops his
ears. Indeed, I can only recognize *his* Eton by
recalling the impressions of my subsequent visits.
Then I see that this master contributed this kind of
culture, that one that ; but I should never have
known it had I not gone back. The doors which
opened for him upon refuges, and revelations, and
intervals of happiness, were doors I never even saw.
Do I regret it ? Hardly ; there was so much outside—besides, I walked in later on. And yet we
are both grateful to our school ! That boys so
different can both be grateful does tell others something important about it.

Some of the most enchanting and penetrating
pages of this book are a discourse upon the value
of that old-fashioned scholarship which trans-
mutes the classics into something quite unlike
themselves ; presenting them not as expressions
of human passions and adventures in thought, but
as those queer static things, *books*. " The Greeks
and Romans, indeed, were remarkably trimmed
and chastened," Mr. Lubbock truly says, " before
they could settle down in the valley of the Thames."
" To what purpose," he asks, " have you loved
those adventures of genius if you aren't a terror
to all quiet minds ? Others may dream and moon
in repose upon a time-approved culture ; but the
learned Grecian is a man, he must be, of a restless

154

and realistic temper, keen, mobile, immodest, grasping the good gift of life with avid hands. There is an image, indeed, of the scholar of Eton ! " And yet Mr. Lubbock has something to say, and to say exquisitely, in explanation of this process of domesticating the Classics, though he marvels at its queerness. But he does not marvel so much at the oddity of the actual process of imparting that culture to boys—and that is what I remember best.

I am again in a large, half-panelled room. At a raised desk sits a man in a university gown, and in front of him sprawl between thirty and forty little boys : the air hums with innumerable subdued noises. One of the boys is suddenly called upon to construe. After a hurried consultation with his neighbour he stands up with an air of apparent alacrity :

" *O Venus*—oh, Venus—*regina*—queen—*Cnidi Paphique*—of Cnidus and Paphus."

" Os, os," interrupts the master mildly.

" *Sperne*—spurn—*dilectam Cypron*—delectable Cyprus—*et*—and . . ."

" Well, go on, go on."

" I can't find the verb," says the small boy— then, suddenly, as though it had been dodging about, " I've got it ! *Transfer !* transfer—*te*—thyself— *decoram in aedem*—to " (his voice quavers inter- rogatively) " to the . . . decorated house ? "

" Come, come. You know better than that. You know what *dulce et decorum est pro patria mori* means : It is sweet and fitting to die for one's country."

" The well-fitted house ? " the small boy sug- gests, smiling to make up for a possible blunder. The master smiles too : " No, no. The word sug- gests reverence, something almost sacred. The adjective together with the noun, the phrase *decoram in aedem* really means a ' shrine,' or, if

155

you like, ' gracious house ' would do here. Go on."
The small boy's eyes meanwhile have been fixed
in absent-minded wonder on his face.

"*Vocantis Glycerae*" (should he risk it ?)—
" of shouting Glycerine." (General titters.)

" If you play the fool you'll sit down and write
out the lesson. Sit down."

" But, sir ! "

" Sit down ! "

" But, sir, *vocantis* does mean shouting or
calling."

" Sit down ! I'll go on construing. Follow
carefully and bring me a translation to-morrow.
This is poetry : ' Of Glycera who invokes thee,
multo ture—with much—or perhaps better—with a
wealth of incense. *Fervidus tecum puer*—with thee
may thy glowing boy.' Who was her glowing
boy ? " (General mild astonishment.)

" Yes, who was the son of Venus ? "

" Oh, Cupid," another boy, lolling on hip and
elbow, answers contemptuously.

" Cupid, of course. ' With thee may thy
glowing boy and the Graces and the Nymphs with
unloosened zones '—are you following ?—' hasten
hither, and Youth, who lacking thee is not charming.' " Here the master coughs, and ends rather
lamely with "And Mercury."

" Quite a party," says the small boy who has
been made to sit down. (Laughter.)

" You will write out the lesson twice."

" But, sir ! "

" If you speak again you will write it out four
times. Come up for a Yellow Ticket afterwards."

Such were our frontal mass-attacks day after
day, week after week, month after month, year
after year, upon the barrier of that ancient language.
How few of us won through to the scholar's ilex-
grove and the placid fields of asphodel !

BOXING

IT is a common device of editors, though it does not always succeed, to send every now and then the obviously wrong man to report on some event. Instead of going to a theatre one week, I went to see Freddy Welsh and Willie Ritchie fight for the light-weight championship of the world. I know nothing about boxing beyond having boxed occasionally with someone as helpless as myself; and all that experience comes to is a vague recollection of a kind of stuffy pain which results from being hit on the nose, and that it is easy to punch the other man's face though not to guard one's own. I recall, also, a pleasant kindling excitement, half temper and half " sporting."

I have known, too, what it is like to be hit hard. One evening at school we had been talking for hours, as boys will, about strength and physical prowess; and to support some argument I suppose, I offered to allow one of my friends, a boy of great bones and thews, nearly nineteen, and several years older than myself, to hit me as hard as he liked. The spot stipulated was the chest, and I hoped by suddenly expanding it to hurt his wrist more than he could hurt me. He took a run, and whirling his fist like a bowler, hit me in the eye. It was an illuminating blow : the next moment I was drowning in a sea of brown mud and fire.

It must have been a knock-out. With this experience in my memory you can imagine my enthusiastic excitement when, in the match preceding the Championship, I saw Danny Cripps

157

stagger up after a clout on the side of the head from Mike Sweeny, before the umpire had counted eight. How, sinking through that buzzing world of mud and fire, he could have heard the counting was hard to imagine. I can only suppose that just as some people can rouse themselves at a certain hour by a resolve firmly taken the night before, so the imperative " I must get up " was lodged in him deeper than waking consciousness.

There was no knock-out in the fight between Freddy Welsh and Willie Ritchie, and there were no falls. The hitting was no doubt harder, though the inexperienced spectator could not be sure of this. He could only see that the blows of Ritchie's which looked most dangerous, missed, and that both he and Welsh could stand a great deal more punching. I am not writing—it would be absurd —for people who know anything about boxing, or for those who want to know what happened each round (they presumably read the sporting papers, where these things are recorded with astonishing accuracy), but for those to whom the next boxing-match, if they go to it, will be as new an experience as this one was to me. Let me first give them a piece of advice. It is no use going to cheap seats—from those the antagonists on the platform look like two little dolls on a napkin. I dare say adepts can follow what is happening from that distance, but the stranger can only get excitement if he is quite near the ring. It is expensive, but you must be close enough to see what is happening when both boxers are hugging and jabbing each other in the nuzzling, tussling way two dogs fight on their hind legs. You ought, indeed, to be near enough to watch their eyes, but this is very expensive. Those sparring gestures when they are apart, bobs and feints, are often beautiful as movements, and often they are not. From a distance there is

158

great monotony in a fight. Your impression of it resolves itself into the recollection of two situations; one in which two men are warily sparring and dancing round each other; and one in which a blow is delivered (you hardly see how) and suddenly they are locked together, jabbing and pommelling and heaving. Then they are separated, and the dancing and pawing recommences. Every now and then there is a dramatic moment which you could not miss though you were far away : a swinging blow and a deft duck and—smack, they are skin to skin, body to body again. Welsh made some wonderful ducks and dives. I remember vividly one passage in which he made a double duck, this side that side, Ritchie's arm going over him twice like Punch's baton over the clown.

The great difference between professional and amateur boxing seemed to me to lie, from a spectacular point of view, in the fact that while amateurs, after giving a blow, step back to get out of danger, with professionals a rush forward is the commonest counter to a return. Sometimes when Ritchie was no doubt intent on some opening, and they were both footing it warily round and round with their arms working, Welsh managed to plant a swift punch in his face. I suppose this would count as a point, but it did not seem to have much effect on Ritchie. Indeed, how the referee decided who had won a particular round puzzled me. One might decide on general grounds that Welsh or Ritchie had had the best of it, and had hit the other man more often; but how far one swinging blow counted against three or four smart punches I could not, in my ignorance of the intricacies of the sport, make out.

Welsh fought in a crouching position, with his head very low ; Ritchie with his arms held farther from his body and his gloves often half open. Welsh

159

nearly always took the offensive. I don't know how risky those head-down rushes of his were. One only saw that whenever Ritchie tried to catch him with an upward blow as he came on, he was always a fraction of a second too late. Would that blow come off next time ? That is what kept me excited, for Welsh was otherwise getting the best of the game. I was near enough to see, but not quick enough to follow, all that happened when they were " fighting in." Welsh was nearly always lower and striking up, and often Ritchie had to content himself with pommelling the back of Welsh's neck. This situation, which was repeated again and again, was thrilling to a spectator near enough to see how much scrooging and hammering went on to maintain what, at a distance, must have seemed a *status quo*. What risks were run when a glove or arm was shifted to get a better opening or to disengage !

The whole spectacle is an exhilarating one : the white square platform with its white ropes under a blazing glare of light, on which these admirable specimens of humanity are perpetually shifting and dodging with steady agility, and beyond them the confused darkness of the crowd with faces set thick as cobble-stones in it. Every now and then a delighted roar breaks out when a blow goes clean home, or is avoided with dramatic dexterity. It is, I suppose, this particular thrill of seeing a smashing blow which humanitarians distrust.

I have myself a strong dislike to vicarious pugnacity—the most enfeebling and commonest of emotions. It does enter into one's enjoyment of a boxing match. There is no doubt about that. But the joy inspired by the exhibition of pluck seems wholly admirable ; and in this world, where things are so inextricably mixed, it is impossible to get the one without the other. After all the satisfaction of

160

seeing a boxer mauled, even if you identify yourself entirely with the stronger (the " sportsman " rejoices when the pluckiest wins), is respectable compared with the quiet pleasure many take at the Law Courts trials where some fellow-creature is often battered out of self-respect and all resemblance to our common humanity.

OLD AGE

READING Volume V of Mr. Buckle's *Life of Benjamin Disraeli* started me thinking about old age.

So far I have never been profoundly alarmed by the prospect of growing old. I was not born with a strong dread of death or of old age. The first book which made the thought of growing old at all alarming to me was *War and Peace*—the epilogue of it. You remember the description of the Rostov family at the end, that family once so gloriously full of life? Then perhaps you remember this description of the Countess Rostov in her old age:

"After the deaths of her son and her husband, that had followed so quickly one on another, she had felt herself a creature accidentally forgotten in this world, with no object and no interest in life. She ate and drank, slept and lay awake, but she did not live. Life gave her no impressions. . . . There was in the highest degree noticeable in her what may be observed in very small children and in very old people. No external aim could be seen in her existence ; all that could be seen was the need to exercise her various capacities and impulses. She had to eat, to sleep, to think, to talk, to weep, to get angry, to work, and so on, simply because she had a stomach, a brain, muscles, nerves and spleen. . . . She only talked because she needed to exercise her lungs and her tongue. She cried like a child, because she needed the physical relief of tears, and so on. What for people in their full vigour is a

162

motive, with her was obviously a pretext. Thus in
the morning, especially if she had eaten anything too
rich the night before, she sought an occasion for
anger and pitched on the first excuse—the deafness
of Madame Byelov. . . . Another excuse was her
snuff, etc. . . . When she required exercise for
her organs of speech—this was usually about seven
o'clock, after she had had her after-dinner rest, then
the pretext was found in repetition of anecdotes,
always the same and always to the same listeners.
The old Countess's condition was understood by
all the household, though no one ever spoke of it.
Only rarely a mournful half-smile passed between
Nikolay, Pierre, Natasha, that betrayed their
comprehension of her condition. But those glances
said something else besides. They said that she
had done her work in life already, that she was not
all here in what was seen in her now, that they
would all be the same. . . . *Memento mori*, said
those glances."

And then Tolstoy adds : " Only quite heartless
and stupid people and little children failed to understand this, and held themselves aloof from her."
That passage frightened me : "What for people
in their full vigour is a motive, with her was obviously
a pretext." Now the essence of what is really depressing in modern psychology is the tendency to extend
to all ages of life, what Tolstoy, with that compassion of his which is one of the most exquisite
things in literature, marked as the characteristic of
old age. The tendency of modern psychology, and
it is reflected in modern fiction, is to interpret
actions and the expression of emotions merely as
pretexts for the exercise of physiological functions.
The next book which made the idea of growing
old alarming to me was *The Old Wives' Tale.*
Arnold Bennett was fundamentally a romantic.

That is to say, his standard of values was not external, he accepted the value given to things by the will as the last word. His favourite character was the miscellaneously - acquisitive, ordinary active man who wants to get on, or wants first this thing and then that ; and the value which gusto transfers to the objects of desire was never criticized by Arnold Bennett. No novelist ever gazed with more mouth-watering, urchin-like naivety into the pastry-cook's window of life. It was the source of his grip upon the imagination of the public.

But there is one element in experience which brings the romantic up short, brings him face to face with a pervasive sense of tragedy (not merely the tragedy of failure to get this or that, a nice house, a nice income, a wife and children)—the fact of old age and death. In the process of time the glow shed by the will slowly fades from things. The reason *The Old Wives' Tale* is Bennett's greatest book is not that he has shown there his powers of description at their best—though he has —but because it has the deepest theme. And in the handling of it he showed himself an artist.

In the first half we follow the adventures of two young sisters, Constance and Sophia. We have followed so breathlessly their divergent careers that we have forgotten how time flies and what it does. We turn a page—at last the sisters meet again ! "They both hesitated, and, as it were, wavered uncertainly towards each other. 'I should have known you anywhere,' said Sophia, with apparently careless tranquillity, as she stooped to kiss Constance, raising her veil." "I should have known you anywhere." But we should not have known them. They are both old women. Constance is just a cosy, tremulous old body ; the proud Sophia is like a blade of tempered steel after her experience, but there is nothing to cut with it. The once flashy

Scales appears again, a shabby wreck, and only to die. The two sisters have ample means ; they live a little longer. "She was a great body for making the best of things," is Constance's epitaph. It is the young generation's turn next. At that meeting of the two sisters the idea of the book has suddenly crystallized ; the last pages make it certain that all who read will understand

Disraeli would not to the last own to a grey hair, but he fought old age with subtler weapons than dye. It was as a septuagenarian lover that he interested me most. The heart does not so soon grow old, but it is painful to have "to lodge the god in ruins." "Well, at any rate, let the ruins be as picturesque as possible," Disraeli seems to have said to himself, "I will live by the youngest part of me still — the heart — and never be without two Dulcineas."

BOHEMIA

THERE is a great difference of opinion as to where the confines of this country begin. I see the smaller Oxford Dictionary defines a *Bohemian* as " a socially unconventional person of free and easy habits, manners, and sometimes morals (esp. of artists, etc.)." This definition leaves much to be desired. " Especially of artists, etc." ; it is precisely the " *et cœtera* " one is curious about. Unconventionality alone does not make a *Bohemian.* It was an unconventional thing to invent " ear-stoppers," and to put them on the moment the conversation became trying, yet Herbert Spencer was not a *Bohemian* ; the most rigid conventionalist would hesitate to call him that. These ear-stoppers were formed by a band, almost semi-circular in shape, with a little velvet knob at each end, which a spring kept pressed over the ears. The device was unconventional ; the effect was comic ; but it was too rational and deliberate a proceeding to be the mark of a *Bohemian.* In fact, I shall endeavour to persuade you that it was the reverse. For Bohemianism must be distinguished from mere eccentricity of behaviour. I remember knowing in my early youth a successful Yorkshire manufacturer who exhibited two odd traits, one of which strikes me now as belonging, like Herbert Spencer's ear-stoppers, to the category of ingenious, rational contrivances, and the other to that of pure eccentricity ; neither marks him as a *Bohemian.* His case is instructive. At the bottom of his park ran an inky canal, down which coal-barges were towed all day. A high wall separated his grounds from the tow-path, and along the top of this wall, which was several hundred yards in length, he placed a row of bottles. The bargees could not resist shying coal at them. In fact, it became their regular practice, a sport to which they all looked forward, and on which bets were laid. Periodically the gardener went round to collect the missiles which had fallen on the park side of the wall, and the ingenious proprietor boasted that he kept one small greenhouse going during the year without its costing him a penny.

His eccentricity was to keep open house at midday on cold beef, which he himself cut into slices with extraordinary rapidity, and flung upon the plates of the expectant guests with a dexterous flick of the carving knife. The slices always landed flat on the plates, and, with the exception of the left-hand corner plate at the other end of the table, his aim was unerring ; for this shot he had visibly to pull himself together, and sometimes he failed. Out of consideration for the feelings of a possibly touchy guest, this place was always occupied by a member of the family, which was a large one. He had, I think, the makings of a *Bohemian* in him, and yet clearly he was not one. He was merely eccentric and ingenious and unconventional.

The way in which a *Bohemian* differs essentially from other people seems to me to lie, not in laxity of morals, nor in irregularity of habits (for some *Bohemians* have clockwork habits), nor in casual manners (for some are punctilious), but in not possessing a sense that everything ought to serve a particular purpose and no other. The *Bohemian* has no delight in allocation for its own sake. Now the run of mankind takes an almost childish delight in contrivances intended to meet the need ot particular occasions ; and their object, as the contents of shop-windows show, is not to make the same things serve many ends, but to have at hand as many things as possible made in such a way that they can only be used on certain definite occasions. The man who is the antithesis to the *Bohemian* is the man who cannot resist a new patent egg-decapitator. He likes his travelling-bag to be constructed in such a way that only a shoe-horn and nothing else will go in a particular place in it. He would, if such a suit could be designed, like to possess one in which the wearer could only go through the motions necessary to golf, and in which it would be quite impossible to shoot or ride. Conventions in dress, dictating a particular costume on particular occasions, delight instead of bothering him. He rejoices to think that he must dress differently for Newmarket and for Ascot. And he treats time and space, as far as he can, in the same way. He likes to arrange his day so that it is difficult to do anything except certain kinds of things at certain hours ; his house so that each room is used only for certain purposes, and each part of each room so that it becomes more fitted for one purpose than any other. His dining-room will be a room in which it is almost impossible to sit comfortably, except round the table ; his drawing-room one in which it would be difficult to concentrate upon work, with a corner of it especially suitable for afternoon tea. On the other hand, the note of the *Bohemian's* house is that any room and anything in it may be used for any purpose as occasion arises, from the dining-room table as a writing-table, to paper-clips as studs, or tooth-brushes as window-wedges. He *prefers* to use his ulster as a dressing-gown, whereas his opposite would like an excuse for having three dressing-gowns, each for a different stage in his toilet. The *Bohemian* does not scorn to use an old hat-box as a waste-paper-basket; and, although his way of life does not conduce to order like his opposite's, it is a mistake to conclude that the one loves order and the other does not. The real difference between them is that the one gets an exquisite satisfaction from thinking that everything round him serves a definite purpose, and is amused by forestalling the minute contingencies of life; while the other is bored by preparing for them, and the purpose things serve is by no means the most interesting quality they possess for him. To the former, the charm of thinking about the hours ahead of him is that each one is ear-marked; to the latter, that they are all empty and can be filled with anything. Æsthetic people are not most interested in the purpose for which things are made, but in their appearance, or the suggestions they may carry for their imagination; they therefore tend to be " *Bohemian.*"

The question, what are the signs by which a traveller may know that he has crossed the borders of *Bohemia*, is difficult to define. The frontier begins at different places for different people. To me it is marked by a house at which one might find any afternoon the master shaving at three o'clock by the drawing-room looking-glass; but to some people such a sight would suggest that they must be nearing the capital. It depends upon previous experience. But if you wish to find out whether or not you are likely to be at home and comfortable anywhere throughout its dominions (this is a practical question often requiring decision), call up to yourself the vision of someone buttering bread with a perfectly clean razor : if the idea sends a shudder through you, you may conclude you will be happier in other social latitudes; but if you can envisage it with equanimity, you may, if you choose, make *Bohemia* your home. As everybody knows, it has as an abode many advantages as well as drawbacks, and having passed this test you may be confident that its drawbacks will not prove serious ones for you.

WORRY

I WISH one of those people who find time to write to me correcting my statements, sometimes sweetly, sometimes with a galling air of triumph, would come to the rescue of my ignorance now. I want to know the title and the author of some verses, but the indications I can give are scanty. They are comic verses; they are certainly not by an author of repute—I should think they were by someone whom no literary man would call a literary man. They have a refrain, " And he worried about it." You remember Socrates' contempt for knowledge which did not, and could not, help a man to live well and choose the better road in life ? These verses are Socratic.

Such contempt for the fruit of disinterested curiosity, for science and erudition, is common to philosophers with a strong ethical bent, and also to cheerful practical philistines of all sorts. Dr. Johnson felt contempt towards science ("A man who grows great in electrifying a bottle ! ") ; though with that imposing and trenchant unfairness which at once attracts and repels us in him, he smiled upon scholarship. No doubt, if pressed, he would have admitted erudition to be also frivolous : still, its pursuit was a highly respectable way of spending time without sin—and that was the great thing. In Bernard Shaw we see (I hope many of us with regret) a similar tendency to pooh-pooh science. He plumps for imaginative intuition as against observation and the accumulation of facts, for genius against detachment. He shocked

171

me once by exclaiming in a lecture that no man
without imagination ought to be allowed to look
through a microscope ; while I felt, on the contrary, that the only type of man I could trust to
tell me what he saw would be precisely the one
Mr. Shaw would debar. But I am forgetting those
verses about which I want information. To give
a further clue to identifying them, I will recall
the circumstances in which I heard them repeated.

It was a village entertainment, the performers
were school-children ; I was staying with the
squire. Though he had merits rather rare in
squires—for instance, if he did make friends with
one of his dependents, in talk with him he ceased
to be the squire—he was extremely lazy and
indifferent about the duties of his position. I
knew him well. The most persuasive wild horse
could not drag him out on a winter's evening to
a stuffy school-room, smelling of warm parents and
children, to listen to hapless little turns, songs,
recitations. His refusal would be partly due to
downright selfishness, partly to an abhorrence of
pretence. Nothing would induce him to pose as the
benevolent patron of the village when he did not
care a damn whether the children acquitted themselves to the credit of the school-mistress and vicar
or not. He had no objection to over-riding or
trampling on the poor ; but patronizing them,
even when a little patronizing geniality would
have been most welcome, was impossible to him.
Now, I took a simpler, a hedonistic view of such
situations. I saw in the mind's eye the decorated
and beflagged school-room ; the empty row of
chairs in front reserved for the party from " the
great house " ; the dumb village audience, the
hesitation to begin. I heard in the mind's ear
the whispered consultations : " Shall we begin ?
Better wait. They are sure to come. . . . Seems they

are not coming "—and I imagined, at least in some hearts, a sense of flatness. It is always slightly depressing to begin one's performance with the impression that it is not considered important (I have experienced this when lecturing), though one gets over it, while an element of august-ness in an audience adds a fearful joy stimulating to performers. In short, when the squire refused to budge I said that at any rate some of us *must* go. We did; and I had my reward. In the course of an entertainment marked by that wooden inability on the part of the performers to make the best of themselves which is the subtle charm of childhood, a little girl in a bright sash got up and recited the poem with the refrain, " And he worried about it."

The story which the verses told was that of a man who might have been quite happy at home, only he had worse cares than any which his wife could succeed in overcoming. He was not the slightest use in the house, for he had been reading in history about the fearful misfortunes which had overtaken mankind in the past—and he worried about it; he had read in the papers about floods in China, earthquakes in South America, famines in India—and he worried about it; worse still, he had read in scientific books how in trillions of years the earth would inevitably grow colder and mankind would be frozen out—and he worried about it. Through the mechanical sing-song of the shrill unmodulated little voice, there rang, whenever she came to the refrain, a genuine and comical surprise. She converted me on the spot to her careless philosophy. I have had backslidings, but on the whole I have followed her pretty well.

Had I not, probably M. Maeterlinck's book, *La Vie des Termites*, would have depressed me. I should have "worried about it." As it is, I can mark

with equanimity where pessimism seems fair,
and where it seems unduly deepened.

After all, one reads such books for information, to satisfy curiosity. If one reads them with
a mind bristling with terror, it is better not to
read them at all : books about insect life do not
suggest an amiable aspect of the *Anima Mundi*.
In this account of the so-called white ants (they
really take colour from the soil in which they live)
there is much that reminds us of human destiny.
They have had to solve the same sort of problems ;
being feeble, unweaponed and unprotected, they
have brought community life to high and terrible
perfection.

But I shall not worry about it.

SUFFRAGETTES

THEY were stirring days—the days of the
Suffragettes. No one knew what they would be
up to next. The crash of plate-glass shop-windows
became a familiar sound ; the sight of a dishevelled woman, half-carried, half-pushed along
between two policemen, tugging and biting in an
anguish of exultation and disgust, became a
familiar sight. In the gutters of the streets all day
long, wet or fine, stood shy girls, selling, in a kind of
rapt miserable patience, propagandist literature; on
boxes at the entrance of quiet squares, in the parks,
bolder spirits were describing to blank-faced or
jeering crowds the horrors of forcible feeding, the
torture of " the cat-and-mouse Act." One morning
we would read that Mr. Birrell had been felled
by five amazons in St. James's Park ; the next,
that Mr. Asquith had narrowly escaped being torn
to pieces on some distant golf-links, or badly
scratched at a Foreign Office party. Interrupted
meetings, well- or ill-aimed brickbats, blazing houses,
damage to property and to male politicians of all
sorts—the changes were rung on every variety of
public nuisance, from the trivial to the dangerous.
Once, pouring from four furniture-vans, like Greeks
from out the belly of the Trojan Horse, a little
female band actually succeeded, in spite of a regiment of police, horse and foot, in invading the
precincts of Parliament. The lobbies of the
citadel rang with the shriek of whistles (in those
days and in such places as ominous a sound as air-
raid signals), when the scene, still classical, turned

into the Rape of the Sabines. Brawny policemen clasped struggling matrons and maids, bore them away, and set them down like dolls outside the gates. The prisons were full ; the tongues of even the most indefatigably-sermonizing magistrates were worn to stumps ; the authorities were at their wits' end, nor had it taken them long to get there. The Hunger Strike was winning. Authority had only one weapon left. It could only pump soup up the noses of women into their lungs and stomachs ; not a pretty form of torture. The object of the police was to arrest as few raiders as possible ; they set these down and told them to go home. The women flung themselves again at the large blue men, battered and swore and scratched—till martyrdom was secured.

They had two weapons ; the power to make themselves an intolerable nuisance, and a hunger for martyrdom ; martyrdom was the most effective, the most precious weapon. The funds behind the movement were inexhaustible. The campaign was a costly one, but the Suffragette coffers were never empty ; they were fed from the most un-expected sources. Quiet old maids who had been content to save for a favourite nephew, or whose public spirit had taken the form of supporting a home for lost dogs, or financing a society for prolonging the close season for lobsters, recklessly contributed far more than their savings. The nondescript women one sees in hotels, turning wearily the pages of out-of-date magazines, sent cheques and curtailed their visits to Bexhill or Torquay. And, more disconcerting, the cry " The Vote, the Vote ! " appealed equally to the daughters and wives of men who flattered themselves they had allowed their womenfolk perfect freedom. Something had come between them and a daughter whose education they had inched and pinched

176

to secure, between them and wives who were
invariably allowed to decide every question of
domestic importance.

One Derby Day, as the horses were coming
into the straight, a woman ducked under the railings
and flung herself before them. She had mistimed
her plunge ; the group of leading horses had already
passed her, and she was struck by one which was
out of the running. She was instantly killed.
This " futile " and heroic demonstration roused a
great deal of feeling. It was tantamount to a threat
to the male population that not only orderly
political life in this country would be destroyed,
but their favourite pleasures would be in constant jeopardy until this matter of " The Vote "
was settled.

Some days later a long funeral procession
wound its way slowly across London from station
to station with bands and banners. I struck it in
Shaftesbury Avenue and walked beside it to St.
Pancras, solemnified by the dull thump of the
drums and the wail of the fifes. What thousands of
women ! What different types ! Old and young,
dowdy and smart, dignified and slatternly,
intellectual, obviously public-spirited, haplessly
the reverse, wearing the badges of the militants,
wearing the ribbons of the constitutional women's
movement, wearing the ribbons of everyday finery
eked out with mourning. . . . I am ashamed to
say I have forgotten the name of the devoted
suicide in the long black box, though I paid
her then the homage of tears. " We are weak, we
are weak," wailed the fifes ; " We are strong, we
are strong," thumped the drums. Thousands of
women, and such different kinds of women ! I became conscious of the vast surge behind this
rackety, screaming movement. What a hetero-
geneous collection of motives, disappointments,

grievances, humiliations, blunders, had contributed
to it and massed these thousands of women together.
The vote was a symbol.

IN GERMANY

SOMETIMES I am transported backwards on the Time Machine against my will. It happened recently while I was trying to read an American translation of Wedekind's plays (*Tragedies of Sex*). Had this translation not irked me I should not now be reviewing memories ; I should be reviewing a book. But its lamentable diction implanted in the text so many false tones that I took refuge in recalling the first time I saw a Wedekind play. That play was the *Erd-Geist*. I saw it so long ago that even in Germany very few had then heard the name of Wedekind.

In my youth I was sent for a term to Leipzig University, in the hope that I should acquire there a thorough knowledge of the German language. Leipzig University was not at all my idea of a University. I found myself homesick and at large in a great town, though at the same time, rather gratifyingly, a rich independent man— the possessor of fine apartments for which I paid the modest sum of 35s. a month. I soon collected a following of needy students, who had discovered that I could afford to be prodigal to the extent of a few guineas. But where was the University ? To me it was a brass plate and Herr Professor Wundt. True, there were the student-members of the corps, who wore white caps, with different-coloured ribbons round them, between crown and peak. These crop-headed, shaven young men lounged round the town in packs, with sticks and canes, drank beer together in the same restaurants, sang songs together, and occasionally went off to the neighbouring town of Halle to fight. (Duels were not allowed in the University itself.) From there they returned, their faces criss-crossed with sticking-plaster. I refused to join a corps ; the offer came too late ; I had already chosen my companions, and they were all social pariahs—musical German Jews, out-at-elbow students, who could not be admitted. But these were faithful to me, and from them I learnt something of the Art of Sponging— perhaps the most valuable accomplishment I brought back with me to England.

Most people are mere duffers at sponging, because, poor things, they have never been in the position to be sponged upon ; they make mistakes because they do not know what it feels like to be a Spongee. They do not understand, for instance, that sigh of slight depression which arises, not from the breast of stinginess, but merely from the monotony of its being always taken for granted, night after night, week after week, month after month, that the rich man will pay. They do not comprehend that it is not only their desire, but also his desire, to forget, as far as possible, this slightly vexatious circumstance ; and, there-fore, that to leap forward with alacrity to pay a penny-ha'penny tram-fare, when on arrival at the theatre the Spongee will of course be left to take all the tickets, is not tactful on the part of the Sponge, but calculated to make the Spongee murmur : " This, at any rate, is not the moment for a display of rugged independence."

I learnt a lot of little things like that from my faithful, tag-rag tail. I learnt too the meagreness of the rewards of opulence. When my followers were courting, it was I who bought large inexpensive bouquets ; when the courting was successful, it was I who paid for small inexpensive opal rings or bright parasols. Thus I knew what it was to have my shoulder frequently patted, to be stroked and told repeatedly that I was a *famoser Kerl*, a *liebeswürdiger Mensch*, a *prächtige Natur ;* and thus I, too, experienced for a brief period all the malease and dubious satisfactions of the rich.

The Leipzig concerts were, of course, magnificent, but the State Theatre performances were of a heart-damping banality, and were spiritlessly acted. After a few experiments I was easily persuaded to abandon them, and our favourite haunt became a long drill-hall with a stage at one end of it. You could sit there, at little round tables, drinking beer during the performance. It was not under control, though there was always a Schutzmann present, in case anything rude should be said about the Kaiser ; and there unlicensed plays could be performed. One evening, before the curtain went up, a bewigged, heavy-eyebrowed man in a crimson satin jacket and limp thigh-boots, with a revolver in one hand and a whip in the other, made a rather ridiculously emphatic appearance in front of it. He began a tirade in verse which I could hardly follow, though it was clear to me the speaker was in a state of contemptuous, wrought-up fury. He hurled his lines straight at our noses as though he hoped they would break them, cracking his whip at intervals and once making everyone jump by firing his revolver over our heads. It was Wedekind himself, taking round the *Erd-Geist*, then only a little side-show wherever he set it up. At Leipzig his audiences were thin indeed—never more than thirty or forty people in the long, grey room, I think. I went, I remember, myself to three out of the four performances. The *Erd-Geist* had fascinated me. It could not be said, however, that these small audiences were indifferent, since the closing act was invariably received with loud hisses ; a gander-like demonstration which prompted me at last to send round a note in school-boy German expressing my strong approval of the play ; and that led to Wedekind and I drinking a silent glass of beer together, nodding at each other over it.

Why did the *Erd-Geist* fascinate me ? I was certainly not experienced enough to see what a dramatic innovation it was. Perhaps " Lulu " herself had something to do with it—Lulu, " the snake " in this menagerie of wild animals (Wedekind insisted that *his* characters were real wild animals, not tame ones like those in other dramas) who poisons, seduces and kills with unaffected serenity. Lulu was acted by a little blonde with a disturbing apathy in every movement, and a " soft un-christened smile " such as I have never seen in an actress since. (I believe she afterwards became famous.) Perhaps I was also fascinated because the play, though mystifying, was at the same time easy for a foreigner to follow : twenty minutes of excited, concentrated dialogue, then—Bang !— a death in a fit, or a suicide, or a murder. A curious combination of crude, energetic realism and of poetic disregard of literal truth, ran through it all. Long afterwards some of Van Gogh's pictures gave me the same sensation. If I had only had my wits about me then, or dreamt I should ever be interested in drama, I might, as long ago as the beginning of the century, have been the harbinger of " Expressionism " to these shores.

DURING THE WAR

AUGUST 4TH 1914

NATURE, I believe, meant me to be a special
reporter, but she forgot to endow me with the
knack of being " on the spot." But sometimes
so much worth noticing is going on everywhere that
it matters little where you are. The night of
August 4th was such an occasion. It does not
disqualify me as a reporter that I was not in the
pushing, yelling, chaffing crowds which thronged
the Horse Guards or in the cheering ones outside
the House of Commons.

I met at two in the morning, in the far and
quiet West, and in a clean, lit, empty, residential
street, an old, eager, one-eyed vendor of papers
with a Union Jack in his billy-cock. A tattered
bill fluttered before him as he shuffled wearily
and hurriedly forward. " Thrippence. Thrippence.
Declaration of War." He was trying to shout, but
he only achieved a quinsied whisper. I stopped and
bought. " It's not in it," he added, confidentially,
pocketing my coppers, " but it's true : God's truth
it is—I couldn't get the latest. I was an hour and
a quarter getting through the crowd." I looked
at him and felt as if I had been in that crowd myself,
and could describe it, too. " If Mr. Disraeli was
alive!" he croaked huskily. After this unexpected
comment he lunged on again with bent knees,
leaving me under the street lamp staring at the
columns of the new, but already familiar, heavily-
leaded type.

Though the region where I parted from my
friends was fairly well known to me, I had lost my

way, and after walking about half an hour I had
come out somewhere below Holland Park. How
late the 'buses were running ! And the taxis were
buzzing one after the other down the main thoroughfare, as if it had been ten o'clock and not two in the
morning. This reminded me of public injunctions,
already emphatic, concerning economy in petrol.
But economy was impossible to-night ; night of
good-byes, of intimacies and friendships huddled
into climaxes ; night of sociable, equalizing forebodings ; night ominous to the solitary, but gay,
positively gay, to the gregarious.

I had noticed on my late ramblings and stray-
ings that " good-nights " from passing strangers had
been frequent, and that they had had a different
ring. People seemed to like being stopped and
asked for a match or to point out the way ; their
eyes were more alive, less preoccupied, more conscious of one. When I joined a group round a
coffee-stall to drink a cup of hot slop, I did not
feel that customary embarrassment at not being
suitably dressed. The silence round me was more
friendly ; some sort of barrier was down ; no one
asked me for money. Beside me as I drank stood
one of those little, odd, undersized fly-by-nights,
her grubby hands resting side by side on the
oilcloth of the counter. She looked up under
her feathers and smiled. It was not the usual
smile.

As I crossed, striking southwards, some idea—
what was it ?—began to peep through these impressions.

A taxi packed with people waving flags whizzed
by, down the now empty road. A girl in a pink
jersey and a man, sitting on the half-open roof,
set up a long hooting screech as they passed : I
felt I had sampled the patriotic enthusiasms of
Piccadilly Circus, What luck ! How depressed I

186

should have been in the midst of them ! There is nothing so heart-damping as being out of sympathy with a crowd.

In a road of modest villas (it was quiet and dark) I passed first one and then another waiting taxi . . . close on three o'clock, and in this region of prudent living ! Suddenly behind some acacias shivering in the night air a door opened. A woman ran quickly down the steps, waving back at a man who was standing in the lighted oblong, signalling and nodding agitated encouragement. In she sprang, flinging herself back with that rapid pre-occupied movement which is equivalent to ex-claiming, "This is life ! " This hectic communal excitement, which overlay gloom and foreboding, which was expressing itself here in intimate ways and elsewhere in confused uproar—my peeping idea had something to do with that.

I had not come up against those blatant mani-festations of it, that swaggering contempt for suffer-ing which suggests such an ignominious combination of cowardice, stupidity, and cruelty. Clearly the great majority (unless they feared too much for themselves or those nearest them) loved war. There was exhilaration abroad to-night, but beneath lay forebodings of dreadful days, and deeper still a dumb resentment at the cold-blooded idiocy of diplomacy. Yet, there it was—and it was a kind of happiness. Why did a declaration of war make people unusually happy ? Was it only love of excitement ? Where exaltation roared and romped and streamed along the streets, it seemed it might be so ; but where I had surprised it, in quieter eddies, there seemed to be another element involved. I caught the idea which had been peeping at me, and the irony of it was enough to make one cry : people seldom experience so genuinely that sense that life is worth living, which a feeling of brotherhood

187

gives, as when they are banded together to kill their fellow-men ; they are never so conscious of the humanity of others as when they are out, sharing risks, to smash the self-respect and mutilate the bodies of those who, but for a few politicians, might just as easily have been hoping with them, dying with them side by side.

Earlier in the night I had seen a party of French recruits doubling through the streets, singing. Everybody had hailed them as they went by. Coming towards me now under the lamps was a man in spectacles, with a small straw hat perched on his big square head. He looked Teutonic. " Gute Nacht," I said, as we passed. He stopped for a second and wrung his hands : " Ach Gott, Ach Gott ! Mein lieber Freund ! "

HOW THEY TALK

"THERE'S no doubt about its effect on *me*," said the literary man ; " I'm done for."

" Oh, nonsense ! " someone murmured sympathetically.

"Can't you write about the War ? " said the cheerful person. " I'm sure you could."

" I can't think of anything else, but I can't write about it. That's the form in which I pay my quota to the general uneasiness and depression."

" I must say, then," said the business man, " you get off pretty cheap. I beg your pardon," he added hastily, " I was forgetting you wrote for a living."

" I had forgotten. For the moment I wasn't thinking of that," replied the literary man, sighing and knocking out his pipe. " The fact is, since the War began my mind has been like a dog on a chain, a dog which is used to scampering about. I feel useless, too—a fly on the fifth wheel of the coach ; and then once or twice every hour of the day I say to myself, ' Think what I am missing ! What I'm *missing* ' ! "

" Ah, I felt like that," said the cheerful person, " till I joined the Special Constabulary." This remark was followed by silence. Then he went on : " Art and Literature can't stop, you know."

" Can't they ? " suddenly snapped a thin man with vivid eyes and a cramped, energetic face. Hitherto his contribution to the discussion upon the

189

effects of the War had been to declare that, so far
as he was concerned, it had made the conversation
of all his friends intolerable. " I always suspected
before I despised the way even decent people felt
about war," he had added, glaring miserably from one
face to another. Now he kept on repeating, "Can't
they ? Can't they ? " leaning forward and beating his knees rapidly with his hands.

" Look at the pacifist," said the business man,
smiling slowly. " He's got more of the wild cat
in him than any of us. Would pussy like a saucer
of warm blood ? "

" You don't know what you are talking about."
The little man turned on him with such ferocity of
disgust that, though no one had moved, each felt
as though he had suddenly sat bolt upright in his
chair. " Perhaps," he went on, controlling his
voice and looking down, " perhaps what you say
about me is true. That's why I understand,
and you *don't*, what war is really like."

" I wish you'd tell me what it is like," said
the literary man, " if you do know."

" If there was the slightest chance of your
understanding, you wouldn't ask. The fact is,
men like you do not know the joy of killing, so
though you understand in a general sort of way
that thousands of people suffer in war and believe
in its atrocities—at least in those committed by
the enemy, yet the inward reality, the horror of—of—
of everything, the sense of *how* these things happen,
is hidden from you. They are not *real* to you.
Consequently, war to you is simply a drama of
courage and endurance against a background of
pain and death, vague as the sufferings in a cancer
ward. At the same time it is all a sort of glorious
game of chess—you don't realize what hell
it is for those concerned who don't go half-frantic
mad, and in another way for those who do.

Naturally," he concluded contemptuously, " you and ninety per cent of the stay-at-homes like war."

" Look here," said the business man, " if you think a battle can be won by men who go frantic mad, you're very much mistaken."

" I must say it gives one a jolly sort of feeling to think of men bearing all that kind of thing," said the cheerful man.

" What about the good-humour of men under fire," asked the literary man, " the shouts of ' Are we down-hearted ? ' and the willingness of each man to go one better in taking risks and helping ? "

" The good-humour and jokes make it all horribly madder," said the pacifist.

" Do you mean to say you think that under no circumstances a man ought to control his nerves? If so, how on earth is the work of the world to get done ? " said the business man.

" It's a question of what you shut your eyes to, and of feeling things in proportion. Nothing is worth the sufferings of war—not even the courage to bear them."

" Everybody has got to die some time," said the cheerful man.

His remark again produced silence. It was broken by one who had not as yet taken any part in the discussion. " What strikes me is that all this time our soldiers are dying for us, we are arguing about their states of mind. Isn't it . . . ? "

" That's what I feel," exclaimed the literary man.

" It's not so much the men at the front as those at home who strike me as detestable," said the pacifist.

"Oh, then, it's not fighting, but *watching* fighting you are talking about!" said the business man.

191

" It is the onlookers who make the wars,"
said the pacifist.

" I thought you people always said it was the
armament-makers. Though you're glad enough
now," the business man went on, with a provoca-
tive chuckle, " that we've got a strong navy—or you
ought to be."

" If Grey . . . " began the pacifist.

" If the Kaiser, swanking ass . . . "

" If civilization is to . . . "

The temperature had suddenly risen. Each
man felt an angry contempt for the other.

" You don't mean to tell me you want
the Germans to win ? " shouted the business
man.

" No," said the pacifist.

" What I can't understand in you fellows is
that you won't let yourselves be natural and
glad, like decent people, at good news."

" Victory is just as horrible."

" You've no guts, then. Have you no feelings
for England ? Germany *must* be smashed."

" There is no such thing as ' England ' or
' Germany '," said the pacifist, " Only Englishmen
and Germans. They're men like us."

" What, those brutes?" said the cheerful man.

" Do you mean to say you believe all those
filthy stories ? "

" Yes, don't you ? "

" I thought war atrocities were all you *did*
believe in, " said the literary man.

" I don't believe they're all on one side. And
I hate and despise the spirit which makes public
men speak of the German sailors as cowardly
' rats ' who have to be prodded out to fight. Our
journalists always say of German soldiers that ' they
advanced as usual with blind, stupid brutality.'
If it had been a British charge, they would

have described it as the coolest feat of arms in military history. And then the gloating over ' mowed down in thousands ' ! Horrible, mean, stupid —stupid ! Think of it ! Fine men with photographs of their children wrapped up in oilskin rags in their pockets, and . . . ''

" I don't suppose the Navy approved of the First Lord's saying that their enemies were cowardly rats," said the silent man. " The military dispatches are not like the papers, are they? And I haven't noticed much of that spirit in the letters printed from men at the front."

" Hardly was Winston Churchill's speech out of his mouth before the German fleet *did* make a sally," said the pacifist, ignoring the interruption.

" You don't mean to say you're *glad* our ships were sunk ? " several shouted together.

" I never said I was."

" You showed it."

" I didn't."

" I won't be in the room with a fellow who dares to rejoice at our disasters."

" I think I shall enlist," said the silent man, getting up. " I expect there is more decent human feeling at the front than anywhere else in Europe just now."

NIETZSCHE AND THE WAR

October 10*th* 1914

DURING the first few weeks of the War Nietzsche's name was bandied about in the Press a good deal. He was frequently mentioned in connection with stories of German brutality. Anyone who had not read him would have thought from these references that his writings were incitements to cruelty and stimulants to domineering megalomania, and that his works were the inspiration of every harsh, swaggering German patriot and every merciless Prussian soldier. This was a silly mistake. In the first place Pan-Germanism is not the note of Nietzsche's writings; he is the bitterest critic of German culture, a more bitter one even than Heine. It is true that in his mouth the adjective "German" is not such a violent term of abuse as the word "English," but it connotes contempt. The word "English" in his vocabulary stood in the region of practice for the commercial spirit which writers like Carlyle, Ruskin and many modern Socialists have inveighed against ; in the region of thought and feeling for the spirit of compromise, timidity, and a belief that humdrum safe happiness is the only thing worth living for. Nietzsche regarded the utilitarian philosophy as the most characteristic of England's contributions to the world's stock of ideas, and the attempts of the English philosophers to botch up a comfortable reconciliation between "egoism and altruism" made him sick. A moral Tartuffism—cant—he thought, was our national vice; and if one is going to bring general indictments

194

against nations, I suppose that old one *is* the most plausible which can be brought against us, just as stinginess and histrionic emotionalism are the obvious faults of the French, and a romantic egotistic density and a follow-my-leader sheepishness the German ones. Nietzsche hated us because he thought us an unphilosophical race—and so, according to his idea of what philosophy should be, we are.

Philosophy was not to him an unusually obstinate attempt to think correctly, but an adventure of the soul. He did his thinking from the artist's point of view, from the ground of mere feeling. It was absolutely necessary to him to attain an exciting, picturesque view of the world; and the very idea that anybody might pull him up and say, "Yes, yes, but is it *true*?"made him lash out furiously in anticipation. The respect for truth for its own sake he dubbed a sort of survival of Mumbo-Jumbo worship. And if you defended the instinct to respect truth on the plea that after all to know it is the condition of walking sure-footedly in this world, he flew at you on moral grounds. "What! you want to walk sure-footedly, do you, you miserable, life-diminishing mediocrity? Don't you understand that tight-rope dancing is the emblem of the noble life, and that you must live from moment to moment *dangerously* to be worth anything? My only difficulty as a philosoper is to pile up the panorama of tragedy, all the cruelties of existence—till exhilaration-pitch is reached at last. I have been blessed myself, having also Hell's phantoms inside me, internal enemies to dominate. Thus I could feel myself to be an ecstatic victor, and wrench at last triumphant joys through the bars of my own sickness and weakness—joys with which your notions of happiness, poor, sleek, smug creatures, cannot compare! Have I not written that you must carry a chaos inside you to give birth to a dancing star?" That is the way Nietzsche harangued us.

But even more than the humdrum common-sensible man he hated the saint, and it is easy to see how he came to do so. The saint is a man who gets along marvellously without feeling himself superior to the universe. The spectacle of a man who accepts destiny, and the tasks it imposes on him—even his own weakness—in a spirit of unshakable acquiescence, was a challenge to Nietzsche's whole philosophy. The saint can't be frightened either into personal cowardice or into a state of blazing egotistic valour; that kind of superb hurrahing anger seems to him a small cramped feeling compared with that which can be attained by going out to meet life and opening your arms to humanity. Now if there really was anything in the saint's way of taking life, Nietzsche's philosophy was scuttled. He had to explain the saint away—and he did it very cleverly.

He declared that the saint lived by a sour-grapes philosophy, invented by the particularly feeble and unpleasant and timorous, in order to get even in the long run with the bold, the handsome, and the intelligent; and to persuade them to let off easily those who were too spiritless and ricketty to hold their own. There are a great many "good" people whom this criticism exposes; but it does not rid Nietzsche of his real adversary.

It is all very well to assert that humility is a kind of sneaking, unlovely self-assertion, that self-forgetfulness is a quality peculiar to people whose selves are so unpleasant that they cannot contemplate them without pain, that pity is a fellow-feeling between the unfit, and that the only reason anyone turns the other cheek is that he is too puny to hit back;—it is all very well saying that kind of thing, and it makes salutary reading for many, but it does not strike at the saint. It leaves quite unexplained the spectacle of a man who, without bothering his head whether or not he is bolder, handsomer, stronger and more intelligent than other people, yet goes his way as unafraid as Nietzsche himself,— and seems into the bargain a much happier man— which is a good *symptom*, at any rate, a kind of guarantee of reserve force somewhere. Nietzsche, like Carlyle, was a tremendous æsthete who mistook himself for a profound moralist. He precipitated himself on certain kinds of beauty in human nature and in the history of man, and became infatuated, not only with them, but with the conditions which made them conspicuous ; though these were not admirable at all. The bonfire of beautiful, flaring, pitiless courage at which he invited poor shivering humanity to warm their hands blazes best in a world which is as poisonous, tangled and dank as a tropical forest. But the advantage the saint has over Nietzsche's heroes is that while being quite as little terrified in such a forest, he is fitted also for a much better country. He does not "shine only in the dark." He is just as free from inner restraints as those graspers and dominators, who have fascinated men by exhibiting the energy which springs from will and conscience pulling together.

The antagonism between the saintly and the warrior ideal is written all over literature, and in some mild form it takes place in everybody's private history. And at certain periods a whole generation will incline to one or other of them. The Germans, we are told, have for years past been fascinated by the ideal of a nation under arms, looking only for qualities in their leaders before which it is possible to grovel. Personally, I doubt the diagnosis ; but if it is more or less true, it is conceivable that Nietzsche's writings may have contributed to encouraging in them an upward-gazing admiration for beaked and clawed humanity. But he is much too critical to be acceptable to more or less beaked and taloned personages themselves. He had not an ounce of exclusive patriotism in him. It was the idea of the aggrandisement of individuals not of nations that appealed to him, and it was to a race of "good Europeans" that he looked forward. True, they were rather Prussian those "good Europeans" —more Prussian than he imagined—a spiked helmet would have become their cast of countenance; but he did not believe they were particularly thick on the ground in Central Europe. This is how he wrote of his countrymen: "When the Germans began to become interesting to the other nations of Europe —it is not too long ago—it took place owing to a culture which they now no longer possess, which, in fact, they have shaken off with passionate eagerness, as if it had been a disease; and yet they have known of nothing better to exchange for it than political and national insanity."

WITH THE RED CROSS 1914-15

I

THE straw palliasses on which we Red Cross men slept had been stacked into sofas for the day and covered with rugs : and I, with a brush borrowed from the nuns below, had finished sweeping a room in a small convent near Ypres, the long low room in which a varying fifteen to twenty of us ate, slept, cooked, washed, smoked, shaved, sang, read, talked, mooned, joked, argued, warmed ourselves, dried our clothes, rested, and, in fact, had our being, when an accumulation of scrap-iron in the corner of it caught my eye. I had promptly popped these bits on the top of the overflowing box of sweepings, bones, tea-leaves, paper, straw, cigarette-ends, and potato-peelings, thinking as I did so, "Lucky, just what I wanted, to keep this muck from flying in my face in the wind outside," when I was arrested by an indignant shout : "Hi! look what MacCarthy is doing! He's gone and thrown all the souvenirs into the dust-bin ! "

They were, indeed, fragments of shell and bomb, squashed bullets, etc., objects with associations. Of course, I picked them out again ; had I not coveted a spiked helmet myself ? But to me a bit of rusty iron was a bit of rusty iron and nothing more, even though it should be the fragment of a shell I had seen burst. Indeed, it would have had to hit me before it could have gathered

199

importance in my eyes. But, free from souvenir-mania in this form, I had it in another as badly as anybody. And although my luggage was not heavy with scrap-iron on my return home, my memory was filled with fragments of events. It is these scraps I have set out for inspection : dusting, polishing, and arranging them to what advantage I can, though not without a misgiving that many will seem to others as inconsiderable as those iron souvenirs seemed to me.

To go out strung-up to endure hardships, to risk his life if necessary, and then to find himself loafing about hotels—that is the first trial of a Red Cross man, and it is not easy to support ; even regular meals may in certain circumstances become a burden grievous to be borne. Imagine the rueful glances he casts at his rolled-up sleeping bag as night after night he retires to an hotel bedroom ; imagine the irony with which his concentrated food-tablets and emergency appliances confront him on the mantelpiece after a day spent in eating, smoking, chatting and pottering round ! No, waiting about is a trial not easy to bear. It is small wonder if someone who left home actually feeling perhaps something of a hero gets restive and edgy under it.

Boulogne was full of Red Cross men more or less in this state when we arrived. The garages were crammed, and along the quays stood rows of ambulances apparently doing nothing. The town was crowded with their owners, drivers and orderlies, many suffering from impatience and irked by the feeling that they had somehow left home under false pretences. Many had been there for weeks (I am speaking now of the middle of October), walking the streets, saluting and saluted, dressed in the garb of soldiers, sipping liqueurs in hotel courtyards, over-smoking, over-talking, scrambling for the English papers, treating nurses to tea or chocolate in the pastry-shops, squabbling, gossiping, damning their own organizers, or laying the blame on the R.A.M.C.—and receiving by every post admiring and anxious letters from home.

I was more fortunate than most. Belonging to a section of the Red Cross attached to the French Army, I got off from Boulogne after three days. But these days were enough to enable me to understand how hard it is to believe that they also serve who only lounge about and wait, and to convince me that those who are incapable of believing this had better not volunteer their services at all. The inevitable intermittence of the work made patience perhaps the most important qualification of all. " Can you stand being bored without getting peevish or slack ? " was one of the questions which should have been put to all Red Cross candidates.

It was a fine house, the Mayor informed me, giving me my billet, but empty ; there would be a bed, certainly, and I could get the woman from next door to make the bed. I went off with my slip of paper to get the key and arrange about the servant.

It was a fairly big house, very bare and cold, with a dishevelled garden at the back ; but it was not quite empty. Sure enough, one room had a bed and a washing-stand in it. Its two large curtainless windows looked out to the back. And there I waited in the dusk for the woman to come as I had arranged. Now if you have a tendency to home-sickness, nothing is more likely to bring on an attack than looking at a damp, deserted garden after sunset ; and there is nothing like home-sickness for making you feel you are not up to your job. I began to have misgivings. I had seen that afternoon some ambulances of the *Service de Santé* drive up to a hospital and discharge their loads. I had seen the canvas curtain at the back of the car pulled apart for the first time, revealing six pairs of muddy boots upright on their heels. Even those heavy-nailed, motionless boot-soles had given me a slight qualm, and as one by one the stretchers were slowly pulled out, it was with a most uncomfortable curiosity that I had watched in each case to see where the bloody bandage would come, hoping it would not be across the stomach or the face. When that look of apprehension which often floats across the features of a wounded man while he is being lowered, has passed, and he lies on the ground at your feet, that first impression, given by those boot-soles, of an extraordinary passivity is renewed. Looking down at him as he lies on his back, his eyes, if they are open, seem to say, " Do with me now what you will." Then two *brancardiers* pick him up, and with stooping shoulders, knees slightly bent, and short steps, they carry him in. One of the surgeons had invited me to come round later in the afternoon and go through the wards, and, if I liked, to watch an operation. Thinking that the sooner I plunged the better, I had accepted ; and it was the recollection of having nevertheless turned tail at the last moment when I heard on the landing of the hospital a curious tapering, whinnying cry—it was this recollection which was making me now, as I waited by the window in the dusk, afraid I should not be up to my job.

I began to reflect on that sympathy of the nerves which incapacitates people from being of any use. It was certainly a sensation which anyone in my position must get under at once ; but had such sympathy in a general way any value ? Some people seemed glad they could feel

202

it. They sometimes appeared to cultivate it. But that was only because they thought it proved they were sympathetic. Yet obviously it had little to do with compassion or fellow-feeling. It was rather a kind of fear ; compassion was often stronger in people who were not distressed by any such physical disturbances. It might be useful, perhaps, that sensibility, to a writer searching for the adjective which would give an extra twist to the screw of horror ; but even to him it was a snare, apt to lead him into the higher sensationalism, of which we had had enough, and more than enough, in literature lately. It was quite compatible with cruelty, if it was not actually a necessary ingredient in deliberate cruelty. Familiarity with painful sights might even change it into that curiosity which watches the cup of anguish filling, watches with the deliberation of a man dropping medicine into a graduated glass. It looked humane, but it was a self-regarding, cold feeling. Practical people despised it ; warm-hearted people particularly disliked it ; benevolent people knew that it was no trustworthy indication of sympathy.

II

We got up as quietly as possible so as not to wake the others who were lying wrapped in rugs like brown chrysalises. The low room hummed with the sound of gentle snoring. It was stuffy ; it was cold. On lying down I had taken the precaution to dry my socks by putting them between my shirt and my vest, but the moment my feet were in my boots again the comforting sense of moist warmth vanished, and the familiar chill struck up my legs.

As we clumped cautiously down the wooden stairs the O.C. was whispering directions to the man on watch to have hot cocoa ready for us against our return. The job would be an all-night one. Outside it was bitter-cold, windy, and pitch-dark ; no moon, not a star ; only on the horizon there fluttered from time to time the lightning of guns too distant to be heard. There had been a booming cannonade round us that evening. Now it had stopped, and nothing was audible but the wind wuthering down the village street and the creaking of bare trees. There was the usual delay tinkering up the machines. I went in again to get extra blankets for the stretchers (two apiece would not be amiss on such a night), to fill the water-bottles with boiled water, and cram more cigarettes and chocolate into my coat-pockets. Then off we started—three cars ; I in the last, since I had been along the road by day-time, and my companion, who was driving, had not. If we got behind—and he was bound to go cautiously—it was my business to remember where the shell-holes came. The road was shock-ingly bad—I knew that—narrow, with mud on each side deep enough to bog a heavy ambulance. I recollected two nasty places in particular : one a shell-hole filled with water in the very middle of the road, which by a miracle of luck was just not too wide for a car to skirt, and one where an enormous crater had broken away a piece of the road just opposite a smaller pit on the other side. What made one nervous on these occasions was the thought of the consequences of an accident. If one gets stuck, let alone the horror of upsetting a load of wounded in the open country at night, a mile or two from help—the road by which the others can be brought may be blocked for hours. Also our section had a reputation to live up to with the French for doing night work along bad roads.

We swished quickly down to the next village with headlights on; but turning into the open country, all lights except the red back-light, had to be extinguished. We were in the dark. The German lines were near on our right, and again somewhere in front of us, a good way off. We started crawling along, straining our eyes ahead into the blackness. The little red light of the car in front, shining like a burning cigar, was a clue to follow, but it was drawing away quickly, and presently it had disappeared altogether. The wind pressed against our eyes. Sometimes the car lurched into deep, soft slush on one side or the other, and had to be righted by a violent twist of the wheel. Was the road curving? And were we coming to the holes? I tried flashing an electric torch intermittently. It illuminated a yard or two of mud and stones just in front, but left us dazzled afterwards with colour blotches, floating on the darkness before our eyes—worse than useless that. Suddenly the whole landscape was lit up by a pale greenish glare. The Germans, on the look-out for an attack, had sent up a rocket. Two flaring stars hung for a minute in the sky as though tied together, dwindled, and went out, leaving us again blinded. "I had better get out and walk in front," I said; "we must be near the first hole"; and, sure enough, I discovered a hole half-filled with straw-water and faggots, but not the one I had expected. More rockets went up, we crawled on and on, then turned abruptly to the left towards a small circle of white light lying on the road. The O.C. was standing there waiting for us, illuminating the large crater with his torch: "Do you see it?" "Right." In a minute or two we were in another village.

Light streamed across the liquid mud from an open door and two broken windows. The house (about the only one still intact) had its back to the enemy's lines, so no precautions had been necessary. On the other side of the road loomed up a shattered church, and opposite the open door stood a large crucifix in a shrine, much bespattered and chipped by shrapnel. The village seemed full of men moving quietly about—French marines in blue overcoats and round flat caps—so they mostly revealed themselves when they crossed a bar of light. One heard the gritting or splashing of their footsteps in the darkness, and saw here and there the wandering spark of a cigarette, which some-times glowed brighter, throwing a momentary gleam on a thick hand, a bearded mouth, and part of a muffler. In the road there was silence ; inside the lighted room a confused noise of talking and moans.

It was difficult for two of us to get into the room with a stretcher, and still more difficult to find a place to put it down. The floor was covered with straw, and the straw almost hidden by the wounded men lying upon it. Close to the door a surgeon on his knees was dabbing at a red hole in the side of a half-naked man, propped up by knapsacks, whose face wore an expression at once of apprehension and of relief such as a frightened child shows when it is at last being cared for. In the nearest corner crouched a young soldier with his cap still on and his face to the wall. He was hunched up like an ape in the corner of its cage, and was talking rapidly to himself. Those whose dress-ings were finished were mostly lying at the farther end of the room. To reach one of them it was necessary to pick your way among apprehensive, tortured bodies, setting down your feet now be-tween broken legs, now beside bleeding heads.

206

And when in order to lay the stretcher it came to moving the wounded man nearest to the one to be taken, then, even if he had been talking or lying lethargic before, he generally began to cry out, either from fear or pain. It takes three men usually to get a badly-wounded man gently on to a stretcher, but here there was often hardly room for two *brancardiers* to shift their feet for the lift. At the door those borne out were covered with rugs, and their few things (caps, pipes), about which they sometimes showed pathetic anxiety, were tucked beside them. Then they were raised again and pushed by their comrades into their shelves in the dark ambulance outside. The stretchers were strapped, with parting words of encouragement; " *Courage, mon vieux*," " *Bon voyage*," etc., and often with assurances that they were lucky to ride in an English car which was going to carry them to bed smoothly and in no time.

But I am afraid the journey was neither very smooth nor very swift. True, we lit up earlier on the way back (one side-light), but the first part of the journey we had to crawl and bump along; and, as on the way there, we had constantly to jump down and peep about for bad places on the road, like someone hunting for a dropped sixpence. The summer lightning of the guns was still leaping now and then on the horizon, but the wind was blowing against the sound, and we heard nothing but the purring of the engine, the swish of the mud, and now and then, alas! when a wheel dropped or the car swerved, an agonized " ai, ai, ai " from the hood behind us. There is considerable skill in driving a car so as to get in and out of a depression with a kind of suavity of movement, and the ambulance-driver may find himself playing at last a sort of game with himself on such occasions—so instinctively

207

does the mind get away from close contact with what is painful. " Here's a beastly place. Can I manage it without a single groan ? Done it ! No, not quite. Well, nearly : count that half a groan "—that is the game.

Once out of the danger zone and in the main road, with our headlights raying out in front along the *pavé*, the old problem presented itself : Is it better to go fast and get the journey over, or to shake less and go very slowly ? We tried both methods that night. If only we could have taken those vile little oblong stones at forty miles an hour, we should perhaps have hardly been rattled, only that was impossible ; but we found going slower than a fairish pace seemed to make small difference to the vibration. The two hospitals for marines were in a little town some miles away. At last we saw the red lamps. One was on the door-step of a small cabaret. There we unloaded. The bar-room seemed already full ; perhaps there were beds and mattresses empty upstairs. Through an open door beyond, two surgeons in aprons could be seen hovering over a narrow operating-table. An elderly doctor in uniform stood with his back against the wall surveying the crowded floor with dazed eyes. I spoke to him. He tapped his forehead and said, " Sleep, sleep—not for two days and nights now." We had to take two of our wounded on to the next hospital. There they were laid in the passage to wait their turn to be examined, while we went into the kitchen and drank cups of black coffee laced with rum before returning again to the ruined village for another load.

Our engine was by this time hot, and it clanked ominously ; we fed it with oil and with water scooped from the ditch. It still clanked, but we got there : crawling along in the dark, afraid every moment if we did not go faster we should

be held up by one of our own cars coming back
again. The room had been emptied and partially
filled again ; but the loading-up went brisker now.
Everybody was working more mechanically; strain
and fatigue are opiates which, if not too strong,
set one mechanically free. I no longer noticed
faces. Nobody spoke more than was necessary.
The bodies of the wounded men were just con-
signments marked " fragile," to be handled and
delivered " with care." One smoked and gnawed
chocolate, handed about chocolate and cigarettes in
silence. Then the return journey—the game of no
bumps, no groans. After several such to-and-fro
journeys things began to telescope together in a
dreamlike way. The bar-room of the cabaret,
however, seemed emptier the last time ; the sleepy
doctor, I remember, was bending over a man lying
loosely with his eyes shut. More coffee and rum ;
back again under a sky now clear and sprinkled with
stars ; a blue-black dome into which there was
beginning to creep a hard sapphirine transparency ;
then at last our own long dim room once more,
with its rows of warm-wrapped sleepers. Ah !
to snuggle down in one's own sack between two
of the chrysalises, to fall really asleep, feeling as
if one had been tossing all night in tumultuous and
distressing dreams ! There is sometimes an almost
mystic comfort in the touch of a pillow.

III

Montdidier, like Rye, is a red-and-grey town
huddled on a hill, which rises from a plain flat as the
Sussex marshes and stretching away on all sides to
the horizon. At the end of several of the quiet
stone-paved streets you see nothing but the sky.
The town has rampart walks and two ancient,
weather-beaten churches, begun in a spirit of

magnificence and brought to completion long afterwards in humility. The older houses, many of them in times gone by urban residences of the provincial nobility, seem as though they now sheltered lives more keenly private. Pull at the iron bobbin hanging beside one of those thresholds, which, though so well kept, look as though they were never crossed, and you divine it will be long before the tinkle brings to the door some little woman in silent slippers and meagre black, whom there and then you may suppose a caretaker, but next day meet hurrying to mass, quite, in her staid and sparing way, a lady. You divine that the grudging peep she would allow you would hint at an unluxurious spaciousness inside, swept and garnished, perhaps a little cold and dim, suggesting prudent neglect and dignified pointful economies. As I walked to bed, when the stones of the lampless streets seemed unnaturally white, and the queer sky-spaces were full of restless stars, the echoes of my footsteps between these silent houses no longer belonged to me in my peaked cap and khaki, but to the impatient pacings of some young hero in a Balzac novel, charged with a double dose of will and appetite.

One night, when a bright moon had put a little ghost in each clean black pane of the windows opposite, and the skeleton shadows of garden trees lay on the streets as clear-cut as on snow, I heard the sound of footsteps approaching, and at that hour and place this was unusual. A short, square, elderly man was coming towards me. When we met, we stopped ; and I observed that his trousers were of some sleek thin material and did not match the rest of his clothes, either in hue or texture. He was clean-shaven ; his cap was pulled forward over his eyes, and round his neck was knotted a not too clean handkerchief.

" Good evening, sir," he said.

I was surprised to hear my own language, for the English army was miles away ; but I was still more surprised by his intonation. It was the respectful and composed greeting of a well-trained servant. What on earth was he doing here behind the firing-line ? How had he got stranded ? Why was he still hanging about ? I asked him to turn and walk with me, and soon got answers to these questions.

He was a coachman (born in Suffolk) who had been thirty-seven years in France, and mostly in the service of a French count, the possessor, among other places, of a château not many miles away. I took out my map. Yes, there it was, the château, in a little green patch which was the park.

" It looks as though it must be now in the hands of the Germans," I said.

" No, sir. The French trenches are at the bottom of the garden. But the Germans have shelled us something cruel ; they're smashing up the whole place. I'd give five pounds to get my clothes. I locked 'em in the dicky of the old coach. Five pounds, I would."

His master, with his two daughters, had apparently stayed on, in spite of intermittent bombardment, for a fortnight. The Count was an old man. He had been unable to believe that his beautiful home was seriously threatened. The Germans had respected all that was his during their first advance, and he had their promise that they would do so in future. But, after their retreat, the French line, as bad luck would have it, was drawn across the bottom of his garden. The terraces in front of the house began to be pitted with shell-holes, and three or four shells had struck the house itself, yet he continued to live in it, and to

211

live, as far as possible, as though nothing very
unusual were in progress ; changing for dinner, so
William informed me, though spending more and
more of each day in the vaulted kitchen at the back
of the house, and at last even sleeping there with the
rest of the family.   Destroy Tilleroy, the treasure-
house of ancient dignities and amenities which
had survived the Revolution ?   Why should this
war be worse than the war of 1870 ?   It was impossible.   Had not a talk with German generals
saved it a few weeks before ?   Nations may quarrel,
but such things are not done.   So the family
had stayed on till the chapel was roofless and the
façade of the house full of gaping rents, the gallery
choked with bricks, plaster and torn fragments
of painted canvas ; while the woods round about
them echoed day and night to the cracking of
rifle shots.   At last the old Count's equanimity had
broken down, and, blighted and bewildered, he had
betaken himself to Paris.   His daughters, however,
were determined not to go farther away than was
necessary.   They hoped to rescue, sooner or later,
some of the things they had been compelled to
leave behind.   Yes, the Countesses were still in
Montdidier, said William, and the bailiff and the
cook and the game-keeper—in fact, many of the
people attached to the great house.   " I'd give
five pounds to get those clothes," he repeated,
beginning an inventory of the articles shut in the
back-box of the coach.   "They are very good
people," he concluded.

It struck me while he was talking that on an
off-day I might help to rescue those abandoned
treasures—one ambulance and a touring car could
take a good many things away.   I told William
I thought he might possibly see his top-boots
again.   But I could not give him a promise.   All
the cars might be wanted every night ;   secondly,

we might not be able to get a military pass to the trenches for such a purpose. Still, would he introduce me to his ladies ? He said he was sure they would be very pleased. They would be grateful, because they had not been able to get a pass themselves as it was considered too dangerous.

We ambulance men had been kicking our heels doing nothing for five days, and the prospect of a little adventure sent our spirits up. Some of us called on the ladies, and we obtained a permit to take them to the château. One evening after dusk we started. We had gone some miles along the road and turned to right and left many times—down lanes, across wide fields and through thick copses—when we were stopped in the dark by a young private soldier to whom we had already been introduced by the ladies. His regiment was holding the trenches at this point, and he was waiting for us by arrangement. Here we left the cars. " *Mon petit*," as the ladies called him, led the way. We splashed along a rutted cart-track, each carrying an empty sack. The ladies were in high spirits. Whatever they might be feeling at the prospect of finding their home irretrievably ruined, it did not affect their vivacity ; nor did they give a thought to the fact that we were now walking within easy rifle-range of the German trenches. They expatiated on the advantages of having a King—look at the King of the Belgians ! on the flight of the French Government from Paris—look at the worthlessness of democratic politicians ! As they tripped along, they talked of the French army, of the certainty of victory, of the Napoleonic campaigns, with a shrug for " Bonaparte "—clearly to them a rather regrettable figure in the annals of national glory. Chattering, smoking cigarettes, splashing into puddles, we made our way further and further into the wood, till

213

le petit held up his hand to indicate that we had better now go quietly. There in the moonlight stood the château ; a long, staid house with rows of tall small-paned windows, throwing the black shadow of its high-pitched roofs and slim chimneys on a formal statued garden, a garden which dropped terrace by terrace to an open sward. " *Ah ! comme c'est triste!* " one of the ladies exclaimed. This was the back of the house—if it could be said to have a back. " You will see two poplars at the bottom of the garden the other side," *le petit* told us. " They mark the line of our trench. The Boches are two hundred yards beyond." Presently we found ourselves on a drive, in front of a doorway flanked by stone lions sitting upright on pedestals. This was the entrance to the stables. The doors, grooved, decorated, panelled and solid, like the doors of some great room, were open, and the yard beyond was crowded with soldiers. In the centre rose a small octagonal tower, and down one side ran a broad, high colonnade. Between two pillars, a Rembrandtesque group of soldiers in overcoats were gathered round a man cutting up a sheep by the rays of a candle. Light streamed from an open doorway at the other end of the yard. It was towards this we made our way, pushing between knots of whispering *poilus*, who were surprised to see women among them. This room, once part of William's old quarters, was now that of the officer in command. Harness was still hanging there, but the room contained a table and chairs of an incongruous magnificence, while a big picture from the château leant against the wall. We were received by the commandant with an ominously guarded amiability. Indeed, I thought at first that we might be refused access to the house. But the ladies conducted the interview with an airy persuasiveness in which the note of

appeal never lost gaiety and lightness. Many
subjects by no means germane to our purpose were
first touched on. Indeed, the talk centred more
upon the commandant himself than anything else,
till, suddenly, he gave us permission and a small
escort. We were told to be quick. In the matter
of candles injunctions were emphatic. A travelling
light would be seen passing the windows and rents
in the walls, and would draw the enemy's fire.
We entered the kitchen by a side door. Stumbling
over broken bricks and splintered boards, we made
straight for the strong cupboard ; and while our
electric torches wobbled their circles of light over
the shelves and the mouths of the sacks into which
we tumbled pell-mell teapots, trays, candlesticks,
and plate of all sorts, I noticed that our escort
kept carefully between us and a gap in the wall
through which the stars were shining. Sub-
sequently, whenever the ladies " pointed," and
started flashing, this human screen invariably
formed itself round them. " More of us have been
hit about the park than in the trenches," one man
whispered to me.

Having emptied the plate-cupboards, we
roamed about the house independently, each with
a sack to fill. The oddness of the assortment of
the objects missing after a burglary will never
surprise me again ; I know now the difficulties of
a hustled burglar. The first room into which I
penetrated was the dining-room ; shadowy as
every object was, I noticed its felicitous proportions.
The carpet was covered with broken glass, which
crunched underfoot. The tall and ample curtains
let in a slip of moonlight, which shone upon a large
oval mahogany table, and gleamed upon a side-
board which I would have gladly put in my sack.
There was an indistinguishable portrait over the
deep stone mantelpiece. Should I attempt to

215

unhook it ? Impossible. Beyond was a pretty
boudoir sadly smashed and littered ; its walls
were covered with close-hung pictures, obliterated
by a thick layer of grey dust from an explosion.
It was a little room of which the furniture suggested
care for both the past and the present, for both
elegance and comfort. A heap of builder's rubble
on the floor was mixed with the broken legs of
gilded furniture. The curly golden mirror was
starred with cracks, and the stuffing was starting
from the damask chairs, which still stood sociably
near each other as though their occupants had just
risen. From this room I rescued a clock, a silver
bottle, a book. If only china had not been brittle
I could have filled my sack. A further door led
into the hall. This was paved with smooth lozenges
of black and white marble, and furnished with one
dark carved wardrobe, gaping wide. Underneath
a crystal chandelier, which hung from the high
ceiling, stood an elaborately painted sedan-chair.
The hall, lit from an upper story as well as from the
ground floor by tall small-paned windows, was
full of an aqueous blue light. And it was here
that I felt overpoweringly, tragically, what a splendid specimen of French seventeenth-century architecture this house was ; that style which, in its
tranquil and severe proportions, expresses Racine
and Corneille, as distinctly as the châteaus of the
Renaissance express an age when the human passions lay nearer the surface, when order was not
accounted strength, nor restraint a sign of inspiration. The wide gradual stone staircase ascended
toward a great blank wall, on which in fanciful
pattern the family-tree towered and ramified.

While in the gallery upstairs I was hopelessly
trying to guess which pictures ought to be cut
from their frames, I heard chattering and footsteps.
Our party was once more united. We passed

together through more beautiful rooms, all be-
grimed and broken ; rooms in which the habits and
possessions of many generations had evidently
harmonized into a charming amenity. On these
thresholds the ladies would sometimes stop for
a moment with quick exclamations of horror. Yet
it was hard to get directions from them. " Yes,
perhaps," " By all means," or " Is it worth it ? "
There seemed no end to things they were prepared
to leave behind without a pang. It was only in
the bedrooms that they flitted, pounced and rum-
maged with real animation. There our sacks
were stuffed with stockings, handkerchiefs and
underclothes. Suddenly I heard a sharp cry of
delight ; one of them had come across a real treasure
at last. She was holding up triumphantly a rubber
hot-water-bottle !

Nevertheless we left heavily loaded with
a good many more or less irreplaceable things.
Some of us carried clocks, others pictures ; one
a silk heraldic banner ; others *bibelots* and candlesticks. If I had felt like a burglar before, I now
felt like a brigand, walking through moonlit woods
with a sack of clinking plate across my shoulders.
The crack of rifles had begun. Those intermittent
sounds reminded me of cover-shooting ; and the
ladies, paying no more heed to them than they
would to sport, had a grateful separate good-bye
talk with each soldier who had accompanied us.

It was not until I got back to Montdidier that
my pleasure in this little looting expedition
vanished. It vanished when I suddenly remembered that I had forgotten William's clothes.
Still, he *had* said he would give five pounds . . .
in a tone which suggested rhetorical emphasis.
Perhaps three would meet the case ? I saw William
again. He took his tip and his disappointment
philosophically ; and he rewarded me with a remark

in which I seemed to hear the strength and the limitations of England. I remembered that he had been in France thirty-seven years; I looked at him—Suffolk was still written all over him; I asked him how he liked the French. "Well, sir," he replied, "at first you don't like 'em much, but after a time you find they're a harmless people."

IV

We were asked to take a French captain in his touring-car to visit the spot where his brother had fallen and was buried. We thought he might prefer a solitary drive ; but he seemed, when he appeared, to be in rather merry pin, so at the last moment I got in too. He was a hard, natty, little man in a fresh uniform and shiny top-boots, and he had a ready shrug for the terrors of war.

It was one of those still November afternoons. The brown copses in the hollows we passed were bloomed with smoky blue like a horse's eye. The captain talked incessantly as we rushed along between the bare road-side poplars. He was at once vivacious, prompt, voluble, and stiff. His tone when he repeated that *la guerre* was *la guerre* reminded me of people who say boys will be boys, and the lightness of his resignation set me wondering how it would wear. For though I could picture him an officer in an office—smick-smack, no hesitation—I could not imagine him at the Front, dealing with men in circumstances which throw one back on human nature as it is.

When we arrived at the village where we were to stop, the captain left us and strode off across the fields to look for his brother's grave. Like all villages near the French line, it was in a great mess, and full of blue-coated soldiers. Twenty or more were standing on the green doing

218

nothing; others were sitting on the churchyard wall; some hung about the slushy road; some came to the windows to stare; some lolled listlessly in the doorways; and from one of the cottages floated the strains of a gramophone—the music of boredom. One or two soldiers asked me the two inevitable questions, "Are then the English near?" and "How long do you think the war will last?"; and I, in return, asked them the two inevitable questions, "How near are the Germans?" and "How long do you think the war will last?" Then I handed round cigarettes till I had no more, and those who got some nodded and smiled, and those who came up too late nodded and smiled. And we all stood together in the mud.

There was a squashed loaf on one side of the road, a tin or two lying about, and on the door-step of the nearest cottage the liquid footprints were mixed with blood. Looking up from this threshold I caught the eye of one of the soldiers. He also nodded and smiled. I began myself to sink into the collective torpor, and to dream also that we were all standing together in the mud. They, poor fellows, had been standing there for close on five weeks, and a little experience had already taught me before that man is not, let alone his other disabilities, an animal properly shaped for standing in the mud. For though after a time the familiar chill about the feet will act almost as a mesmeric suggestion that one is a cart-horse, the delusion is never complete enough. Four legs are too badly wanted, and men cannot stamp and snort for no reason. A sudden sound does not startle them into momentary clumping activity. Above all they cannot put their necks across each other and rub and rub. Only that gesture could express and relieve the mutual feelings of men who, having surrendered their individuality, find

219

themselves day after day, week after week, standing together in the mud.

For us two Englishmen, however, there was this afternoon a distraction in store. Someone shouted " Messieurs les Anglais ! " We instantly swung round our haunches and pricked up our ears. An old priest was eagerly beckoning from a window. We went up to it. " Are the English near ? " he asked. I told him that we were not serving our own soldiers, but attached to the French Army; our army was miles away. "How long do you think the war will last ? " he enquired animatedly. Coming from him the question seemed like a fresh one, and we entered his little white-washed sanctum to discuss it. We talked it out over coffee and cognac, and concluded, with a sense of having eliminated the influence of hope, that it must be over in February, 1815.

As it was one of our duties to enquire, wherever we went, after the many English who had disappeared during the retreat from Mons, I went on to ask him if there were any English graves or identification-badges in the village. Had any English passed through ? " No : not a single one of them. But what do you think I did ? " he asked, gazing at us whimsically. " When the Uhlans came I rushed out into the road and waved my hat shouting, ' God save de King ! ' Yes, Monsieur, I tried to embrace an officer ! " At the recollection of this awful *gaffe* his eyes and mouth became as round as a schoolboy's, who sees his booby-trap fall on the wrong head.

" And how did they behave ? " I asked.

" How did the Boches behave ! " He raised his hands and eyes to Heaven. Then jumping up he pointed to the smashed lid of his bureau. " There ! They took all the money, all the offertory money, all my little treasures ! *Les Boches !*

Voilà les Boches, voilà, voilà, encore les Boches."
And at each exclamation he thrust at us crumpled
manuscripts, torn books, and photographs with
heel-marks on them. " They turned out every
drawer ; they threw the things about the floors,
and trampled on them ; they pulled down the
books ; they took all the money ! Peuh ! *Voilà les
Boches.* Peuh !" He sat down with the emphasis
of an immense contempt.

" And where were you while all this was
going on ? " I asked.

" I ? Oh, I was lying in the nettles at the
bottom of the garden," he said simply.

Seeing us look rather surprised, he began to
laugh ; to laugh so immoderately that he doubled
forward in his chair till only the top of his touzled
white head was visible. " Yes, I and my old
housekeeper spent the night hiding in the nettles."

We were sorry to part from this most sweet old
person who was without a sense of dignity, though
with a little pains he could have emulated the port
and presence of John Bright ; but the captain had
passed the window, and we rose to go. On the
drive back the captain continued to talk as he had
talked on the way out. His *tenue* was as rigid and
precise as before. His ideas on every subject were
done up as neatly as packets of French chocolate,
and as convenient for polite handling. Together
the two men seemed to me to represent two sides
of the French character with which we are most
out of touch. I could not help contrasting them,
wondering vaguely beside which I would sooner
fight. Of one thing I was quite sure, that if the
captain did hide in a bed of nettles he would not tell
anyone.

V

The road to the mill was a narrow lane with
low hedges on both sides ; it ran across some water

221

meadows, divided here and there by lines of pollard willows. We had gone about half the way when a dagger of white fire, a yard or so long, suddenly leapt from a gun behind a willow-clump, and there was a crash which made one's whole body blench. Another followed, and another, and another. Half-a-minute's pause, and presently the dusky fields behind us were scattered with winking flashes : and the shattering whacks condensed into a solid element of uproar in which, for the first moment or two, one existed only with the confused consciousness of a man who has taken a bad header into deep water. Then, as a diver collects himself and accounts for his sensations— the confusion, the pressure, the noise about his ears—so one rose out of that submerged condition into an ordinary awareness, which included, alas, an uncomfortable certainty that one was wishing oneself anywhere but among the guns. There is, however, a sort of opiate in enormous uproar ; it prevents you from imagining you *could* be anywhere else. The Germans were replying, it struck me, very feebly. I saw the smoke of explosions now on this side of the lane, now on that, but I could not hear them. It was nothing to what our cannonade must have been to them. If anyone wants to know what the ordinary man feels, who is unaccustomed to finding himself on the edge of a little modern battle, and is bound to remain inactive, I can tell him : " So this is IT. Am I going to become unbearably nervous ? " That is the form fear first takes. I was very glad of distraction, though in this case it came in a way which held up the cars. A long stream of muffled, great-coated figures were hurrying across the road in front to the attack, and we had to pull up. As they swarmed past the car I shook hands with some of them, and bawled *Bonne chance* ! The faces of some were tense with a kind of exhilaration, others seemed going forward in a sort of moody stupor. I plunged for handfuls of cigarettes (the blessed cigarette which seems never to come amiss even to a soldier before a charge, or indeed afterwards, when, perhaps, he is mortally wounded) and handed them out till my pockets were empty. They smiled and hailed us with any scraps of English they could remember. " Good-night," " very well," " old England," " good luck." One Marine, evidently very much pleased with the idiom, shouted laughing, " It's bloody f——ing cold " ; it was his *moriturus te salutat.*

VI

" Talker " was, of course, a term of contempt. The first time I heard it applied to anyone out there was in the streets of Amiens.

I was walking with one of our own section of the Red Cross, one whose irreproachable military bearing was wont to make us all feel the civilians we were. Indeed, no stranger who saw him imperturbably turning out his toes would have guessed that he, too, was a " sutler and campfollower." Our cars were waiting in rows in the street, and we were passing them when a French officer ran up behind and plucked me by the sleeve. It was not his white face or the blinking glitter of his eyes which struck me first, but his manner. It was so oddly, in its deprecating urgency like a beggar's. He wanted a lift in the direction of Paris, couldn't we give him one ? He kept repeating : " I must get home. I'm tired, tired. I must get home." . . . " There are only three of us left," he went on rapidly, " a captain, a major and myself. It was awful. It lasted for days. I must get home. My nerve has gone. I didn't mind at first ; I was very brave at first. But I can't bear a noise now ; if a horse stumbles, I shake all over. I'm no good at all. If I hear a gun, I run away ; I run—I can't help it. Can't you take me home ? Trains are so slow. I'm no use. I've been sent back to rest."

But it was impossible to give him a lift ; we were due in an opposite direction. My companion shook his head and strolled on ; the Frenchman, with his reiterated " It was awful ; I must *rest.* You have no idea . . . only three officers left," gradually fell behind.

" What a pity one of us can't take him ! " I said.

" Oh, he's a talker," my companion replied.

Since then I have met several " talkers." They are common. I remember asking the way, my first night at Montdidier, of a dark form in an almost dark street. At the sound of my voice he turned upon me with a sudden clutch of alacrity. He began telling me at once he was back for three days from the trenches ; he would show me the way—yes, he would accompany me. Might he dine with me at the hotel ? He joined the four of us at our table, and we drank together two bottles of rose-pink champagne, and listened while he talked. Talked ? His tongue went like a clock when the pendulum is off. He reminded me both of a schoolboy just home for the holidays and a man who has seen a ghost.

I have met " talkers " in khaki, too, since then, and sometimes I have wondered if my companion on that stroll through the streets of Amiens would continue in all circumstances to turn out so imperturbably his toes ? I have concluded he might. But would the word " talker " in his mouth suggest that particular shade of contempt ?

By the by I have found a nickname for him,

" The Ibis."   It has caught on, though nobody can see the point of it except myself : *in medio tutissimus ibis*—he reminds me of the school-boy rendering of that tag, " In the midst stalked the Ibis, the most cautious of birds."

OUR LEGENDARY CONTEMPORARIES

I

THE OLD EMPEROR

AT a table spread with a fine linen tablecloth, by the open window of a high, quiet room, sat a clean, old bald man in a green uniform, with an order round his neck. Opposite him hung a full-length portrait of a splendid lady with a proud, energetic face crowned with many coils of dark hair. The golden and lapis-lazuli clock upon the carved mantelpiece marked the hour of eleven. Outside, on the terrace, a sentry walked backwards and forwards, the sun glinting on his bayonet and buttons. The soldier was tired of thinking himself a lucky dog for not being away with the army in Galicia, for not having wife or children or even a sweetheart, and he could think these thoughts no longer. If he could have whistled, he would have felt better ; but as it was, he had nothing to do but eye disparagingly the statues and flower-beds which rayed far away in all directions from the palace into the vistas of a beautiful, boundless park. He was thirsty, too, which reminded him that neither beer nor life were what they had been ; and this made him feel sad. At each end of his beat he stopped, clicked heels, shouldered arms, and turned like a doll; in becoming a mechanism for a moment, he forgot all this. The wind and sunshine played with the trees and fountains.

Inside the room there was no sound but that

of the slow suction with which an old man was
imbibing a creamy gruel from a wide cup, which he
held shakily with both hands to his face. He would
have liked to put it down ; but he was determined
to go on drawing in the thick liquid till he could
see the gold crown and double-headed eagle at the
bottom of the cup. " I can see the heads already,"
he said to himself, tilting it up more and more,
swallowing, and gazing into the cup. " The tops
of the wings. . . . Yes, that's enough." Replacing
it carefully, he wiped some drops from his white
moustache and clean-shaven chin. Then, leaning
back in his chair, his eye caught the shine of silver
on the table, and he stared at it inhibited.

How long he remained in this condition he
could not have told. Two men were whispering
near the door ; one was in black knee-breeches
and white shirt-front, the other in a uniform
covered with orders and medals. At the sound
of voices the old man wrenched his eyes away from
the silver and looked up. The man in uniform
withdrew, closing the door gently behind him ; the
other, making two bows, advanced towards the
table.

" Will your Majesty grant an audience to
General Count X ? He wishes to tell your Majesty
the news of a glorious and complete victory which
has just reached us from his Highness the General-
issimo."

" Let him come in."

The officer advanced, bowing, and, after con-
gratulating his Imperial Majesty upon this latest
triumph of his arms, proceeded to give an account
of the victory. As the old man listened he drew
more vigorous breaths. He held himself more
upright, and the deep fold across the chest of his
uniform straightened itself out ; and when the
General had finished speaking his eyes beneath their

227

saurian lids rested on the speaker with an almost threatening animation.

"You are to understand, once and for all," he said excitedly, "I trusted Count Bismarck. Austria may lose battles, but she cannot be beaten. And if the King of Prussia has had the insolence to press for one inch of territory, let him understand that the terms are *impossible*. Let him remember that there are other Powers who wish him no good. France . . ." But, catching the glance exchanged between the other two, he suddenly collapsed, dwindling into himself again. He began nervously pushing away the cup in front of him, muttering : "Very glad ; very glad indeed. God be thanked ! Gallant fellows ! Tell the Archduke he has done . . . I expected. . . . Praise be to God ! I must get a little sleep, a little rest."

"Majesty has not forgotten Majesty's orders for the day," said the man in black respectfully.

"No, no, no." He reached out his hand and struck the spring of a silver bell.

"Your Majesty, I have them with me. In accordance with your wish, the authorities of the Empress Elizabeth Hospital are expecting you at two o'clock. Count X. will have the insignia of the Order which your Majesty graciously wishes to bestow on the Herr Professor." And he gently pushed across the table a few sheets of glossy paper inscribed with sentences written in a clear, large hand. "The notes which your Majesty ordered to be drawn up."

The old man's eyes travelled over a statement of the number of patients treated in the hospital, a reference to the righteousness of the cause, and an expression of gratitude to God for having manifested on so many glorious fields His championship of the Empire ; and, having turned the page, they rested for a moment on a phrase or two : " . . . the burden of many years and many personal sorrows which it has been my lot to bear." He nodded and made a gesture to indicate that the interview was over, asked that his physician and valet should be sent to him, and lay down on a large, cool red leather sofa.

From a warm half-sleep full of fancies, he woke lightly. His physician was feeling his pulse, and presently beckoned impatiently to a servant holding a glass on a tray. The august patient appeared refreshed. There was a different look in his face now, a look of slyness and hardness. Pressing both knuckles hard into the sofa, he raised himself into a semi-upright position and, reaching out for a gold-headed cane, which was instantly put into his hand, he made his way slowly to the door. At a side entrance, where he received his military cap from one man-servant, while another laid a cloak about his shoulders with the tenderness of a dressmaker shrouding a delicate dress in tissue-paper, a powerful motor was standing. It drove smoothly away with him into the town.

Under the trees of the boulevards children were playing : long-legged little girls in tartan frocks and boys in socks and sailor suits were running about, skipping, or chasing hoops along the broad gravel walks ; and on the benches in the shade nurses sat side by side, rhythmically pulling and pushing their prams backwards and forwards as they talked. Nothing here was changed, except perhaps there were fewer children. In the streets there were certainly far fewer men who were not in uniform. As the royal motor passed a pavement café, two young officers dressed in light blue and smoking at a little round table sprang to their feet and saluted. They were discussing and comparing the Russian and the Prussian character. They instantly resumed their conversation. " Yes," one was saying, " a touch of orientalism has its drawbacks in war ; but if a man can't understand the meaning of the word vanity, he is, for all his qualities, a vulgar soul."

The old man in the car was pleased with the soft pressure of the summer air against his face. He had been touched by the sight of the children on the boulevards, they reminded him of his address to all the children of his Empire ; and, above all, he felt his mind was now firmly seated in the actual. As for the little ceremony before him, what surprise, which could possibly shake his poise, could be lurking for him in that. Suffering ? Had not *he* suffered enough himself in all conscience during his long life ? He knew all that by heart. The steps of the hospital under the awning were lined on each side, with doctors and surgeons in uniform or frock-coats, and behind them rose a bank of nurses. Up the druggeted staircase he went slowly with bent knees ; the Professor was a little behind him, and they were followed by a cortège of high officials, generals and doctors. On the first landing the doors of one of the great wards stood open : a long, cool room, a stretch of shining floor and two rows of beds. It might be the place of pain and distress, but to look at, it was a beautiful " symphony in white." All eyes were fixed on him with a stare which knew no shyness ; some were feverish, bright eyes, others slow, sleepy eyes.

Leaning on his cane and stopping at each bed in turn, he asked the same questions when he stopped, and made, hardly varying the words, the same little speech. " You have suffered for God and the honour of your country. Your Emperor is grateful to you and will not forget." In one there lay a smiling man who at intervals, regular as clockwork, turned his head to one side and snapped the air as a dog snaps at a fly. The old man stood and looked

230

at him. " Do you know me?" he said. Then, getting
no reply, he turned to the Professor, and asked what
was the matter. The Professor explained that the
man had lost a portion of his brain.

As he moved up the long room, stopping at
each bed for a minute and saying the same words,
some saluted him theatrically, others only smiled.
He stood calmly with his hands upon his cane, as
though his mere presence were a force which left all
well behind him as he passed. At the bedside of a
young man, the Professor explained that this one
would soon be as right as ever again. " And you
want to go back and fight for us ? " The young
man lowered his eyes : " No." " Ah, brave
soldier ! I knew you would say that," and whether
he had understood or not, the old man proceeded
composedly on to the next. The tour up one side
and down the other was almost completed, and he
was about to leave the ward, when he was arrested
by a voice : " Majesty ! Majesty ! " It came
from a bed near the door, whose occupant did not
raise the blanket ; he had only one arm, and the
hand of the other was missing. The Professor
pressed forward with a smile : " One of our most
astonishing surgical triumphs, your Majesty." But
the Emperor did not seem to hear ; his eyes were
held by the eyes of this torso of a man propped
up against a pillow. " Majesty, you are all-
powerful ; tell them to put me out of my misery."
The old man's hands began to tremble on his cane,
and he turned quickly round. " Take me home.
Please, please take me home," he muttered, and,
clutching at the arm of an equerry he shuffled
quickly out. Down the stairs the voice pursued him,
" Majesty ! Majesty ! Tell them, Majesty . . ."

II

THE OLD MASTER

"The Master's" study was half a museum and half a library. On the black oak writing-table, gleaming in the wintry light from the windows, stood an antique bronze statuette, about six inches high : an engaging little naked Venus. At her feet lay his ink-pot, a lump of hollowed jade, its natural bosses and depressions smoothly moulded into a vague conglomeration of flowers and human forms. On a renaissance cabinet near the wide stone fireplace (itself removed from the retiring-room of an ancient castle, and carved with roses and myrtle) stood another Venus, represented with a beard and male organs of generation, with a sceptre in her hand and the body and breast of a female ; on the pedestal were cut in faint red letters the words "Duplex Amathusia." On one side of it were a number of turquoise-blue Egyptian gods with animals' heads : on the other a Spanish saint, carved in wood, the swirl of whose gilded garments expressed his ecstasy. Two queer Thibetan masks frowned and grinned above the door, and the wrinkled head of Homer stared blankly from the top of a bookcase running the whole length of the room. The serried rows of sleek books, some thick, some thin, rose one upon the other from unwieldy folios to a top-shelf of many tiny volumes, which looked as precious to the eye, and felt as pleasant to the touch, as enamelled boxes. The receptacle which once held the face-powder of Ninon de Lenclos now held the Master's cigarettes, and his biggest armchair was upholstered with the vestments of an Abyssinian bishop. The pictures were all small and old. Of two of the most notice-able, one represented a sweet-faced, exquisitely clean old monk on his knees, gazing up into the still vault of heaven, and the other a Holy Family with St. Anne hanging out the under-clothes to dry. The library was composed of only two kinds of books : well-attested masterpieces in all languages and of all ages, and a choice collection of the most extravagant examples of human enthusiasm and aberration.

The Master came in, and sitting down heavily by the fire, he threw on a faggot to make a blaze. It crackled upwards, brightening his worn, plump face, and, leaning back, he held out towards the flames his large clean hand. It made him feel happier. But when the golden twigs crumbled to red and white ashes, depression rolled over him again. He sighed and looked helplessly over his shoulder at his writing-table. He could only think of two things now, his childhood and the war. All day long he thought of nothing else. Except for the miserable people lugging, that very moment, their children and bundles along frozen roads, with pictures behind their staring eyes of charred homes, of faces, once responsive, last remembered as yellow objects, dirty, mauled, like turnips sheep have left half-eaten, or as terrible masks with lifted lips and goggling eyes, expressing, violently, nothing —except for those wretched ones, instinctively flying to preserve lives they no longer wanted, he was perhaps as miserable a man as any. Not that the war had touched him nearly. He had no sons ; he mourned no friends ; his contemporaries were all old men ; his life went on as usual. One or two of the young men who used to come to see him, to listen to him and laugh with flattering alacrity, would never come again : that was all. He remembered one in particular ; how he had, while on leave, come up with an introduction to this very room, glowing and clean as though he

had just come out of a kind of moral bath ; and
how they had talked together about Theocritus.
Soldiers were the only people he could be sure now
of talking to as though nothing in particular were
going forward. He had never written or said a
word that could help them or could ever occur to
their minds in these days. Yet they seemed to
treat him as though he were quite a sensible man.
Indeed, all that he had written had been distinctly
to belittle the profession of arms ; yet of all kinds
of people soldiers seemed the least inclined of any,
if they had been at the front, to suspect him of
being " unpatriotic." The majority at home
treated him as a pernicious fool, and he was constantly coming across passages in papers and
magazines in which his " literary extinction " was
mentioned gleefully as one of the signs of the times.
The tone of these references implied that he would
feel this acutely. He did mind ; but so little in the
way the writers thought that they made him smile.
He minded in a much more dreadful way. It was not
the eclipse of his importance at the moment he
cared about. Something else had happened ; his
own feelings had shown up his work. All his life he
had spoken as a wise man ; in the lightest passages
in his books, in the lewdest, his own wisdom had
always been implicit. He had only had one thing
to say. No writer had touched on more subjects ;
but none had repeated himself more often. His
message was that man was a little creature, and if
he would only be humble enough to know that
pleasure was good enough for him, and learn that
his troubles came from turning up his nose at the
gifts of that good Goddess, mother of the arts, all
would go well. She bestows them lavishly ; so
lavishly that no one need ever be very eager to
grasp one particular pleasure or to snatch it away
from some one else. Miss pleasure here, you will

find it there : if only you understand it is that you want, and that is good for you. Pleasure will make you kind, too. You will throw no stones at your neighbour and you will live on easy terms with yourself. True, pleasures do not satisfy ; but if they do not, is there not " sweetness and youth " in desire ? And if Nature has made you that anomalous creature, a thinking man, why, what an inexhaustible spectacle lies spread before you : the strange paths men are impelled along by motives they do not understand ; the extravagant distortions of natural beings into which they puff and pinch themselves ! It needed only a little detachment, and the folly of the world became a spectacle hardly painful, even subtly flattering to one who looked on. This had been the drift of all he had ever written in history, fiction, criticism, and verse. But this wisdom did not work with him now. The world had claimed him as part of itself. He had never chuckled savagely over the welter of the world, like Swift or Voltaire ; he had preferred to smile and to pity. His detachment had charmed. It had persuaded a whole generation that nothing was quite so wise as to see folly everywhere and forgive it. He could see men's folly clearly enough now, in all conscience ; but it no longer seemed his part, or anyone's, to forgive it—individuals perhaps, but not *it*. Yet when he had heaved himself up, and gone to his table, the words, when they came, fell into their places with the accustomed suavity, and pity and took on the old detachment. He could not bear what he had written.

" So this is how I used to write about the struggles and catastrophes of the past," he thought. " My God, how much I have left out!"

THE HARVEST OF A QUIET EYE

I ATTENDED the Labour Congress (August 25th 1917) at the Central Hall, Westminster, with a view to describing the proceedings, but my impressions were so numerous and varied that as soon as I had walked down the marble staircase of that useful but cumbrous structure out of the shadowy, noisy hall into the sunny, noisy streets, I knew already that as a reporter's " piece of graphic " my article was doomed to failure. One must have some kind of focus ; I had none. The only way of dealing with my impressions would be, I realized, to talk about myself. And so I shall. Before the proceedings began I settled into my seat with the excitement of a girl at her first ball. You may open your eyes at this. " Certainly," you will say, " the occasion was an interesting one ; but, surely . . . " No, it is not an exaggeration ; let me explain. The word " Labour " in the political sense, to a man like me, is a word of mysterious significance. It suggests to me hopes for humanity, fears for much that makes life delightful to me, the righting of enormous wrongs and the infliction of many injuries on individuals with whom my nature is in sympathy, the possibility of a dull, lustreless civilization, but the only chance of a really noble and dignified one. Therefore to me the spectacle of " Labour " in council was moving and august, and the commonplace appearance of the delegates could not hide that from me. The subject under discussion also interested me, and the manner in which it would be

236

discussed and the conclusion which would be reached upon it would be some measure, I thought, of the diameter of the brain of this leviathan, Labour. I regret to say it turned out to be some thirteen hundred thousand inches shorter than I hoped. " Canst thou take Leviathan with a hook ? " After it was all over, the answer to Job's question, I feared, must be in the affirmative ; though it could be added, with truth, " but the hook is very liable to come out before the monster is fairly landed." When we all dismissed for luncheon I was in good spirits ; but when the Conference was over I was in dreary spirits. It was not that at 1 p.m. I was full of hope that the voting would be to my mind (the miners' rock-over to an anti-Conference attitude precluded such hopes), but I had just heard a speech which had put a glow into me : a sharp sensible speech with self-forgetful passion in it, very different from the mouldy *bravura* of personal explanations. That phrase is not a direct dig at Messrs. Henderson and Barnes, who on this occasion were right to put their own cases. But I have often noticed at public meetings of every kind, and the Conference was no exception, that when the speaker turns from what he stands for to defending his own conduct, a peculiar energy is infused into his gestures and words. He seems to speak with freshness and will, while the audience wakes up with an eagerness which seems to say : " Ah ! ah ! this is the real thing." Undoubtedly they share emotionally the same sense of proportion. When the speaker is a working man, transition to this deeper animation, because the method of oratory is then simpler and more transparent, is still more noticeable. The people's orator cannot resist the cries of " Good old so-and-so ! " " Stick it out ! " etc., etc., which his first words about himself elicit ; and on the whole I prefer the bursting

237

vehemence of self-justification which follows to the polished perturbation as of one unaccustomed to speak of himself, or to the self-contained detachment as of one who does so only as a necessary duty, so familiar to us in the orators of the governing classes when they begin by saying : " To touch on a personal matter." I was struck on this occasion by the absence of shyness and nervousness in the speakers ; the naturalness with which most of them began to speak and the naturalness with which they stopped. This was heartening to me. For apart from that estimate of our civilization which is summed up in the saying of Tolstoi's, " The rich will do anything for the poor except get off their backs "—an arrow I shall never be able to pull out of my conscience—the principal consideration which makes me democratic in feeling is a preference for the plain clap-trap of the semi-educated to the more insidious and perfect humbug of the well-to-do. If a man is going to pretend to be better than he is, *sans peur et sans reproche*, perfectly pure, perfectly disinterested, adequately informed on every necessary point, quite unbiased in judgment and all the rest of it, I prefer that the result should not be much more plausible than a child dressed up as a Red Indian.

But to return to the subject of personal explanations, which were so important a part of Tuesday's proceedings and form invariably so large a part of public life. When we are all in heaven, and when the works of the Recording Angel, miraculously indexed, and doubtless, if I do not misunderstand human nature, by far the most popular volumes in the heavenly library, are consulted by orators, I can imagine most of them passing a perplexed hand over their foreheads as they read the fascinating pages containing their own records, and muttering to themselves : " Why, I thought

I spent my whole life in advocating this or that,
attacking this or that ; but, good heavens ! what
pages and pages and pages there are merely about
how I behaved in such and such circumstances,
how right I was to do this or say that, in spite
of appearances ! Perhaps these repeated and repeated explanations were necessary, but I never
guessed they would in the end bulk so large." At
this meeting everyone was expecting a personal
explanation from Mr. Henderson. It was necessary.
All I wished was that his statement had not been
so " statesmanlike," and delivered at moments in
a manner almost archidiaconal. I wanted him to
speak more out of himself. I wanted him to say
straight out : " I feel bitterly about the way I
have been treated. One of the things one can't
get over in Mr. Lloyd George, when he has tripped
one up and sent one sprawling, is the advantage he
takes of one's own decency. He counts, and knows
he *can* count, on certain people ' playing the game '
whatever he does. But instead of that making him
treat them with more consideration, he takes it as
a pull he has over them. And the damnable truth
is that in the political game it *is* a pull. He knew
I was helpless. Partly because I am the sort of man
who hates to appear to act as though paying off
scores, chiefly because I believe for the good of
the country and the success of the war it is absolutely essential that Labour should work with the
Government. Because of all this I am most
anxious you should not try to turn him out ;
but if you feel, as I do, that he would never have
slammed the door of the Cabinet in the face of
Lord Curzon and sent Barnes out like an office-boy
to fetch him in at the end of two hours, and if
you think, as I do, that expresses his attitude
towards Labour as opposed to Wealth—well, put
it in your pipes and smoke it till the proper time

comes." Such sentiments might be divined in what Mr. Henderson said, but he spoke more in grave sorrow than in anger, and for this I was sorry. I missed the democratic frankness, the democratic passion. That was the flavour which exhilarated me in a speech which soon followed ; the speech which sent me out to luncheon in a glow.

Several speakers had spoken after Mr. Henderson, and the motion before the Congress was that the Labour members of the Government should be at once withdrawn. I had looked away from the platform to survey the restless rows of simmering delegates behind me, when a curiously urgent, slightly veiled voice made me turn my head towards it sharply. A long man, flat-chested, with a loose flop of greying fair hair and moustache to match, was standing on the platform, grasping the rail in front. The hank of hair kept jerking upwards and falling forwards as he stooped to emphasize what he was saying, or drew himself suddenly up, like the crest of some excitable bird. What he said was perfectly clear, and each sentence masterfully emphatic. I turned to my neighbour : " Who's that ? " " Don't you know ? " he said. " That's Bob Smillie." Of course, I knew him by name, and I remembered his *mot* too, about those recruiting-posters, representing a nonplussed but able-bodied and still-in-the-flush-of-youth papa being posed by a boy with the question, " Daddy, what did you do in the Great War ? " " If my son asks me that," he said, " I shall say, ' My boy, I tried to stop the bloody thing.' " What he was saying was perfectly good sense. Referring to Mr. Henderson, he said : " resignation " was in his case a soft word for " chucked " ; and presently there was a loud roar of laughter at the story of a lodger, thrown out of the first-floor window by his land-lord, who picked himself up, saying that he would

THE HARVEST OF A QUIET EYE

not sleep in that house another night. But the object of his speech was to prevent the motion recommending the withdrawal of Labour from the Government being put : " You know perfectly well that the delegates cannot vote in favour of it without consulting their societies…It will be lost by an overwhelming majority. It will be said *that* is the voice of Labour. Labour has again and again been made a fool of in this way." When he slewed round to my side of the hall and I could see his face, the crying face of a man in almost mortal distress, I saw in it the same vehemence that I had felt in the swing and jerk of his gestures. Friend Smillie, I know nothing or next to nothing about social questions or what goes on in your world ; a compliment from me to a Labour Leader is worth precious little. But were I suddenly endowed with creative power to plant men, I think I would risk it, and lay down at once 20,000 replicas of you. No doubt I should have to temper the results of this fiat by a numerous creation of other reformers who would see the many-sidedness and intricacy of things ; but I swear you are the vital ingredient in the mixture which can move the world.

Mr. Will Thorne made an impression on me of the kind which it is delightful to receive, but not so flattering to make ; for those human beings who are privileged to make that impression, from a kind of modesty perhaps which is itself part of that power, are absolutely unconscious, or even rather contemptuous, of its effect on others. It is possible that Mr. Will Thorne's conception of himself is as a sort of Danton or firebrand, and that he conceives his rise to eminence as due to the violence of his views and the revolutionary recklessness of his spirit. He hinted, indeed, that the intransigence of his Internationalism and Socialism, after the war, would be something horrific. But, if I may judge from the impression he made on me (these notes, remember, are only snapshots of men seen once like characters in a play, and have no more authority), he was always elected because no one could help liking him confoundedly ; especially after they had laughed a little at his simplicity. There are people whom, when one has once laughed at them, one can never like quite so much again ; there are others to whom afterwards it is impossible not to remain attached. I could not help thinking what a splendid Duke of Beaufort he would have made. He would have roared at you loud enough to make you jump in your saddle if you rode too near the hounds, but it would leave no soreness or sense of humiliation behind. In fact, I saw him best in some such circumstances, the amplitude of which would give wing-space to the sweep of an easy kindliness, a simple loyalty, and a still more simple obstinacy ; I saw him better thus, at any rate, than in the bewildering, cross-purposed world of politics.

I admired Mr. Purdy in the chair. A good many things must have astonished the Russian delegates on the platform, but none, probably, more than the way in which Mr. Purdy controlled an assembly which at times reached a pitch of disorder dismaying even to a ragg'd fourth-form master, by tapping the neck of a water-bottle with a penknife. The English are a race with a great calm and sense of order at the bottom of them. They are also a reasonable people. I only wish they were not so self-righteous. In that respect they are mad and most difficult to deal with.

Before the voting took place I went up into the gallery that I might see the many as one. It was like looking down on the hide of some agitated

animal, bristling in places, smooth in others, un-
dulating with the play of muscles beneath, an
animal emitting an extraordinary jumble of pur-
rings, snarlings and yappings. When the result of
the voting was given out, both sides were pleased,
and the uproar was commensurate. The strains
of " The International " and " Keep the Home
Fires Burning " struggled for predominance among
miscellaneous bawling stronger than either. But
the excitement was by no means over. There
were the amendments to discuss, among them the
question of proportional representation at Stock-
holm. Before this was put to the vote there was
a virulent and hearty pandemonium—both adjectives are required. I could not make out what it
was all about. I perceived, as in the end did the
chairman, who was as busy as a conductor at a
Wagnerian climax, that Mr. Ben Tillett was anxious
about an amendment of his. One of the small
impressions I carry away with me is the picture of
him advancing up the gangway, in a neat grey
suit of remarkably smart cut, bawling to the point
of congestion and with both hands round his mouth :
"Point of Order." Suddenly he sat down with the
reposeful satisfaction of a man who has made a
great speech.

NOVEMBER 11TH 1918

The maroons went off as I was pulling on my
boots. It was eleven o'clock, and the war was over.
I went to the top of the kitchen-stairs and shouted,
" The war is over ! " The washing-up clatter
stopped for a moment ; someone exclaimed,
" Thank goodness ! " As I slammed the front
door I said to myself " The war is over." I
repeated it again ; but meeting with no response,
I began to abuse myself. " You clod, you dead-
alive lump, the war is over !" Still no response.
" Well," I thought, " at any rate I can go out
and see how happy people are ; that I shall enjoy."
In the street men and women were walking briskly
with the same intent. Each looked to see how
pleased the other might be, and each, having
caught a reflected ray, beamed on the next passer-
by. Apart from the few self-generators of high
spirits, who were hooting and hailing others intermittently from bus-tops, most people, it struck me,
were out to gather emotion. Here and there a few
flags fluttered from the windows, and women came
to doorways or up area steps to smile on every one
that smile they usually reserve for their own
children. A drum-and-fife band followed by some
soldiers turned the corner ; I felt inclined to cry.
Should I follow, and in tears ? " No. This time,"
I thought, " I'll be on the hub of things ; so on to
Buckingham Palace." Many were bound in that
direction. The crowd, at first loosely-flowing,
began to congeal, then to solidify. Its current was
strong enough, however, to sweep me some way up

the Mall, in spite of the stream flowing down it. I caught at a cannon, crowded with people, and mounted. At last I could look round. The Mall was choked with vehicles invisible under their loads; on the pavements and between the traffic, heads were set as thick as cobble-stones, and above them fluttered innumerable handkerchiefs and little flags. The statue of Queen Victoria caught my eye; up it black figures were swarming like ants over sugar. One youth, looking as small as a child's doll, already lay comfortably cuddled within her fat marble arm, another was pulling himself higher by the help of her nose and her veil. The chaotic din of yells, cat-calls, tin-noises and squealers swelled now and then to a roar. Near me a block of Canadians kept chanting with rhythmic persistence, " We—want—King George." And there, sure enough, far away on the Palace balcony, appeared a little group of figures, male and female. One was doubtless the King; he was probably making a speech.

A crowd is usually the most incomprehensibly patient of beasts; but that day its particles were restless, and longing to disperse, move, recongregate, no matter where. It began to loosen and swirl, and I, too, was washed gently on under the Admiralty Arch into Trafalgar Square; caught now and then, like a straw on a rock in a stream, then pulled firmly away, on down Whitehall, where the housetops were trimmed with people, and the windows were blocked with faces. Sometimes a snowstorm of paper wavered down on our heads; it pleased me to fancy the scraps were once copies of D.O.R.A.

But it was time for me to exercise initiative; and like a swimmer who makes the bank but touches it lower down-stream than he intends, I landed and reached my destination. There, in a high-perched room looking over the Thames, I was absorbed into private life. I became as a plant in a parlour-window whose leaves are still, though outside the wind is shaking bushes and trees to their roots. And looking out of the window I had to tell myself yet once again that the war was over at last. There was the river, there the black boats and the barges punching up or gliding down tide ; there the familiar silhouette of warehouses, factories, chimneys, there the rayless London sun, " shining like a new penny in a basin of soapy water." Yet how often I had looked on that scene, feeling far happier than this ! The distant howl, it is true, brought a faint glow of emotion. But it is lucky I haven't, say, a toothache, I thought ; it would need but a little trouble to cover up all my joy. Then I thought of the recumbent figures in hospital-blue on Carlton House Terrace, pulling themselves by cords from their pillows to wave for a minute at the crowd in the Mall below ; of the lorry-loads of nurses I had passed, jigging and cheering ; of one anxious, impatient face—a woman's—in a taxi with luggage. Communal satisfactions are only a background to other feelings ; that it should be well with the background is often vital to real happiness, but the sentiment of life within is so near and dear, that whatever impinges on this takes precedence, though not always in judgment, always in feeling.

When London went to lunch there must have been many luncheons close replicas of mine—luncheons with discussions about what this would mean to Germany or that to us ; discussions more giddy than usual, stimulated by rather more wine, with the Kaiser and Hindy and Tirpy and Ludy bobbing up in them like apples in a warm, spicy posset ; conversations almost entirely inane, childish, but pleasant. The company I was with being well-to-do,

246

the word " Bolshevism " also recurred, a name for
a thing like the fog now at the window. For the room
grew dingier and darker, the fire redder and redder,
and the windows as brown as transparent brown
paper, through which could be seen the black,
dripping branches of trees. But the fire was
ruddy and warm. It would not be bad after all
to end nodding over a pailful of coke, guarding
tools with a sack on one's shoulders ; not so bad,
at least so it seemed when in each of us was a glow
that the infection of public rejoicing could turn
to a blaze. We had all become shadows where we
sat—just shadows, each with three points of light,
two eyes, and one spark of a cigarette. Someone,
with whimsical solemnity, thought fit to pour on
my head a small libation of wine. I was thinking
this was the last armchair I had sat in before going
to France—what years, what ages ago ! Time !
Time ?—yes, of course Time like an ever-rolling
stream bears all its sons away—" I must be off."

The park was empty ; the paths were shining
wet ; I walked in a bubble of mist. It was a
No-man's-land of ghosts ; not of the ghosts I would
fain have talked to, who still look wondrous like
themselves, but of wispy, whimpering ghosts,
anonymous ghosts—multitudes of them. And yet
on the other side of No-man's-land I ran into
a crowd, streaming home as from the Derby ! Such
a jolly crowd, every man and woman of which had
apparently backed the winner ! Then (for me),
tea and exclamations : exclamations of whose
banality it was impossible that day to tire : " Isn't
it marvellous ? Isn't it *incredible* ? Isn't it. . . "
but words break down in gestures. It was pleasant
to savour thus the inexhaustible obvious ; but it
was to the night I looked forward.

To set out with the expectations of a child at a
pantomime, but never to be sure if the curtain had

247

EXPERIENCE

actually risen, whether or not what you saw might
not prove to be only a drop scene ; to push on and
on, to wander hither and thither, in search of the
spectacle, and then to discover that you, in virtue
of being one of thousands and thousands, you just
doing that, *were* the show—such in barest analysis
was the night's experience.   To become as a currant
in a vast human plum-pudding, gaily bedecked,
danced round by the flames of harmless good spirits
and offered up at the table of the *Padre Eterno*,
serves, as metaphors will, to bring back its sensations. A great gregarious good-humour was
abroad, a solid fraternal satisfaction. It softened
and made friendly-pathetic the squeakiest, thinnest,
most self-assertive monotonous manifestations of
joy. How inexpressive a creature is man ! Left
to himself, without the help of art, which he
despises, he can only kick up behind and before,
scream, " Ow-yow, tiddle-diddle-ooo ! " and change
hats with his female.

On November 11th they said " We are so
happy ! We will show it and romp." They did,
and were happier still. On November 12th they
said, " We were so happy last night ! We must
romp again." They made gestures more violent,
lit fires, knocked hats off and charged each other
in the streets. Were they happy ? Perhaps. But
I know I came between two men, facing each
other, with the sulky semi-consciousness of bulls
in their eyes, and with split lips and dripping
noses. On November 13th they said, " We must
pump up jollity to the last dregs of all." They
rushed about dragging cannon to batter in doors
of hotels, tore clothes off the backs of women, and
tied one, it is said, to a lamp-post and danced round
her. I deduce that they were not nearly so happy.

Unshaded street-lamps and lit windows, long
unlighted, were enough that night in our eyes to

248

make a glorious illumination. Piccadilly was a ball-room, where strangers ran at each other with a cry, hugged, took the floor, and twirled and jigged to no music, or only that kind which from earliest ages has been famed for keeping off devils.

We did miss a band. I met only one, it was a Belgian military band, travelling inside a 'bus. Behind the quivering windows they were blowing and banging it out, their energetic faces looking like dashing portraits by Franz Hals ; while from the top of the 'bus men in steel hats and blue-grey coats leant, shouting, shaking hands with the air. Trafalgar Square was more sombre ; processions of munition chits with flags trailed about, singing nasally, lazily, sometimes jeering and laughing at passers-by. A great revolving crowd of black loiterers sat about, ran about—did nothing, did anything—as happy and easily-distracted as dogs. The door of St. Martin's Church was open ; there was a thanksgiving service going on. The quavering, throbbing and whining of the organ, and the people at the foot of the portico steps dancing " Nuts and May", harmonized into a single appeal which made me feel I should like to go in, sit still and remember. Pews, a slightly foggy atmosphere, bright lights and soporific warmth—how familiar it all was ! The service was composed of hymns and improvised prayers ; the former were rather lugubriously triumphant, the latter moving because spoken naturally. We prayed for many kinds of people : the dead, the bereaved, the wounded, the saved, the relieved, for statesmen and Christians and reformers. I waited for the clergyman to tell us also to pray for our enemies; he was, I thought, the sort of man who might. But he did not. At the close we sang, " God save the King," and fixing my eyes upon the Lion and Unicorn above the altar, whereon stood a small brass cross, my thoughts turned to " a highly respectable First Cause," whose views on Alsace and the Suez Canal were sensible and positive. Then I was once more absorbed into the paganism outside.

And so home, through the streets which were easy to traverse in the wake of charging wedges of humanity, among people who laughed when they were jostled, on into the quiet West, where the houses were dark, and dusky flags hung limply from the windows, as though in dumb show saying " It is finished."

DIGRESSIONS OF A REVIEWER

YOUTH AND LOVE

I HAVE just been reading Cobden-Sanderson's journal; the charm of the earlier pages is that the moods which they record are those of a young man not yet by any means used to life. Reading them brought back my early twenties to me. Others, too, will recognize these humiliations, self-reproaches, and moments of superb superiority, which are characteristic of a youth who does not know whether he is truest to himself when he is bone-idle, or when he turns to some distasteful work. He only knows that he is a most unsatisfactory person, though blessed with visions compared with which a career or a cause seems of slight value. He suspects that he is a muff and a waster, and as often that he is a poet, only—unfortunately, and as it were, accidentally—an inarticulate one. Still, what does incapacity to communicate matter at those times when he knows himself to be so happy a combination of seer and saint, and life lies spread like a map before him? Feeling, vision, are the important things.

And yet it does matter, matter very much, when he must descend from the mountain or cannot find his way up. How enviable, how admirable, then, do those appear who are not (surely *they* cannot be ?) blessed with such " openings " ; those whose thoughts never tempt them to understand Creation, but who, on the contrary, with modest resolution settle down to their jobs—marry, get on, get something (damnable, suspect, honourable word !) at any rate *done*.

Then woman comes on the scene, a complication, a solution ; half disastrous compromise, half rocket of salvation. One of the most exasperating yet charming things about her is that she seems naturally more at home in the world. To her it is all simple and glorious, if . . . of course there are " ifs." They are the important things to tackle, and it is up to him to do it.

When she first appears she is only part of the general field of contemplation, a feature in that fresh delightful region upon which he is too often tempted to dwell when he should be raking the wide horizons. But once on the height, how small a part she seems of all that really matters ; strangely delightful, but still how small a part— till things go wrong between them—then, to his dismay, he discovers that she is essential, and that thinkers are not detached. During the days which follow, visibility is very bad from the heights. Ah, how preferable was friendship ! But, since she is essential, she must understand what is greatest in him ; and at this point begins what may prove love's sweetest or bitterest comedy. She must understand that most valued, yet perhaps dubious, side of him, or how can she be comparable to a friend ? If one of them at least has not humility, Heaven help them both !

THE PEERAGE

A NEW edition of that useful and entertaining work, *Burke's Peerage*, has recently appeared It is a book to be dipped into rather than read from cover to cover. When I turn these crowded pages I am reminded again, as I am whenever I try to get on a six o'clock 'bus in the Strand, that I am, at heart, a Malthusian. There are too many people in the streets, too many in the peerage. The population question is the one question on which I *cannot* see the other side. Every bachelor, every spinster, is in my eyes, *ipso facto*, a martyr in the cause of humanity, for to have children of one's own is a source of happiness. I would, if I were king, even at the risk of cheapening a little further that honour, give them each an O.B.E. We shall never be happy, kind and sensible, till we are less thick upon this planet. We shall never have a civilisation of which we can be proud, never a State which we can each feel is a greater self, until the newspapers can report, with pardonable exaggeration as a most significant event, that " a vast concourse of over five hundred people assembled to support the policy of the Government."

There are even too many peers. The eighty-first edition of Burke has convinced me of this. It has 2,789 pages ; the first edition published in 1826 had 400. To each name a number is attached, representing the precedence to which that person is entitled. However large your dinner party, the King, of course, goes in first ; but I have failed to discover who, if you invited the whole peerage,

would go in last. Mrs. W. H. Williamson, I know,
goes in 160,089th. I have not carried my researches
further.

The interest of this great book, which satirists
in their bitter way used to call the Englishman's
Bible, is various. First and foremost it appeals to
genealogists. Ancestor-worship is a passion of
maturity. The young rarely have it, but it often
breaks out in later life in people who were once
extremely bored by discussions as to who was
so-and-so's great-great-aunt. Another source of
interest is looking up the real ages, when they are
given, of ladies who give the impression of only
having left the schoolroom a year or two ago. Then
for those with literary sensibilities, there is pleasure
derivable from the magnificent massing of high-
sounding and glorious titles in the person of one
man. This always gives me a thrill. The owners
of multiple titles ought never to be announced by
only one of them. I should like to hear, for
instance, a butler roll out the words :—" The
Duke of Hamilton, of Brandon, of Chatelherault ;
the Marquess of Douglas and of Clydesdale, the
Earl of Angus, of Arran, of Lanark and of Selkirk ;
Lord Avon, Lord Polmont, Lord Machanshire,
Lord Innerdale, Lord Abernethy, Lord Jedburgh,
Lord Daer, Lord Shortcleuch and Lord Dutton " ;
and then—instead of a crowd of grandees, see a
solitary unassuming gentleman, perhaps with a
mother-of-pearl stud in his shirt-front, enter the
room. It would appeal to my dramatic sense.

As the peerage and baronetage is so large now,
I have decided to be unmoved by any title which is
post-Waterloo. This increases my natural respect
for the remnant.

ELOQUENCE

I DO not know who coined the phrase "verbal imagination"; eloquence is one of the gifts of nearly every great poet, and eloquence is so astounding a faculty that, in its perfection, it can even make a poet, without other gifts, resemble a great one. Shakespeare undoubtedly had it, but in him it was subordinate. Victor Hugo had it, and in him, though it did not stand in the stead of imagination, it was a dominant faculty. His style was a rushing torrent of condensed vivid images and apocalyptic epigrams. The marvel of it was the way in which one metaphor grew perpetually out of another. In Swinburne's poetry too (no wonder he admired Victor Hugo), we are both exhilarated and fatigued by this miracle of the inexhaustible bottle. At first it seems a marvel that these poets can go on so long; soon—that they should ever stop. Both poets are in pursuit of an unending crescendo; and, like Wagner in music, they reach so early what, it seems, must be the emotional climax, that you are astounded they should be able to proceed at all. Yet on they go. To continue to rise ever higher and higher may be impossible, but they seldom flag.

HENLEY

HENLEY as a critic constantly surprises me. He writes like a man from whom one does not expect justice : with defiance, with pride in his prejudices. Yet when you examine his work, you are impressed on the whole by its fairness. He mounts the judgment-seat with the airs of one who does not pretend to be impartial ; but his speech is a speech from the bench. He delivers himself with the gestures of an advocate, but in substance his address is more judicial than you had foreseen. Again, he writes with the determination to be trenchant and picturesque ; he loathes tame statement. You expect him therefore to be slap-dash and inaccurate ; he turns out to be learned and painstaking. Painstaking passion is his note as a critic.

CREDIT OF WORDS

THE credit of words depends upon the prestige of
writers who use them, and therefore it is up to
(do you deplore that expression ?) careful writers to
adopt useful words and phrases which have kept bad
company. " Sense " used as a verb, meaning to
apprehend vaguely, is a vivid word : " they met,
and he instantly sensed an enemy " ; " view-
point " can be useful, too, especially when " point
of view " would introduce another " of " into the
sentence. We should overcome reluctance to
accept English compounds, for we feel no such
aversion from learned foreign ones. " Airman "
has at last ousted " aeronaut," and " hand-book "
was once thought vulgar.

INVECTIVE

THE late Lord Morley, when he was editing the
Pall Pall, was amused by a young journalist who,
when asked his particular line, replied " Invective."
" Invective ? May I ask against what ? " " Oh
. . . anything—general invective." One recognizes
that impartial faculty for getting angry. It can
produce sneers, tropes, tremendous metaphors ;
out of it some pages of memorable prose have been
written. Such anger is delicious to experience,
for it is accompanied by a glowing sense of superiority,
and it can be an immense stimulus to composition.
But it can only be cultivated at the sacrifice of
some spiritual honesty: that is the price which must
be paid. Success depends upon rapidly draining
into general channels the contents of your private
reservoir of resentments, vainglory, thwarted ambitions, wrongs and grudges. Such emotions are
ductile. It is particularly easy to make, for
instance, a little current of envy turn furiously the
mills of righteous indignation. But then the writer
must be unconscious of the sources of this energy.
Hence the necessity of a certain dishonesty or
lack of self-awareness which, whether inborn or
acquired, may sooner or later make a fool of the
specialist in invective.

Again, invective which has become a habit is
apt, like charm, to lose its virtue, for both depend
for their effectiveness on spontaneity. Personal
charm which has been extravagantly used for
personal ends, from winning hearts to securing
corner seats in railway carriages, in time grows

blowsy. It gradually loses the brave delicacy and sweet candour proper to it, though its possessor may be quite unaware that this is happening. In the same way the adept at invective does not notice when something has crept into his style which makes it ineffective. His attack may still amuse, even impress the detached reader, but it has become incapable of giving pain to the victim, which is its proper end. A self-delighting exuberance in animosity, a too obvious contentment in the sleek sarcastic phrase, actually bring balm to the wounds which deadly statements ought to inflict. The victim is relieved by observing that the writer is licking the chops of his own malice, and executing a war-dance instead of thrusting at the vitals of his enemy.

Swinburne was master of a glorious exuberant invective, but I doubt if his fiercest tirades gave much pain even to Dr. Furnivall or Robert Buchanan. The first effect of his " Under the Microscope " is to convince the reader that it must have been immense fun to write it ; he is sure that the author, after giving rein to his emotions, must have enjoyed a sunset-calm of mind. This, of course, is fatal to the proper purpose of invective.

261

JOURNALISTS

JOURNALISTS often write in each other's company at the same table or in the same room, and I, a journalist with a hitching pen, have thus had chances of studying the human countenance during the stress of composition. The face of one engaged in writing is seldom cheerful. Clutton-Brock, whom I love to remember, wrote in rapid spurts with brief pauses. He looked worried but eager—a terrier watching a rat-hole, you would have said. He wrote close, not on alternate lines ; for, happy journalist, his sentences came from him in the right order. Between the spurts, if he looked up and caught upon my face that foolish blankness which accompanies search for the elusive word, his lips would part, his eyes and white teeth shine at me for a moment, and he would nod encouragingly —perhaps whisper softly the word " Garbage " (Authors, when they meet at parties, speak of each other's work in tones of melancholy reverence, but it is not thus we treat each other in Fleet Street). Sometimes " Y. Y." came up to finish his essay in my room. It was a sign that he was behindhand with his copy. Now, though the charm of his writing is that of effortless and cheerful communication, his aspect at such moments was that of a harrowed solitary whose life has never been visited by a ray of sunshine. I have watched Bernard Shaw writing amid chatter in the hall of an hotel. He sat collected, still—no fakir more self-withdrawn; but what he was writing read next day like the words of one gesticulating on a platform in an ecstasy of humorous exposition. Hilaire Belloc will bend over verses of towering extravagance a visage charged with resolve to resist to the uttermost and the last. Maurice Baring, whose ideas out-race the most illegible pencil, and after whom typewriters hammer in vain, wears in the act of writing an expression of agitated resignation. Indeed, the only thoroughly cheerful countenance I have seen opposite me under these conditions was that of G. K. C. in his youth. His script was as leisurely as a fair copy. Never hastening, never stopping, but with gurgles of delight, he would cover the requisite number of pages. His hand never moved from the paper ; he finished in a surprisingly, in an enviably, short time.

Now peep into a little room the other side of my landing. . . Do not reproach me for indelicacy. It was not a condemned cell I callously bade you enter. The man you saw within, gazing so wistfully at a patch of sky, was a leader-writer, one who had just triumphantly hit one nail on the head, and was about, with a deft tap, to drive in another. Indeed, if you judged journalists by their expression during composition, you might form too dismal an estimate of their profession. It is not so bad. It allows more freedom to impulse (a most important element in a happy life), and it encourages a greater variety of interests, than most professions. Of course, it has its drawbacks, among which I count as serious that of not providing pensions for the old and tired. Sooner or later I shall have to seek another calling ; I have my eye on it.

I shall open a School for those who write Letters to the Papers—so many newspaper correspondents are apparently unacquainted with the guiding principles of this art. Men write letters to the papers for various reasons ; to further

263

causes, to advertise themselves, to display their knowledge, to correct other people's facts, to rebut their arguments, to apologize, to give pain, to appeal for money, to flatter, to thank, to report whatever has startled, pleased, interested or disgusted them, or—because they have nothing else to do. In each case the motive of the letter should decide the manner of it. The writer should first be clear, not only about his own motives, but about the view the public are likely to take of himself in relation to the matter in hand. This is a fundamental condition of writing a good letter to the papers. You would think this was generally understood. It is not.

One of the disappointments which Lord Oxford met with during the last few years of his life was his defeat as a candidate for the Chancellorship of Oxford University. It was an honour he coveted, and it would have been an appropriate one. He was defeated by Lord Cave, who thereupon wrote to *The Times* a letter which badly needed revision. Lord Cave's ostensible motive was to thank those who had successfully supported his candidature. Nothing could be more gracious. Yet it was not a good or a gracious letter that he wrote. By way of stimulating future business, I will make a few comments upon it, showing how useful, even to the eminent, my School will be.

" SIR, — Now that the election for the Chancellorship of the University of Oxford is over, will you permit me to express through you my thanks to those who gave me their support ?

" My candidature was not proposed or supported by any political organization. The appeal to accept nomination came to me from heads of colleges, professors, and other leaders of Oxford thought—and in such terms that no man could

have rejected the appeal who was not prepared
to put his personal inclinations and love of ease
above the opportunity of public service ; and the
subsequent arrangements were in the hands of
a small body of resident graduates, assisted only
by a few friends in London. They were handicapped
by the delay in nominating me and by the acknow-
ledged pre-eminence of my distinguished opponent ;
and I shall always remember with pride and gratitude the confidence and consideration which in
these circumstances they were good enough to
extend to me.

"For myself, I will only add that, while I cannot
hope to be so good a Chancellor as Lord Curzon—
who always seemed to me to be the ideal holder of
that historic office—I desire nothing so much as
this, that I may be able in my time to render some
service, however small, to my beloved University.
—Yours faithfully,

Cave.

House of Lords, S.W.1, July 3.

The first sentence is a trifle pompous, but
otherwise no exception can be taken to it ; and the
last paragraph is appropriate. In the first sentence
Lord Cave fulfils his ostensible object in writing
to the papers, he thanks his supporters ; in the
last he expresses with becoming modesty the zeal
with which he enters upon his " historic office."
Had all the rest of the letter between these two
paragraphs been deleted the result would have been
quite suitable. In its present form it would undoubtedly have been returned to him, had it been sub-
mitted to the School. But we should, of course,
have had to explain to Lord Cave the drastic
excision of what he wanted to say. Some blunt-
ness would have been necessary. We should have
justified the cut on the ground that the body of

his letter showed first an incomplete awareness of his own position, and secondly, a complete unawareness of the general view taken of his relation to the matter in hand—namely, his success in competition with a distinguished ex-Prime Minister (all Prime Ministers are not distinguished) also remarkable for those very qualities of mind which a University honours.

The public, it is true, was not surprised at Lord Cave's election, since it knows that appointment to this honourable office is almost always determined by political loyalties ; and when voting-day had been fixed so as to suit the clergy and inconvenience two-thirds of the electorate, the result was certain. Thus in the general view, Lord Cave, whose chief claim to intellectual distinction rested on his being a successful conveyancer, was in the rather uncomfortable position of having beaten the obviously better man. In such circumstances silence is always golden. But silent he could not be. Instead, he devoted (as you see) the greater part of a *letter of thanks* to suggesting that politics had nothing to do with his triumph, and that his victory would have been even more overwhelming had there not been delay in nominating him !

We should never have allowed him to make this mistake ; nor should we have permitted him to state that only the victory of his unselfish devotion to public service over his " personal inclinations and love of ease," had enabled him to stand in the first instance. The Chinese have a proverb, " A red-nosed man may be teetotaller, but no one will believe it." The world is cynical, perhaps too cynical, in judging human nature, but the writer to the papers must take that into account. The public could not well believe, even if it happened to be true, that an energetic and successful lawyer was indifferent to a great but not arduous post which, in normal circumstances, it would have been unreasonable on his part to hope to win. Besides, it is always ungracious to accept the windfalls of fortune with a too dutiful smile. From such howlers we could have saved him. That *The School for Press Correspondents* is wanted and will acquire a good clientele I no longer doubt.

PAIN

I HAVE lately experienced a sensation I had quite forgotten—pain, and once more I have almost forgotten what it is like. How odd that so unique and overwhelming a sensation should leave so vague a recollection ! It is not perhaps surprising that very acute pain should be irrecoverable by the imagination, for it disintegrates the personality. It is a delirium, and destroys the world. But a pain one can manage, a simple, stale, grinding ache, varied by hot shoots—a pain like that ought, I should have imagined, to have left behind it a clear impression. Yet I have to pinch my injured limb to convince myself that such a feeling exists.

It is a habit of mine to examine whatever happens to me and to squeeze a little information out of it, though why I do this I hardly know. Now from my recent experience the conclusion I have drawn is that boredom is a large part of the total unpleasantness of moderate pain. Pain (I am not speaking of extreme pain) is the most *boring* thing in the world. Though the sensation itself is utterly unworthy of serious or of prolonged attention, while we are feeling it we cannot attend to anything else. It is abominably monotonous. At first sight it is some slight alleviation to watch the pain carefully, for what seemed a homogeneous sensation turns out to be a composite one. It has a rhythm in it—a crescendo, a sparkle or twist of greater acuteness, a diminuendo : " Here we go up, up—Ah !—Now we go down, down, down."

PAIN

Imagine watching so simple a phenomenon hour
after hour! It is intolerable, an outrage. Yet
you can't get away from it; you are a slave.
If you violently wrench your mind away and clamp
it upon something else—a thought, a bottle, a
flower by your bedside, you pay for the little outing.
Very soon you feel the tug of the chain, and back
your mind must come to this boring, empty thing.
And you will be punished, too, for having distracted
yourself; for you will fear, when you attend to it
again, that the pain has meanwhile become worse,
that it *is* getting worse. And when fear enters
your soul, then you are in a bad way.

HANDY WORDS

DURING the war a pretty word for a girl came into general use ; a soldier would speak of her as his " bird." It was an old expression. I came across an earlier revival of it in a poem by Thomas Campbell :—

> And by my word, the bonny bird
> In danger shall not tarry.

Such slang words often have better pedigrees than correct ones ; " bilk " for instance, was used both by Spenser and by Dryden ; and " snag " and " squelch " are good English, and so is " swank," in the sense of hale and hearty. Burns uses it. In the matter of words we are sitting upon a chest of fine old coins, complaining of our poverty, and yet never attempting to pass them. If one or two ever get into currency it is thanks to gay, illiterate persons without pretence to education, who love a vigorous word. We literates trade with greasy paper-money, and coffer up neglected gold. What a charmingly expressive word for a retiring, absent person the adjective " yonderly " is, for example— a yonderly man ! " Mim," meaning prudishly or very discreetly silent, is another word I should like revived as a feminine refinement upon " mum." It survives only in that nursery rhyme which used to be sung to some of us while we were jogged on the knee :—

> To market ride the gentlemen,
> So do we, so do we,

Then comes the country clown,
  Hobbledy gee !

First go the ladies, mim, mim, mim ;
  Next come the gentlemen, trim, trim, trim ;
Then comes the country clown,
  Gallop a trot, trot, trot.

I want " Scritch," too, as well as " Screech " ; it
suggests a more subtle sound. Coleridge, by the
bye, revived it,

    Perhaps it is the owlet's scritch,
    Or what can ail the mastiff bitch ?

A " Moonflaw "—meaning a wild, lunatic fancy—
and " Moonling "—" I have a husband and a two-
legged one, but such a moonling "—are both, as
Polonius would have said, " good." Then there are
all the old compounds beginning with " mis "
which we have allowed to drop out of use. We
" misgovern," " misprint," " mislead," but what
a handy word we neglect in " mislike," which, being
less positive than " dislike," expresses a common shade
of aversion. I like the word " to gowl," too, which
means to weep from rage or spite ; it is a fine
sulky word.

BORROW AND BELLOC

IF ever a man succeeded in getting himself into his books it was Borrow—and a queer self it was. He has the art of riveting our attention upon it. He is as circumstantial as Defoe, yet he prepares his effects theatrically ; he is full of mystifications, and yet he is open ; he jumbles together the matter-of-fact and the romantic in a narrative only credible because all these things are happening to *him*. To such a man, you say as you read, any adventures might happen ; with such a traveller any conversation might take a fantastic turn. You cannot think him truthful ; yet you surrender your notions of probability. He moves through life an heroic figure to himself, and anything—a tinker, a gipsy, a pedant, a pedlar of Bibles—to his chance-met acquaintances. The irony of the contrast is a luscious delight to him, and that delight is shared by his readers, whom he is most careful to let into the magnificent secret. He flourishes a robust common sense in your face ; yet what attracts him most is mysterious. He is an intense egoist ; yet he perceives everyone he meets to be unique and interesting. He takes his readers into familiar country and also into a world of marvels such as nature-lovers never see. There were deep pits in his temperament ; this swashbuckler was subject to agonies of fear. In *Lavengro* he apostrophizes his sacred terror thus.

" Oh how dare I mention the dark feeling of mysterious dread which comes over the mind, and which the lamp of reason, though burning bright

the while, is unable to dispel! Art thou, as leeches
say, the concomitant of disease—the result of
shattered nerves? Nay, rather the principle of
woe itself, the fountain head of all sorrow co-
existent with man, whose influence he feels when
yet unborn, and whose workings he testifies with
his earliest cries, when, 'drowned in tears,' he
first beholds the light; for, as the sparks fly upwards, so is man born to trouble, and woe doth he
bring with him into the world, even thyself, dark one,
terrible one, causeless, unbegotten, without a father.
Oh, how unfrequently dost thou break down the
barriers which divide thee from the poor soul of man,
and overcast its sunshine with thy gloomy shadow!
In the brightest days of prosperity—in the midst
of health and wealth—how sentient is the poor
human creature of thy neighbourhood! how instinctively aware that the flood-gates of horror
may be cast open, and the dark stream engulf
him for ever and ever! Then is it not lawful for
man to exclaim, 'Better that I had never been
born!' Fool, for thyself thou wast not born,
but to fulfil the inscrutable decrees of thy Creator;
and how doest thou know that this dark principle
is not, after all, thy best friend; that it is not that
which tempers the whole mass of thy corruption?
It may be, for what thou knowest, the mother of
wisdom, and of great works; it is the dread of the
horror of the night, that makes the pilgrim hasten
on his way. When thou feelest it nigh, let thy
safety word be 'Onward'; if thou tarry, thou
art overwhelmed. Courage! build great works—
'tis urging thee—it is ever nearest the favourites
of God—the fool knows little of it. Thou wouldst be
joyous, wouldst thou? then be a fool. What great
work was ever the result of joy, the puny one?
Who have been the wise ones, the mighty ones,
the conquering ones of this earth? the joyous?

I believe not. The fool is happy, or comparatively so—certainly the least sorrowful, but he is still a fool; and whose notes are sweetest, those of the nightingale, or of the silly lark ? "

It is impossible to say what his books are about ; but to read them is to enjoy an outing from civilization and convention, and in the company of an erratic, learned, solitary, sociable companion whom—though he talks to you frankly and incessantly—you understand almost as little at the end of the journey as you did at the beginning.

There is one modern book which, though it has not the same flavour as Borrow's books, will, I think, take the same kind of place in literature,— *The Path to Rome* ; and to read it is also to enjoy an invigorating spiritual and physical outing. Just as Roman Catholics enjoy Borrow in spite of his aggressive No-Popery, so Protestants can enjoy *The Path to Rome* in spite of its militant Catholicism. Belloc, too, has the power of riveting attention on himself and yet remaining enigmatic. His book is as full of fine writing and courageous gusto—of descriptions and energetic reflections. Also it is full of good stories, including the immortal one of the Duke of Sussex, the Engineer, and the simple-minded Frenchman, wherein is discovered the correct theory of the Simple Human Sense of Authority.

CONVIVIALITY

I WAS never " a gay young dog," though I will not go so far as to boast that I was, at any time, capable of pronouncing the most famous restaurant in the Strand " Roman-o's," as Sir John Simon once did in Court, thus unconsciously testifying to an exceptionally well-spent youth. I have always had friends among the race of " gay young dogs," and I have thought it particularly amiable of them to tolerate me, so few were the good points we had in common. I have envied, without attaining, the grace of unconscious candour which is their prime virtue ; but I never could contribute to festive hours anything more positive than benignity. It is almost impossible for me to get drunk, though it is true that on a few occasions in my life, after an Alice in Wonderland dinner-party, I have had to jump into my bed as it passed my corner of the room ; but the seat of reason has never been shaken, neither has memory been disturbed. This characteristic disqualifies one from sharing the pleasures of rampageous conviviality, which depend upon complete self-forgetfulness.

CENTENARIES

THE custom of observing literary centenaries is growing. It is a sign of the large number of literary journalists there are about, and of the attitude of editors and the public towards literature. It is hard to place a literary article if there is not some pretext for presenting it to the public. There is no reason why people should be more inclined to read Crabbe or Chaucer on an anniversary,— and they do not ; but if an article can begin, " Last Thursday two hundred years ago Cowper was born," that apparently removes a feeling of impatience which editors dread in the public when they are addressed on topics which have no pretence to be burning. In 1921 I showed up an article beginning " A hundred and twenty-one years ago the poet Cowper died," but the formula had no magic in it. I saw I should have to wait ten years before I could triumphantly begin " Two hundred years ago the poet Cowper was born,"—and be printed.

SENTIMENT

OUR contemporaries are down on bad sentiment, but lenient toward poor humour, which is really as contemptible and for much the same reason. You can win nowadays quite a respectable reputation if you " run about the city grinning like a dog," but if you shed a few easy tears you are thought an ass. Consider how Sterne with his Maria, his dead donkey and his Le Fever would be despised if he were writing now. He escapes censure only because we do not choose to believe he took his sentiment seriously ; he is so clever, and so clever in a way that suits our taste, that we refuse to believe he was not ironical in such passages, though anyone with an historic sense knows he thought them highly becoming and exquisite.

CHURTON COLLINS

I HAVE been reading Churton Collins' " Illustrations of Tennyson," an investigation into the sources from which the poet drew inspiration. It is an amazing product of scholarship and memory. What learning! one exclaims as one reads it, and —with greater astonishment—What a memory! For Churton Collins belonged to the old school of bookmen who carried their knowledge about with them, not to the type of the latter-day literary man, who is unable to quote fifty consecutive lines of Homer or Shakespeare, but keeps his erudition on his shelves. I do not mean to insinuate that he does not know what is inside his books, he does ; but when he comes to writing he is helpless without his library. Now, " Illustrations of Tennyson" is a book which could have only been written by a man whose library was in his head.

Churton Collins had a magnificent verbal memory. As he read Tennyson, he recalled all the passages he had ever come across in Latin, Greek, Italian, French or German literature which resembled the poet's thoughts, similes or phrases. He evidently remembered, too, where such parallel passages occurred, so that he could verify them. The result was a book which is an anthology of a rare kind, full of beautiful fragments from the world's literature, some of them taken from far-out-of-the-way sources.

The results were not pleasing to the poet. He did not like appearing, to use his own simile, as

> A full-cell'd honeycomb of eloquence
> Stor'd from all flowers.

" It is the business of critical justice," said Johnson, " to give every bird of the Muses his proper feather," and Churton Collins had attended to the business so thoroughly that Tennyson felt like a plucked eagle. His critic had shown how deeply indebted he had been to earlier poets, especially to the ancients and even to the obscurer classics. The number of imitations, analogies, adaptations and straight transferences which Collins noted is astonishing. The poet was often shown to have improved immensely what he had borrowed, even in the case of Homer ; but neither this admission nor a most respectful preface propitiated Tennyson, who was not content to be compared even with an enchanted island—if the point of the comparison lay in his being *full of echoes* as well as of

> " Sounds and sweet airs, that give delight."

I infer that it was after the publication of this book, not in defence of Gosse, that Tennyson growled out, when Churton Collins' name was mentioned : " He's a louse in the locks of literature."

EMERSON

I KNOW many who will at once turn over any page on which the name of Emerson occurs. His tender idealism, the benign didactic loftiness of his tone, that serenity which smiles upon evil as " undeveloped good " and passes over difficulties, are miles away from prevalent moods. There is no great Victorian preacher on whose behalf it would be more hopeless to start a cult; indeed, any critic who lights Emerson's candle now is in danger of extinguishing his own. But what do our little dips matter ? One thing is certain : Emerson wrote so well that he will reappear before other courts for judgment. His philosophy may seem to this generation mere philomory ; his candid detachment irritating ; his purity too crystalline to be true ; his culture the kind most irritating to modern artists :—

> In the room the women come and go
> Talking of Michelangelo—

his pretty fancies (butterflies incased in little glittering blocks of ice) at once too intellectual and too homely to merit admiration ; yet return he must. Such is the reward of writing well. Style alone gives this privilege of appealing from one generation to another, of winning fresh hearing for ideas though they have been repeatedly turned down.

BOSH

THERE are books which belong entirely to that day-dream world into which it is often restful to nestle down, away from reality—and away from literature. For literature and indeed genuine art in any form, even when its theme is most remote from reality, has an odd way of seeming real—of making us feel more alive. We do not turn to it when we want to fade out.

Anyone with the habit of self-observation, when searching his shelves, must have often caught himself avoiding not only masterpieces, but even the works of any writer who has a position in literature. There are moods when we want to read bosh. With some people this is the only mood in which they ever open a book, and this is their misfortune ; but we all feel that there is not as much first-rate bosh as we want. The supply of second-rate and third-rate is almost unlimited, but first-rate bosh is nearly as rare as a masterpiece. The purveyors of it therefore deserve very well of mankind. Next to the writers who have created beauty, and fired and renewed our love of it, or have recorded their own sense of the meaning of life, next to these, the prime entertainers should be ranked as benefactors of mankind. They are always handsomely rewarded as far as money is concerned, but they are too little esteemed. A fairer sense of proportion would give them more respect than the majority of the almost-artists, for they provide something which men genuinely need.

281

There is a type of reader who puts any book which aims at merit of a serious kind above rubbish, and despises rubbish, even when it is as good as *Sherlock Holmes*. For my part, I think it fair (and possible) to be as critical of bosh as of literature. It is no use comparing them, because the test is different, but each within its own category can be as rigorously tested. *War and Peace* is a stupendous work of art, though it has faults which any one can see ; *Sherlock Holmes* is first-rate bosh, though it also has faults any one can see, but it is — well, first-rate bosh.

POPULAR WRITERS

I DO not think popular taste has deteriorated. The best modern writers do not appeal to that taste, partly because there are so many half-good writers successfully competing with them to satisfy it ; partly, too, because the best authors of to-day do not happen to possess the splendid though popular qualities of Scott and Dickens, but different ones. Lord Rosebery once said that the stamp of merit on a book was " the thumb-mark of the artisan." He ought not to have said anything so sycophantic. Popular taste is a good judge of creative power on a huge scale, of what is exciting and of what is human, but it is very dense in all other matters, and it likes barefaced imitations of the qualities it understands as much as those qualities themselves. The great majority are more easily taken in than the over-refined ; nor are they so easily scared out of their mistakes.

There are silly books which run through the rabble of readers, devouring their hundreds of thousands. We are told that the victims of these books love Shakespeare. Would they, I wonder, if he were not the best advertised of all authors living or dead ?

Another point: if you want to learn to write well, it is often more practical to turn, not to the masters, but to the popular writers. The contrast is so instructive between the way they let themselves go, splurging and splashing about, piling it on and spoiling their effects, and the way that on rarer occasions they put down the perfect statement and leave it. In the stories of careful, conscious writers everything is apt to be so evenly well-done that it is hard to discriminate between what is necessary and what is not.

From the barbarians one learns also that it is above all important to be really excited oneself by whatever one is describing.

If I were in charge of an Academy for Literary Failures, part of the curriculum would be to make newcomers prune, without destroying, stories by writers of good bosh. It would be no use to start by choosing, say, a story by Turgenev as a model, and telling them to imitate its economy, delicacy and balance.

THE SENSE OF SECURITY

I NEVER know whether to damn the age or to praise it : I can't marshal the data. Many people, however, appear to have little difficulty in doing so, and in concluding that the twentieth century is damnable and decrepit. Many of these obviously start by idealizing the past. It is rare, of course, to find anyone glorifying their own times ; and there are few periods in history which wear a cheerful self-satisfied aspect. The age of Elizabeth, which shines so gloriously in our eyes, was eaten up with remorse and self-contempt—an ugly, thrusting, vulgar, cruel muddle it seemed to the Elizabethans themselves. But the age of Queen Anne was, I think, a fairly self-satisfied age ; and so, indeed, was all the first half of the eighteenth century. Men thought themselves rational—and, on the whole, they were justified. Of course, they did not consider that they were men of a noble stature compared with the race they invented and called " the Romans " ; still, when they compared themselves with their ancestors, Elizabethan or mediæval, they were satisfied. Then in the middle of the Victorian era people were again, on the whole, pleased with the way they were getting on. Of course, there were grousers who pointed at the ghastly condition of the slaves of the manufacturers, or at the massive stupidity of the middle and upper classes ; but there was a lot of hope in the air. Men believed they were at bottom good and wise ; barbarism was over ; all that civilization wanted was to be cautiously and gradually tidied-up, and then it would progress from triumph to triumph. They had stopped writing coarse books ; they had eschewed duelling and cock-fighting ; virtue and getting-on in life were widely respected ; they were daily growing richer, and men of science were doing wonderful things. Only the abnormally timid dreamt of serious upheavals. Indeed, the sense of security was so powerful an ingredient in the social atmosphere that those who have been brought up, even within whiff of it, have been unable to reconcile themselves to post-war conditions.

MODERN POETRY

THERE are fashions in poetry. These fashions are strong modes of feeling, and it is impossible for the sensibility of a contemporary not to be coloured by them, unless he confines his reading to the poetry of the past. The leading fashion in poetry is now tolerant of obscurity to a degree unwarranted by examination of the poetry which mankind has seen fit to treasure down the ages. Modern poets are apt to be mannered and subtle in the expression of emotion to a pitch exceeding even the seventeenth century. Dread of the commonplace, lack of faith in common ideas and moral values, have driven them back upon idiosyncratic associations and subjective themes ; upon shivers of queer disillusionment—*Hi ! Hi ! Hi ! les amants bizarres*—upon sudden mystic exaltations, meaningless in any philosophic sense, or upon attempts to create a childish wonder-world out of an odd collocation of images. Like other fashions this one will soon pass.

THE SOCIAL ENEMY

NO one loves Liberty who fears Licence ; so far as I know this is an original aphorism.

Such lovers of liberty are intolerant only of intolerance, and the only kind of moral indignation they permit is that directed against moral indignation ; in this they revel. This general attitude is instantly sympathetic to me.

The Enemy is an active spirit which animates certain, often capable, and nearly always unfortunately, self-assertive people. It is best suggested by an example. I will take a quotation from Mr. Haynes' " A Lawyer's Note Book."

" He only wished to add that he could not concur in the reason given by the magistrate when he said that there was strong public feeling that these regulations should not be unduly maintained and enforced. In his (Mr. Justice Avory's) view this sort of legislation, which was intended to restrain the vicious propensities of those who indulge in the eating of sweetmeats up to bedtime, must be maintained and enforced to keep such vicious propensities in check (Mr. Justice Avory as reported in *The Times* of April 14th, 1923)."

The occasion of this *obiter dictum* was, no doubt, that petty piece of oppressive legislation regulating the sale of sweets, the object of which was, however, in no sense moral. But observe the gusto with which the learned judge gives it a moral interpretation and finds an excuse for bringing down the pedagogue's cane ; then ask yourself what sort of community ours would be to live in if Mr. Justice Avory was autocrat of it, or, still more awful thought, if it was composed of people like him.

And there is a more immediate warning to be drawn from this passage. A great deal of social legislation has been passed, and a great deal more threatens to be passed, which has been, or can be, partially justified on inoffensive grounds, but behind which the driving force is really this detestable spirit. It is not apprehensive, human affection, which makes Mr. Justice Avory delight in depriving a flapper of an evening feast of chocolate ; I think we may be sure that he is not deeply concerned about her little stomach. But when he imagines her popping one cream after another into her mouth, what I fancy he feels is a kind of sudden anger, which would be expressed by exclaiming, " She must be stopped making a little beast of herself ! " We have all experienced this emotion ; many people feel it when they see a kiss. We can recognize it easily if we like. It is a wholly delicious feeling when we have the power to interfere ; and even when we have not, there is still a not uninteresting glow in it, though perhaps too much like an itch to be entirely pleasant. Nothing could be more opposed to a natural movement of human charity, or friendly concern for another than this emotion. It is in reality an intensely egotistic, self-assertive emotion. Controlled, as it often is in decently self-critical people, it often turns into patronizing contempt (that shows how little real regard for others enters into it) ; and when it is uncontrolled, it masquerades as concern for the happiness of those who have excited it. Lust does not more readily conceal itself as love ; jealousy counterfeit more cunningly a sense of justice. And this spirit is the Enemy.

THE PRIVY PATH

WHEN I come across some profound piece of criticism into which the critic has, I feel, been led by surrendering to his own temperament, I wonder if my own method of criticizing is not mistaken. One cannot get away from one's own temperament any more than one can jump away from one's own shadow, but one can discount the emphasis which it produces. I snub my own temperament when I think it is not leading me straight to the spot whence a general panorama of an author's work is visible. This point is often some obvious little knoll or terrace, which almost everyone would mount to get a view. Perhaps the other kind of criticism is more valuable, in which the critic wanders down a vista which he is impelled by a personal impulse of curiosity to explore, ignoring what lies to the right or left of him, or what others see when they just look round them. But again how often the most alluring and mysterious little path in a garden leads only to the gardeners' privy!

THE LAST OF ALFRED DE MUSSET

ONCE out in the street I withdrew my mind from the play I had just seen, " Madame Sand," and thought about Alfred de Musset. I found myself in memory sitting in a small orchard at the end of a straight, sandy path, down which a gaunt old gentleman, my grandfather and my best link with the past, was proceeding towards me with a bottle of wine under his arm and two glasses clinking in his other hand. It was exceedingly hot. The blossoming apple trees, though charming, threw a very thin quality of shade upon our round iron table and chairs. Earlier in the afternoon we had quarrelled over the respective merits of Victor Hugo and Ibsen as dramatists. My grandfather could not hear Ibsen mentioned in the same breath with even Schiller, let alone Victor Hugo : " Ibsen's world," he had shouted, " is a world without honour," while I had maintained that the motives and emotions of Victor Hugo's characters were theatrical and fictitious. For an hour I had lain, extenuated, on a velvet sofa, while the old man paced the little sitting-room haranguing me, It was an oven in spite of the closed green shutters. Every now and then he would stop in his stride to stroke my cheek with his long hand and call me repentantly " angel," before again becoming stormy and abusive. At last we had compromised over Alfred de Musset. He was romantic enough for anything, and I was prepared to admit that he was adorable. So my grandfather said, if we moved to the orchard, he would tell me a story about him, while we drank together the cup of peace.

" When Musset died in 1857, Sainte-Beuve wrote that people felt as though they had buried their youth with him. It was a generous tribute, but it corresponded little to realities. As far as I remember about fifty people followed the coffin down the Rue de Rivoli, and at the Place de la Bastille I don't suppose there were twelve of them left. The Academy was not there in force—though Mérimée and Sainte Beuve attended. But, mark you! when more than twenty years later, in 1880, some young men organized a fête in Musset's honour, there must have been five thousand people in the hall of the Trocadéro ! You see, long before his death Musset had become a dim figure—he was forty-six when he died. His great power lay in his sensibility and he had an extraordinary precocious gift of expression. He wrote beautiful verses very young. J'ai dit à mon coeur, à mon faible coeur. . . . Musset is in that line. Yes, love is the only good—from 1830 to 1840 he was obsessed by that idea :

> Le seul bien qui me reste au monde
> Est d'avoir quelque fois pleuré,

—you remember ? And how he sometimes wrote with the natural elegance of La Fontaine ?

> J'ai vu verdir les bois et j'ai tenté d'aimer

Well, then, towards the end of his life he went utterly to pieces. He drank too much. He hugged his own sorrows—rightly, for they had inspired him ; but at last they failed to do so any longer. He became neglected, dilapidated—and he was forgotten. . . . My story has to do with that.

The great lady of the world of letters was

then the Princess Mathilde Bonaparte, who collected authors. I suppose one evening at her salon the conversation had turned on Alfred de Musset. One can imagine how they would talk, how half pensively and half mockingly they would all agree that Musset had expressed the sorrows and ecstasies of their youth. What ages ago all that seemed! She declared she would ask him to dinner.

Now Musset had once been the ideal dandy, and he was still as proud of being a man of birth and a man of the world as he was of being a poet. He had long ceased to go out in society and this invitation must have been an event of some importance to him. He was determined to shine, and I am afraid, as you will gather, he must have prepared himself for it too well. When the evening came (seven was then the fashionable dining hour), Musset did not appear. The company waited an hour and then went down to table, where his chair next the Princess was empty. They had just sat down when he entered and took it without a word of explanation or apology. He was deathly pale, and when offered soup he asked for brandy. " In this," he said abruptly, holding out a tumbler. The footman hesitated and looked towards his mistress : " Give M. de Musset what he asks for," she said. He drained off half a tumbler and was immediately and violently sick. There is no need to describe the scene. He was supported out of the room, and he lay down in the Princess's boudoir till dinner was over. Then he came up to the drawing-room, and leaning his elbow on the mantelpiece discoursed delightfully for half an hour, made a formal bow—and disappeared from the world of salons and dinner-parties for ever.

THE LOVER OF LIFE

I HAVE been re-reading George Wyndham's letters, and thinking about him. What a lover of life he was ! The contagion of another's enthusiasm roused his own ; he loved that reverberation, and sought to create it in conversation. He was extraordinarily, almost femininely, appreciative. To such a temperament to appreciate, to enjoy, whether it be a fine day, a book, a charming face, a ride, a friend's wit, a gesture of affection, amounts to an obligation, and to fail to meet it is to fail to live. It is not of such stuff, of course, that the workers of the world are made, nor the creators. If such a one possesses facility and gifts (Wyndham's gifts were indisputable) he may be profusely productive, but he will remain an amateur (not necessarily a dilettante) to the end. He may work with spurts of energy that shame even the concentrated ; but, presently, he will hear life knocking at his study door. At the first gentle tap he may shake a resolute head, but who can resist opening for long if instinct tells him that on his threshold stands not that old bore, Experience, but an ever radiant princess with a smile for him—specially kind for him ? Such men inevitably squander themselves, and are alternately reproached for wasting their gifts and for pretending to possess more talent than they have. The gesture with which they scatter largess (let the word stand for affection as well as talent) to some seems generosity, to others ostentation. But the fact remains, men often love a lover of life more than those (it may not be fair, but it is so) who devote themselves steadily to their service.

THE PLEASURES OF DISGUST

HAVE you ever been irritated by the pretensions and confusions of modern life ? By the mediocrity of its sentiments and the meanness of its types ? Have you ever felt disgusted with the faces in omnibuses ; the restaurants where you feed, the rooms in which you sleep, the conversation of artificially amiable people, the mechanism of your own body, the messiness of food, the dreariness of professions ? Then (this sounds like the beginning of an advertisement of a quack medicine), if you read Huysmans, you will find that whatever has disgusted you in these things is described with an atrabilious vehemence, an extravagance of acrimonious precision, at once exaggerated and acute, which will bring you a little temporary relief. Two elements enter into this relief, the glow of satisfaction at finding branded what ought to be branded, and the reflection, " Well, *I* at any rate can stand life a little better than that." If you read Huysman's description of being shaved in a cheap shop, you will be amazed at your past fortitude. We are apt to associate travelling in " a sleeper " with luxury and comfort ; after reading Huysmans one realizes that to spend a night in a wagon-lit is torture ; his account of such a night eclipses in horror Poe's *Pit and Pendulum*. There is no greatness of mind in Huysman's indictment of Life ; but to the shivery fastidious it is a keen pleasure to find their complaints stated by one more shivery and more fastidious than themselves—and with such a fury of contempt. I find it myself a most refreshing change from the cheery pooh-pooh attitude. The fun of reading Huysmans is the fun of seeing the ugly, dank, flaccid thing, presented not as it is, but as even uglier, greasier, meaner.

MEMORY

THERE is no doubt that Conrad possessed a memory of most unusual retentiveness. Only in course of time could he forget what was not significant to his imagination or consonant with the prevailing mood in which he wrote. When he attacked a theme near to him in time, the process of selection was too intentional to be really successful, and much more laborious. That, I believe, is the chief difference between the journalist, when he has a genius for reporting, and the artist. The fresher impressions are in the mind of a reporter, the better use he makes of them ; in the evocation of incidents, and facts in their immediacy lies the merit of his work, while the artist's success depends upon steeping them in a mood, characteristic of his whole response to life ; details and incidents must stew first in that emotional part of him which we label roughly memory. William James, I seem to remember, distinguishes between two kinds of memory : one is that retentiveness which enables a man to remember things, whether he is interested in them or not. (This is the examination memory.) The other kind of memory functions only when a fact is associated with a number of things which concern him nearly ; emotion is an essential part of it. The model journalist has a fly-paper memory to which things stick of their own accord. The other kind of memory is indeed the mother of the muses.

THE TWO MINUTES' SILENCE

I ASKED a friend of mine (I had better tell you he was a Catholic) what he thought about the yearly ceremony of the Two Minutes' Silence. " It is a substitute," he said. " People would like to pray for the dead, but they think it wrong. It is a makeshift ; just as M. Coué's knotted string with his injunction to assert at each knot, ' Every day in every way I get better and better,' was a substitute for the rosary, while psycho-analysis, a method for getting things off the mind, is a substitute for the Confessional. Only, of course, telling beads does not compel one to assert what may be a series of thumping lies ; and the man who employs psycho-analysis gets no absolution except from himself."

Touching Armistice Day, and this new ceremony, I will quote from a source I have rarely tapped in these pages, the daily papers. On the evening of that day, under the heading, " Men who Broke the Silence," some curious incidents were recorded which I record again here, since they offer an opportunity for each reader to discover something about himself. After reading them ask on which side your sympathies lie, or in what proportion they are divided, and you will then discover something about yourself which may prevent your future reactions from surprising you :—

Several incidents marked the Great Silence, one in the City threatening to develop seriously.

A young man in Moorgate Street wearing a
" Trilby " and a brown linen coat of the kind
usually worn by warehousemen, took no notice
of the signal, but continued on his way. People
at first looked at him in surprise, and one or two
tried to trip him up. The offender paid no heed
to the booing directed at him, but pushed his
way through the crowd and walked across the
road. One man said to him, " Take your hat
off, or something will happen to you." This
warning was also ignored.

Immediately the silence was over about 200
people made a rush for him. He stopped to try
and argue with them, saying, it was stated by an
eye-witness, that he was at liberty to please
himself as to what he did.

A boy grabbed his hat from his head and
threw it in the street, where it was soon kicked
and torn beyond recognition. Several people
aimed blows at him. One, delivered by a tall,
strong man, hit the offender on the jaw and
seemed to have loosened several teeth and
made his mouth bleed freely. The crowd was
now thoroughly roused, and the man sought
refuge in the first door-way that presented itself.
This happened to be the entrance to a large office-
furniture emporium.

The crowd tried to follow him, shouting
threats. Many women were among the pursuers,
and one of them who was particularly angry
led the chase.

The manager of the shop, realizing the situation, conveyed the man through the premises
and let him out at the back door into another
street. Meantime the crowd in front of the
premises had grown to considerable proportions.
Ultimately the police had to be summoned to
clear the pavement.

Another young man, who persisted in making his way along the Strand with his hat on throughout the Two Minutes' Silence, was mobbed and taken into custody for his own protection. He was a seaman, aged twenty-six, from Great Yarmouth, and he was charged at Bow Street with insulting behaviour. It was stated that when the crowd attempted to mob him, he took off his hat and coat and offered to fight. The magistrate said he had behaved very foolishly. " Why ? " he replied. " Why all these demands ? It is not an order. People can please themselves." He was bound over.

Two 'bus drivers abused by the crowd for not shutting off their engines retorted that they were ex-Service men, and refused in spite of menaces to do so.

Now, which do you sympathize with, the non-conformists or the people who mobbed them ? The answer you make to yourself will throw light on your attitude towards all sorts of moral, social and political questions. It is interesting to reconstruct the scenes in imagination. In the case of the 'bus drivers the wrangle seems to have gone on, probably noisily, during the silent minutes ; in the others, one can imagine the people in the streets frozen to impatient immobility, flaming with righteous indignation within, till like released terriers after a rat, they dashed at the non-conformists. Which do you sympathize with—" the tall strong man " who hit the offender on the jaw and loosened his teeth, or the man in the brown linen coat ?

My sympathies are on the side of the latter. Non-conformists are often excessively disagreeable but there is salt in them, and a community without a sprinkling of them is damnable to live in—" Read Trotter's *Herd Instinct*," as Tarlton would say.

Lovers of liberty are often asked what they mean by liberty. An important part of what they mean is that the public should never be able to impose complete uniformity, either in opinion or in the expression emotion.

MAKING SPEECHES

WHAT daunts me when I get upon my feet to speak is not that I am unaccustomed to public speaking, but that all my previous speeches have been failures. And yet I think, or rather, to use the formula of words which was constantly on the lips of that cautious metaphysician Sir William Hamilton,—" It seems to me that I think I believe," that there is the making of a speaker in me. In the first place, why otherwise should I continue to be asked from time to time to address audiences if there were not still a faint glimmer of hope animating those who know me that I *might* be worth hearing ? And secondly, I am certainly endowed with two-o'clock-in-the-morning eloquence—solitary eloquence. But I believe this faculty is not uncommon. When kept awake by indignation or anger I am able to give absent persons a trouncing, which in my opinion falls little short of Chatham or Cicero in that line. Quicken me at that dark hour with a small personal grievance or a gigantic public scandal (like the behaviour of the British in Ireland), and off I go. Sentences of trenchant invective, unforgettable sarcasm, polished irony and thumping directness flow from me easily. Yet at an earlier hour, in the presence of other human beings, it is as much as I can do to stutter through the tamest statement of my case. How is this ? What is the explanation ? What paralyses me— the sound of my own voice or the eyes of an audience ?

I took up Mr. Ruffin *On Forms of Oratorical*

Expression and How Delivered in the hope of learning how others had overcome these inhibitions. Nothing certainly would be more useful (or delightful) than to be able to make a speech. The object of this work " is to foment and encourage the spirit and study of the art of public speaking." It is not " fomenting " I need ; but the book is advanced for me. I have never read one so full of hard words. Yet I was as surprised as M. Jourdain when he found he had been talking prose all his life, to discover that I had been achieving unawares *Enantiosis* (if you say " He's no fool," that is *enantiosis*), Enthymema, Homœoptoton, Homœoteleuton, Pathopœia, Paraineticon, Polysyndeton, Synchoresis—I was surprised to find how I had been performing feats of that kind all my life. If you say, " We shall miss our train ; we shall be late for dinner ; they will be furious," and add bitterly, "All right, all right," implying, " have it your own way and be damned "—that is Synchoresis. It is amazing the degree to which rhetoricians have classified and distinguished forms of speech. Indeed, from one aspect this book reminds me of a rock garden full of labels with long strange names on them attached to inconspicuous flowers, and where the labels are always much larger than the flowers. (That sentence, by the way, is an example of Homœteleution ; you observe both parts of it end with the same word). Of course it does not do to think to yourself, " Now I am going to bring off Enthymema," which indeed you do whenever you say, " I shall take my umbrella, for I think it will rain " for you are suppressing a statement implicit in your reasoning that umbrellas are useful when it rains ; but, if you catch yourself using such forms in a speech, Mr. Ruffin will tell you how best to deliver them.

He analyses the endowment of various famous

orators, and the qualities which enabled them to sway their audiences. You will find this part of the book more interesting ; but it will probably fill you with despair—and so will the pictures of the countenances of these orators. Take Henry Clay. I daresay you could manage most of his favourite forms of oratorical expression, *Anaphora*, *Apostrophe*, *Asteismus*, *Apodixix*, *Asyndeton* (he favoured the A class), and *Epagoge*, *Eperotesis*, *Ethos*, *Sermocinatio ;* but if your countenance refuses to " beam with animation," your eye to smile or dart flashes, your body, " in moments of vast passion to bend almost double," your " homely mouth to shrink and curve in passion almost to a Grecian chiselling," these achievements will avail you little.

At the end of the book will be found practical general hints to speakers, and, immediately before the end, descriptions of the impression made by such modern orators as Gladstone, Bright, Spurgeon, Bryan, Harding, Lloyd George. Their methods are analysed and specimens of their finest passages are quoted. These passages are often fifth or sixth rate from the point of literature. It looks as though, with pen in hand and plenty of time and a passion, many a writer, hardly known to fame, could *write* purple patches as good as theirs. Take Bryan's famous speech on bimetallism—the one which ended, " You shall not crucify mankind upon a cross of gold." It drove his audiences (he repeated it hundreds of times) almost wild with enthusiasm, but it is merely a trenchant piece of bombast to read. It is the voice, the man, the giddy whirl of excitement round the speaker, that make the difference. Oratory is a hot-house plant ; an orchid that shrivels to an ignominious object in cool air. Yet it is a splendid art—finer than acting, to which it is sister.

I heard Gladstone when he was a very old man. His voice then was like the dashing of a cascade at the end of a cavern ; but old—very old—as he was, there was still surprising animation in his gestures. His great speeches, however, still read well. It is so easy to hear the voice as you read (I cannot supply Spurgeon's or Bright's), for Gladstone's sentences are obviously spoken oratorical sentences, not sentences composed with a pen by a man who imagines himself in the act of speaking, nor are they like Spurgeon's and Lloyd George's speeches, mere talk. They are marked by the delays and circumlocutions of elaborate improvisation like the later style of Henry James. They have dignity of form. You cannot help reading them aloud in your head. (The way to read the later Henry James, by the way, is to read him aloud ; sentences which puzzle the eye, in spite of involutions and clauses, then become clear to ear.) There is a tremendous solemnity about Gladstone's sentences ; gravity is their characteristic as definite as fire is the characteristic of that long-dead orator, John Donne, in whom Mr. Ruffin would be interested.

I have not read Mr. Ruffin's book properly— only dipped in it, and I may be doing him a wrong in saying that among his hints to speakers he has not emphasized the paramount importance of sincerity. Sincerity can be faked, but it is hard to fake it, and the worst of learning the art of oratory is that it is apt to destroy sincerity until that art has become second nature—and even then the art may be more obstrusive than sincerity. There is a story of Carlyle carrying a motion against Gladstone at the meeting which founded the London Library. " Down he came," grumbled Carlyle, afterwards describing the occasion, "like Apollo with his shining bow and quiver ; and I a poor simple Orson, with no winged words at command. . . ."

This was repeated to Gladstone, who exclaimed: " Simple Orson, indeed ! It was the most wily speech I ever heard in my life." Several famous writers are really orators on paper. Carlyle is certainly one ; to-day Mr. Wells, I think, is another. The oratorical temperament is excited by words. The born orator is even more excited by his speech than by his subject. He may have learnt his speech by heart, repeated his phrases, as Canning did, again and again in front of a looking-glass, but no sooner does he begin to utter those words, than he is fired like a poet when he first grasps a glittering conception.

HIGHBROWS

PERHAPS the most important benefit we derive from reading Mr. Aldous Huxley's book of essays, *Music at Night,* is an increased awareness of the privilege and advantage of being a "Highbrow." In one essay, called "Foreheads Villainous Low," he discusses the new stupidity-snobbery and ignorance-snobbery which make people apt to congratulate themselves upon the lowness of their brows.

"It is not at all uncommon now," he says, speaking of a shy reference to Mantegna in one of Mr. Ernest Hemingway's novels, "to find intelligent and cultured people doing their best to feign stupidity and to conceal the fact that they have received an education." This is the new snobbery. Twenty years ago it was still a compliment to say of a man that he was clever, cultivated, interested in things of the mind. To-day the candidate for such praise is terrified of being labelled "Highbrow." I can still recall the look of astonishment which appeared on the face of a fellow-journalist when, defending some article I had written, I once said, "*Of course* it was highbrow; I am a highbrow." "Well," he replied, "you're the first man I've ever heard admit that he was a highbrow."

The first! Think what that implies. That I should have admitted that my self-respect as a journalist depended upon my being a cultivated writer who cared for things of the mind struck him as a daring confession, instead of a boast which at diffident moments I might easily think excessive.

I cannot imagine being ashamed of such culture as I possess.

What I am ashamed of—considering that I have done nothing all my life but read, talk, listen and write, is that this culture still has such yawning gaps, such shaky foundations.

What is the cause of this ridiculous diffidence which afflicts intellectuals to-day? Why should they allow every muddled ignoramus to assert his superiority? Why should they be afraid of betraying their own? In the essay "Foreheads Villainous Low" Mr. Huxley answers those questions. He attributes primarily the arrogance of lowbrows to-day, and the sycophancy of highbrows, to universal education, a tree only planted fifty years ago. Its first fruit, he says, has been contempt for culture. "When culture was confined to a few, it had a rarity value comparable to pearls or caviar." But "when finally the Many were given the education which, when it was confined to the Few, had seemed so precious, so magically efficacious, they found out very quickly that the gift was not worth quite so much as they had supposed—that, in fact, there was nothing in it. And, indeed, for the great majority of men and women, there obviously *is* nothing in culture. Nothing at all—neither spiritual satisfactions, nor social rewards."

True, certainly true, but let us stop and see how far these truths take us. Culture has no longer the same prestige-value that it once had; and education, though professional democrats still prescribe it as a remedy for every social or individual ill, is, as the Many have found out for themselves, far from being "a magic elixir." To put it bluntly, culture administered as education has bored them, and brought in very meagre returns. They have begun to clamour instead for useful or technical instruction. Therefore, those who reveal culture and their faith in it in every line that they write, appear to the Many to be fraudulent and pretentious bores—for that is what they mean when they call them "Highbrows."

Mr. Huxley has discovered the cause of the confidence of such people to-day. They are backed up by the spirit of a commercial age.

"Mass production is impossible without mass consumption. Other things being equal, consumption varies inversely with the intensity of mental life. A man who is exclusively interested in the things of the mind will be quite happy (in Pascal's phrase) sitting quietly in a room. A man who has no interest in the things of the mind will be bored to death if he has to sit quietly in a room. Lacking thoughts with which to distract himself, he must acquire things to take their place; incapable of mental travel, he must move about in the body. In a word, he is the ideal consumer, the mass consumer of objects and of transport."

There you have it! "In the modern industrial state highbrows, being poor consumers, are bad citizens." No wonder, then, the highbrow is made a universal butt, and the timid highbrow disowns his distinction. Nevertheless his advantages are obvious. To be a highbrow is the cheapest, safest way of living a contented life; and intellectual and æsthetic interests are the only cures for that uncomfortable itch, envy, which robs even the successful of half their satisfaction. The man who is rich in mental possessions is not likely to be depressed by the lives of the wealthy, on the contrary, they tend to add to his entertainment.

This is, of course, annoying to those rich people whose pleasure in their possessions is largely dependent upon being envied for them, and naturally

annoying to those who want to sell the highbrow
something, or to organize a good time for him.
But there is a wider reason why he exasperates,
and a deeper one. The world of culture is a closed
society, and any closed society is intolerable to a
democratic age. Aristocracy of birth has lost prestige and the aristocracy of wealth lacks mystery.
Anybody is in it the moment he has made money,
and out of it the moment his money comes to an
end. It is a precarious distinction.

The only exclusive world remaining to-day is
that of the highbrows. Into that you cannot buy
your way. You cannot even, alas, be certain of
qualifying as a highbrow by hard work, by reading
the best books, looking at the best pictures, hearing
the best music. You may get an entrance on those
terms, but you will be found out when you are there.
No wonder highbrows are jeered at and abused!
I have watched the embarrassments of those trying
to be gentlemen, and of those pretending to be
rich; but, believe me, these were nothing to the
bewildered misery of those trying to live beyond
their intellectual means. The robust lowbrow knows
this by anticipation, so he contents himself with
shouting sour grapes over the vineyard wall.

The intellect creates a hierarchy according to
the intellect, the heart desires equality for all.
They are incompatible aims. But the highbrow
journalist can do two things for those outside the
wall. He can point out that the qualification for
becoming a highbrow is to care for the things of the
mind, and that the amount of knowledge of literature, of art, and of philosophy required is actually
small: interest is everything. Granted interest,
knowledge grows. Then he can warn the outsider
not to be unduly intimidated by the shibboleths of
highbrows. Mr. Huxley's essay on "History and the
Past" opens with an amusing comparison between

Culture and the special knowledge which a united family accumulates.

"Do you remember Aunt Agatha's ear trumpet? And how Willie made the parrot drunk with sops in wine? And that picnic on Loch Etive, when the boat upset and Uncle Bob was nearly drowned? Do you remember? And we all do; and we laugh delightedly; and the unfortunate stranger, who happens to have called, feels utterly out of it. Well, that (in its social aspect) is Culture. When we of the great Culture Family meet, we exchange reminiscences about Grandfather Homer, and that awful old Dr. Johnson, and Aunt Sappho, and poor Johnny Keats. 'And do you remember that absolutely priceless thing Uncle Virgil said? You know. *Timeo Danaos* . . . Priceless; I shall never forget it.' No, we shall never forget it; and what's more we shall take good care that those horrid people who have had the impertinence to call on us, those wretched outsiders who never knew dear mellow old Uncle V., shall never forget it either. We'll keep them constantly reminded of their outsideness."